ANXIETY FOR BEGINNERS

ANXIETY FOR BEGINNERS

How It Feels to Live with Anxiety
and How to Make the Best of It

ELEANOR MORGAN

HarperCollinsPublishersLtd

Published by HarperCollins Publishers Ltd

Originally published in the United Kingdom in 2016 by Bluebird, an imprint of Pan Macmillan.
First published in Canada in 2017 by HarperCollins Publishers Ltd in this hardcover edition.

HarperCollins books may be purchased for educational, business,
or sales promotional use through our Special Markets Department.

HarperCollins Publishers Ltd
2 Bloor Street East, 20th Floor
Toronto, Ontario, Canada
M4W 1A8

www.harpercollins.ca

Library and Archives Canada Cataloguing in Publication information is available upon request.

ISBN 978-1-44344-891-8

Printed and bound in the United States
LSC/H 9 8 7 6 5 4 3 2 1

For Matt and Pam

CONTENTS

ANXIETY FOR BEGINNERS

PART I
SOMETHING'S WRONG

A TORNADO IN A TOILET STALL

WHEN I WAS SEVENTEEN, I LOST PART OF MYSELF to a toilet stall. A part I don't know if I'll ever get back.

It was a sticky summer afternoon, somewhere in that liminal haze between lunch and the last bell. Back-to-back biology. Leaning across the lab bench marked with the compass carvings of bored hands, I saw the blackboard starting to blur. It fizzed like TV static. I felt tired—way too tired for not having done any PE that day. The teacher was talking about mitochondria. "They're the powerhouses of cells!" she may or may not have said.

I'd been struggling to concentrate. *Mitochondria.* The word twitched in my head. I mouthed it under my breath: "Mi-to-chon-dr-ia." The look of it in chalk, all frills and layers, made me want to gag.

Something weird was happening in my guts. *Shit,* I thought. *I'm going to puke. I knew I shouldn't have had two sausage rolls.* The prickling sensation you get behind your ears when you're about to vomit spread all over my head. I didn't recognize it at all. This feeling crawled up the back of my neck and into my hair like lice. It reached my hands, made them go numb. *Fuck.*

It quickly became very frightening. Within seconds I was convinced I was about to detonate there on my wooden stool. Something had to come out, somewhere—

"Excuse me, miss."

"Yes?" The teacher walked over.

"Can I go to the toilet, please?" I whispered.

"If you must. Be fast."

The distance between that lab bench and the toilets must have been ten metres at most, but it felt like hundreds, a wilderness of parquet flooring. As I closed the stall's little door behind me, I anticipated the kind of vomit that sounds like someone emptying a bucket of water on the floor. I bent over, but nothing came. Just waves of nauseating pressure that never crashed. When I realized I wasn't going to be sick, I put the seat lid down and sat and looked at the floor the way I had a thousand times before on toilet trips to kill time when I was bored.

Only, the floor now was different. It had the same wet clumps of toilet paper, tampon applicator tubes and empty crisp packets making Hansel and Gretel–esque trails into the neighbouring stalls, but it was moving. Actually *moving*. A noise left my mouth—one I'd never made until that day—and then I felt a cold, black fear like I'd never known. My head swam. The walls were like putty to my touch. Nothing made sense to any of my senses. This was possession, pure and simple. I wanted to climb out of my skin like you'd climb out of a pair of trousers. That's how I can best describe an experience that words cannot give true descriptive power to. In the space of a few minutes death became a certainty. What else, if not death, could be the end point of such physical and mental free fall?

I wasn't hyperventilating, but I couldn't quite breathe deeply enough. Inhaling, I remembered my dad talking about animals dying alone. He said he knew a man whose dog had gone into the garden shed and curled up in a ball among the tools to die by herself. I thought about lying in a ball on the wet floor in the jeans I'd safety pinned at the ankle so they were tight like Nick Valensi's from the Strokes. *You're going to die. This is it. Your clothes are going to reek of piss.*

I wanted to shout, but who for? The teacher? My lab partner? My mum? Who would hear and how would they help? I didn't shout. I just sat. Eventually, after what felt like a lifetime, the floor stopped moving and my guts merely fizzed, rather than threatening to detonate. I had no idea how long I'd been in the stall, but surely I *had* died and come back to life.

Walking out to the sinks, my legs felt hollow. *What the fuck just happened?* I burst into tears, running the water as hot as it would go over my hands. Looking in the mirror at my face, I looked . . . the same. My clothes, hair and shoes all looked the same. But how? When I glanced at the stall through its open door, I just saw a manky school toilet. How had it been the centre of a storm just moments ago? I was shaking, but I started to feel myself again. I—the person who'd walked into that science lab, laughing at Charlotte O'Neill's impressions of our weird art teacher—was "back" from wherever I'd been. But some kind of switch had been flicked.

I went and sat at my bench again, convinced that whatever had just happened was visible all over my face to everyone. A few girls looked up from their Bunsen burners, but people skived all the time and a long absence mid-lesson was nothing new—I myself had gotten away with it. Maybe I wasn't in the toilet as long as I thought. My concentration was hazy for the rest of the lesson, though, and when it came time to go home, I still felt strange and couldn't stop thinking about the "experience," as I referred to it in my head.

I walked past the skate ramp, where I spent most of my evenings, sitting with others reading *The Face* and desperately trying to like the taste of beer and fags, and thought: *Jesus, it would be awful if that weird thing happened here in front of everyone. What if I couldn't stop it happening so quickly? What if everyone saw me?*

Those two words—"what if"—would come to define the next fifteen years of my life. They would haul me out of lectures, off Tube trains and away from dates. They'd boot me out of nightclubs and cut short conversations at parties. They'd paralyze me in restaurants, pin me in bed, shred my social life and so wear out my mind with secrets that twice my exhausted psyche would give up. Of course, I didn't know any of that then.

It was a hot walk home. The kind of hot that scorches the grass yellow and makes the air smell like hazelnuts. Running my hands through the pampas grass that kissed the corners of the swimming pool behind my house, I had no idea that what I'd experienced was a panic attack. Things would change— Jesus Christ how they'd change—but at the time I knew as much about a "panic attack" as I did about the formula of a carbon atom. Whatever it was that had happened to me earlier that day had left a gash in my mind. There was no going back. I struggled to eat dinner, remembering the nausea. In my top bunk that night, I fell asleep imagining my evenings at the ramp and how, if I ever felt that ill again, I'd have to get away so no one could see.

What if it happened out of nowhere again somewhere else? What if I couldn't be alone? What if I died next time?

What if.

"TWO LITRES OF PUS"

THAT FIRST PANIC ATTACK CAME SHORTLY AFTER I returned to school following months at home recovering from a spectacular ruptured appendix.

It was a strange experience and one I have only sketchy memories of after a certain point. Over a few days of increasing pain and digestive symptoms that both my mum and I attributed to "a nasty period," my appendix became infected, exploded and turned a good few inches of my bowel gangrenous. The surgeons had to remove all the poisoned bits, along with the two litres of pus that filled my abdominal cavity. That's more than a giant bottle of Coca-Cola, if you want perspective. When my mum took me to Emergency, holding over five feet of teenager in her arms like a pike, my body was raging with peritonitis, septicemia and a body temperature that broke the measuring equipment.

I remember very little, other than a portly nurse saying, "Yep, you're cookin' nicely," but was told later that my eyes had been rolling in my head, I had been having seizures and, basically, had been snuffing it. Fast. The last thing I remember is my belly being the size of a house, and having waves of pain that made me flail at anyone near my bed in an appeal to make it stop.

After several hours of overnight surgery, I came to on the ward covered in wires and big splashes of iodine solution, with a huge drain thing full of coral liquid hanging out of the right side of my body. Mum was asleep on a chair beside me, her hand on my shin. She woke up and told me what had happened. My father was there, too, she said, but I should go back to sleep. I had a flashback of Dad in his work suit, leaning on the bed bars and playing hangman with me on the back of his newspaper. I begged him not to do a funny one in case it made me laugh and hurt too much. (The words were "drum kit.")

I healed well over a few weeks. Being young and sporty saved my life, or so the surgeons told me in their "you really should be dead" speech. But those weeks were bleak as hell. Unable to move without help, I ate, bathed, went to the toilet (all kinds of joy there) and vomited in the same hospital bed, or on the floor beside it in that bucket-emptying way. Every available space in my room was taken up with flowers from visitors, and the smell of them all, in my fitful daytime sleeping, was heavy and toxic. I was toxic.

Sometimes stuff would leave my body while I was in the company of other people. One of my best friend Kate's favourite stories from that time is the day almost my entire family—siblings, grandparents, aunts, great-aunts—were hovering around the bed and I lost control of my bowels into the bedpan that pretty much stayed permanently under my bum, just in case. I was looking my granddad in the eye as I shat myself. Horizontally.

Mum must have sensed something had happened (perhaps through her nose), because she herded everyone out, saying I "needed to rest." The nurse came in, took the pan away and wrote some notes in my chart. I looked later and saw that she'd written "offensive green stool" in small, ornate writing. That detail is also a favourite of Kate's. She once threatened to get the words tattooed on her arm.

Once I could sit in a chair, walk to the bathroom and eat and drink regularly without messy consequences, I was allowed to leave the hospital. After lunch on that day, Dad drove me home in the big, navy Volvo, and I just couldn't comprehend that I was sitting in a *car*, rather than on a hospital bed or wipe-clean vinyl armchair. The fabric of the passenger seat, worn bare by years of fidgety child arses, was so soft. Chrissie Hynde was singing through the stereo for someone to stop their sobbing, and my pale body (I looked like E.T. when he gets sick and turns white) was pointed towards the open window. It was sunny and the breeze was thick around my shoulders. Dad glanced over and smiled at me. It was dreamy, being in that car. A warm hologram.

"I can't believe it, Dad."

"Neither can I."

It was another few weeks before I could dress myself properly. Walking around the house meant steadying myself on kitchen counters, sofa arms and door handles like an old lady. Physiotherapists and nurses came to the house. "Oh, *bless* you," they'd coo when they saw me propped outside on a bench with pillows and magazines. I hated it. I hated being pitied. When my scar got infected and there was talk of me returning to hospital, I wasn't having it. My bedroom might have smelled like a post mortem, but I wanted to go back to school so badly: back to hockey, swimming, and crap pasta, plastic cheese and ketchup in the canteen with my friends. To soaking toilet rolls and lobbing them at the ceiling. (Looking back, this remains an inexplicable pastime.)

Through sheer iron will, I forced myself to move despite the pain. Battling the nausea that came with eating anything bigger than a sandwich, I got stronger and regained some weight. My legs stopped resembling two greying pipe cleaners. I walked the dogs up and down the lane and finally got fit enough to go back to school. To sixth form! (Eleventh and twelfth grades.) I'd been planning my first-day-back outfit for ages—down to the bracelet.

That first day was predictably slow and overwhelming. By midday I was exhausted. Everyone wanted to see my scars— dark, Frankenstein slashes that they were—and *everyone* fussed. Teachers stopped me in the corridors. "Eleanor, are you all right?" they'd ask in coffee-breath whispers.

I was polite, but they did my head in. In that first week or so back in the fold, I was defiant. Defiant through the tiredness, the soreness and the endless, machine-gun questioning. I couldn't play any sports yet, which infuriated me, but I was back with my friends at eye level, rather than looking up at them from a hospital bed or a couch. I was no longer the invalid—at least, not on the surface.

I'm explaining all this because I believe that this period of readjustment to Real Life was when my problems with anxiety really kicked off. I *had* experienced some anxiety as a child, which had mostly mirrored my mother's concerns with germs and contamination, and had once resulted in a short-lived period of trichotillomania (pulling out of hair). But I did everything other kids did and had never been reserved or held back by nerves. I have no memory of struggling with life until after my appendix burst.

Within a couple of weeks of being back at school, I found that the symptoms I'd learned to deal with in my recovery—the nausea, the sleepiness, the weak limbs, the bowel upsets, the light-headedness—started to feel ever so slightly less than manageable. I was in high school but again felt as I had when I'd just started school: excited, but wary of the long corridors and assembly halls . . . the open spaces. It was as though I was getting smaller, like Alice after she drinks the shrinking potion.

Wall edges got sharper; the sound of doors closing grew louder and made me jump. Smells like drying paint and new furniture were more overpowering than usual. The volume on every sense got dialed up a notch. Not to the point of real discomfort, but to a level that made me feel I had to be careful. Of what, I didn't have a clue. It was a quiet dread, with no name.

I started spending lunchtimes inside reading, saying I was tired even when I wasn't. I'd make excuses for not walking home through town with friends, saying I had to get back and help my mum with something, and I would walk the long way round, by the river, alone, thinking, thinking, thinking.

I still messed about with my friends, stayed reasonably engaged in class, laughed a lot and spent the evenings on the landline talking utter shit with people, but something was holding me back from being entirely . . . *there*. Actions and interactions didn't feel quite so easy. I was withdrawing.

Something was wrong.

TAKING ROOT

A TRAUMA INVOLVING A TOTAL LOSS OF PHYSICAL function and a pretty solid staring contest with death are bound to have some psychological impact on a young person, at least for a while. Through a trusting, open dialogue with a therapist, I've realized just how significant the trauma was for me. The anxiety that began to creep in when I was trying to readjust to normal life became woven into the very fabric of my existence as an adult. It would, at times, make life feel like a joke I wasn't in on.

It took me nearly fifteen years to begin working out what may have made me the way I am and to start tackling it. Fifteen years is a long time. A lack of trust in therapy (I had some dire experiences), along with fear and an unwillingness to accept myself as unwell, played a large part in making my relationship with anxiety so drawn out and difficult. But it was also due to a lack of understanding generally, I think—my own, my parents', my caregivers'—of the ways in which anxiety, a feeling we all know, can knock you clean off your axis.

Here is the reality: in 2016, anxiety disorders are the most common kind of mental health problem and, overall, one of the biggest burdens of illness in the world. A major study conducted in 2012 by researchers at the University of Queensland, surveying nearly half a million people across ninety-one countries, suggested that, globally, one in thirteen people suffer from clinical anxiety. And yet anxiety remains a riddle to so many—including those who suffer with it every day of their lives.

There are things we do know. We know that anxiety is not a tangible "other": an infection or something that buzzes around us, waiting to sting. For some of us, though, if the right factors are at play, our normal responses to the stressors of life— which include anxiety and fear—can become dysfunctional.

The fight-or-flight response is a part of every human body and is at the root of how we respond to fear and stress. This handy reflex works by stimulating the heart rate, dilating air passages and contracting blood vessels. All this increases blood flow and oxygen to our muscles so that we are ready to run from something life-threatening: a wild animal, a fast car, a dangerous person. It's pretty important as far as physiological responses go. However, for me, and for the millions of other people out there with anxiety, the fight-or-flight system short-circuits. Many factors can contribute to this happening: genetics, trauma, drugs, hormones, physical illness. Although the *exact* cause of any anxiety problem cannot be isolated, we know that the response—one wired into our psyches and bodies as a natural, helpful response to life—ends up being unhelpful, because it is triggered unnecessarily, all the time.

There are all kinds of metaphors associated with this short-circuiting, but I like the one about records: if we think of the brain as a vinyl record with grooves the needle slips into to play a track, people with an anxiety disorder have—for whatever reason—etched grooves in their mind that they slip into on a hair-trigger of fear. We develop thought patterns, rituals, avoidances and obsessions relating to where and how we've felt anxious before, and at the slightest threat of experiencing that anxiety again, the fight-or-flight response kicks in. For example: there is a road in Dalston, East London, which I can't walk down without feeling a little itch in my gut. I had a very bad panic attack there once that created a traumatic memory of that place—a groove. This means that now whenever I pass that spot my subconscious brain tells my conscious brain, "Hey, we need to be on guard here," and I start to feel anxious.

I can't really do anything about this knee-jerk synaps-ing—it happens at too deep a level. I can, however, control my response, which is something I've been taught how to do in cognitive behavioural therapy. For fifteen years, though, I would respond to even the smallest niggles of anxiety with spirals of disastrous thinking:

Oh, I feel really uncomfortable all of a sudden. I had a panic attack there once, on that corner. What if I had one there again—wouldn't that be an arse? Oh god, it was so awful—I couldn't see straight and my arms and legs felt so hot and tingly I felt like I was having a stroke, and I had to run into an old man's pub to use a horrible toilet and, oh god, what if it happens again? Will I be able to get to a toilet in time? Oh god, now my stomach hurts and I feel sick! I hate feeling like this! Why can't I stop it?

When we consider how anxiety has become tattooed on society, it's right to question why we need a system as sensitive and prone to glitching as the fight-or-flight response.

Charles Darwin, who reportedly suffered from a crippling panic disorder for years that often left him housebound, argued that to a degree, it is highly evolved to be "on alert" most of the time. But a system that is controlled by one of the most primitive parts of our brains is often a bit simplistic in the way it interprets danger.

Mark Williams and Danny Penman explain this in their best-selling book *Mindfulness: A Practical Guide to Finding Peace in a Frantic World*: "The brain makes no distinction between an external threat, such as a tiger, and an internal one, such as a troubling memory or a future worry. It treats both as threats that either need to be fought off or run away from."

Sometimes the "dangerous" person is us. The dangerous thing is not a wild beast but a thought or a recollection.

I've negotiated an anxiety disorder for my entire adult life. Twice, it got so bad I had what I can only refer to as a "breakdown," even though we're encouraged not to use that word these days. Depression and anxiety share many of the same symptoms, but during those two periods of my life I was trapped by a new, thousand-volt level of anxiety with a thick duvet of helplessness on top. These were times defined less by sadness and more by living in fear of the next minute, and what physical symptoms it would bring.

Am I losing my mind? Should I call an ambulance? Could I take a load of sleeping pills that would make me sleep for days but not kill me? Am I going to have to go onto a psychiatric ward?

These were questions I asked myself when stuck in a cyclone of negative thought, my ability to be rational sweating out through my warm spots.

While staring at pictures of myself as a child or even as a teenager, before the whole nearly dying thing, I've asked out loud, "Where did she *go*?" It's like there are two versions of me—Version 1.0: Pre-Anxious; and Version 2.0: Anxious.

I miss Version 1.0 like a limb.

After that first panic attack in the science block toilets, I thought about nothing else for the next fortnight. It happened again a few times, and each time, the fear of it happening anew cranked up a gear until the fear became a steady hum. A literal hum, too, right behind my ears. At night I'd cry, wondering what the hell was going on inside me. But telling my parents or friends was out of the question. Actually talking about it made it seem more real. I became convinced it was a physical problem, anyway—something related to my damaged insides. For obvious reasons, this was scary to think about.

Three weeks of misery slowly passed, and after experiencing one totally sleepless, sweaty night, I turned up at the doctor's office on my own at 8:30 in the morning. I pleaded with the receptionist to let me see someone, not really knowing what I was seeking help for. Luckily, someone was available: a doctor I'd not seen before. I told him what I'd been going through and he sat back in his chair, pursing his lips. "Based on your medical history, I'm going to run some blood tests," he said, "but I think what you're experiencing may be panic attacks."

He gave me some leaflets and referred me to a counsellor, who turned out to be an old lady working in a musty room in the community centre next to the Shell garage. She smelled of my grandma, Oil of Olay and wool.

This sweet lady's modus operandus was to say, "It'll be all right," and give me a couple of elastic bands to wear on my wrists. She told me to snap them against my skin every time I sensed the onset of an attack, which for me meant starting to feel nauseous, dizzy and full of pins and needles. She told me there was nothing to get "stressed" about.

I don't remember the elastic bands alleviating the physical symptoms at all, but I knew no better and they at least made me aware of a flow of energy that needed catching. Somehow. However, despite this woman's kindness and my GP's commendable act of referring a seventeen-year-old to a therapist rather than immediately putting her on medication, I can't help but look back with resentment at the laid-back attitude of it all.

Still, through the combined distractions of preparing to leave for university in London, herbal sleeping tablets and a slightly better understanding of the nature of panic attacks and the claustrophobic loops of anxiety they cause (I had become very good friends with the now-defunct Ask Jeeves.com), I did get slightly better. I realized that with the "right" things in place (avoidances), I could get through a day like anyone else. Or at least in a way that wouldn't make my anxiety noticeable to anyone else.

Once I got to university, I created no support network for myself in my new surroundings, despite a mini crisis mere weeks before arriving. Through sheer bloody-mindedness and a heavy backpack of stigma, I told myself I'd be fine. I *had* to be fine. I had a name for these episodes now, anyway, and that was the main thing.

On my first night in residence, before heading down to the common room to meet loads of other freshers and whoever was playing the spellbinding acoustic version of "Stairway to Heaven" I could hear coming up the lift shaft, I wrote "UR

OK" in tiny biro letters on the base of my thumb. I rolled my eyes at myself and the American teen movie cliché of my act, but I wanted to have something to remind myself when I looked down that I was all right, that I could do it and that I was the same as everyone else.

By this point my parents knew about the anxiety, mostly because I'd had to explain the abundance of fawn elastic bands I'd left in my wake the summer before I left home. The stationery stores in Bishop's Stortford didn't know what had hit them. They were nice-ish, my parents, if a little confused about what was going on. I couldn't answer when my dad asked, kindly but slightly despairingly, "What do you have to be anxious about? You've got it all going for you." I was anxious of being anxious and frightened of having a panic attack the minute I left the house, but I just couldn't put that into words then. Without ever having needed to understand anxiety, I guess they didn't know what they were dealing with.

Once out alone in the world, I'd say I was fine when my parents would call. I couldn't be arsed to talk about being anxious, mainly because I couldn't bear the idea of them worrying. I found it suffocating—that invalid thing again. Of course the reality was that underneath the excitement of independence and beginning to discover myself and what the world had to offer, I lived with a constant fear of having a panic attack when I left my little room and was out and around other people.

In lectures, supermarkets, train stations and pubs, the fearful thoughts were like a second heartbeat. I could be like everyone else, absolutely I could, but only if I had everything aligned in my head. Only if I could get out if I needed to. If I couldn't get out, then the "what if" spiral would begin. Not having a clear path of escape—even in the supermarket on Victoria Street—became a trigger for real, all-body fear.

As for many others with an anxiety disorder, my life became defined by "safety behaviours" relating to where, when and how I'd felt anxious in the past, behaviours that helped me navigate living in London on my own. Places got red-flagged if I'd had a panic attack there or been close to experiencing one: *No, you shouldn't walk through Green Park to get to that seminar because you had a panic attack there last week. Find another way.*

This internal dialogue became never ending, and something my therapist now refers to as "The Chatterbox." But back then, even when the endless "chatter" exhausted me, I didn't think about therapy seriously. In fact, while trying to find my place in the huge, sexy city of London, around loads of sexy, brainy people, I felt ashamed that I might need therapy; fearful that it would make me less than whole, different from everyone else having the time of their lives. On the occasions that I did contemplate talking to someone, usually at night, I'd quickly shake it away: *You're not crazy, fool.*

I got through those first two years of university with all my caveats and avoidances. I had an absolute ball at club nights at Trash, Nag Nag Nag, Misshapes and Kash Point, all meeting points for every shade of "other." They were heaven, those nightclubs, teeming with cool kids who were realizing they could paint themselves however they wanted and be both outsider and insider—part of something, a feeling of beautiful havoc. For me, it was like all the fashion and pop culture magazines I'd obsessed over in my teens come manifest. I'd never seen boys snogging boys on dance floors, while other boys kissed girls, and girls kissed girls up against the wall.

Trash, in particular, was a club night with so many firsts for so many different people. Even the regulars felt a buzz of relief once they'd passed the door girl's inspection. If you didn't look right, you weren't getting in. The Yeah Yeah Yeahs were big when I started going. I remember queuing from really early on the Monday night they were due to play a "secret" show. As they tore through the baggy garage loops of "Date with the Night" at deafening volume, and Karen O turned every set of genitals in the room inside out with her screaming and charging, I thought: *It's happening. Look at me, here, doing this.* Reading about a band in the *NME* in a park in Bishop's Stortford was one thing, but being in a club and watching them play so close that you could smell their BO was something else.

It was in those clubs that I met my people. Met myself, really. When I think about late-night London in the early 00s, I feel giddy. Only, I wasn't always mid-crowd in nightclubs or gigs. I liked to be at the side of the throng, gently engineering whichever group I was with, to stay near the toilets and exits. To feel safe, I had to know where they were in every place I entered, especially considering that at the sharp end, my anxiety mostly manifested with gut issues. I was terrified of shitting myself, basically, even though it had never happened. It still hasn't. But anxiety doesn't believe in evidence. I would come to be reminded of this over and over and over.

If I couldn't see a toilet, or at least a Fire Exit sign, I was screwed. My night was spent gently obsessing about how I could get out if I needed to. Although there was something paradoxically comforting about surrendering your body to a crowd of jerking figures in a dark room, every voice swallowed by the thunderous volume of the speakers, if I got too hemmed in I'd start to panic and would end up doing a French exit, legging it without saying goodbye to anyone.

I'd walk home to my student accommodation (right by Victoria Station) trying to breathe deeply and pull back the gallop of my thoughts. *Well, it was good while it lasted,* I'd think. *But thank god you got out when you did. Imagine what would have happened if you hadn't.*

I now know that every time I fled in a panic like that, I was telling my brain that there was something to fear; that every place, other than home, my small room, had a whiff of danger about it. I was making the anxiety worse but had no idea.

Open spaces were a navigable, but often daunting, prospect. If I did have to walk through Hyde Park, say, because my friends fancied it, I'd mentally keep track of all the bushes I could hide behind—just in case. I had to sit at the end of the row in every lecture or cinema—just in case. If I ever took the Tube, I'd stand by the door, facing it—just in case I had to get out fast.

Every next second and its potential escape route had to be mapped out, because what if I couldn't get away?

Anxiety feels like a "what if" disease.

CRACKING

B Y THE TIME I GOT TO MY THIRD YEAR OF UNIVERSITY, I'd "what if-ed" myself into a terrible state. At twenty I had that first "breakdown" I talked about. I put that word in quotation marks because it's a term often rejected in modern psychiatry in favour of "crisis," for example. The words "nervous breakdown" still, somewhere, summon those whispers and rumours around school about teachers or friends' parents. Summon images of fainting, jerking, stupor. But my fear of having a panic attack had become a 24-7 obsession.

I feared walking to the big Tesco in Hackney that was two hundred metres from my house, let alone going to lectures. I needed a "get-out" plan for every possibility, even if I was just nipping across the road for milk. Eventually, the volume of misplaced adrenalin I generated became unsustainable for my brain. I broke down like a clapped-out car.

At twenty I had my first episode of depression. It happened very quickly: proper depersonalization (a sense of detachment from your surroundings, as if nothing, not even your body, is real); fourteen-hour stretches of sleep; a total lack of appetite. I just couldn't move, because every physical movement felt like a hallucination.

For a few days I lay still on my bed listening to *Moon Pix* over and over on a boiling hot Discman. I'd read that Cat Power (aka "Chan" Marshall) wrote the album in the midst of a breakdown, so somehow it felt apt, even though I'd previously had no understanding of what a mental breakdown would actually look or feel like. Marshall's voice, a misty searchlight, was an echo: the voice I couldn't find even in myself for how I was feeling. There's one song on that album, "No Sense," with a dragging, Al Green–like guitar refrain, that's a bullet in the back on the rare occasions I listen to it now. I actually interviewed Marshall a few years ago and told her this. She got tearful and then it got a bit awkward.

Summer winds tapped my neighbour's eucalyptus branches against my window and I became more and more worried about what to tell my lecturers about just not turning up anymore. I lost fourteen pounds in under two weeks. I'd stare at my flat mates making dinner and think: *How are you doing that? How are you just making food and talking to each other? How are you hungry? Can you see the delirium I feel inside as I try to laugh with you about our landlord? How are you concentrating on the TV? How are you opening the patio doors to smoke and not collapsing in the sunlight?*

I finally went to my GP, and it took me nearly an hour to get there. "There" being under a kilometre away. The doctor prescribed sertraline, a SSRI (selective serotonin reuptake inhibitor) antidepressant frequently prescribed for anxiety disorders.

He seemed surprised as I was talking, saying, "Well, you look well." Why? Why was he surprised? Because I'd showered and had clean hair and clothes? Because I wasn't sitting on the chair rocking, clawing at my skin? Because I could string a sentence together? What does "not well in the head" *look* like? I said none of those things, of course. Instead, I managed something along the lines of how I felt I wasn't living, just existing—like my salad days were limping by like, well, wet salad.

Proust, in the second volume of *In Search of Lost Time*, writes the following on adolescence:

> In a world thronged with monsters and with gods, we know little peace of mind. There is hardly a single action we perform in that phase which we would not give anything, in later life, to be able to annul. Whereas what we ought to regret is that we no longer possess the spontaneity which made us perform them. In later life we look at things in a more practical way, in full conformity with the rest of society, but adolescence is the only period in which we learn anything.

The spontaneity of semi-adult youth that Proust describes had seemingly escaped me. I was twenty and I felt so old. Knackered. Desperate.

"I'm not living the life of a young person anymore," I told the doctor.

His reply was something like, "What does that mean to you?"

To which I answered, "Wanting to do things and actually being able to do them without chickening out or running away."

I gave an example: going to Tesco without worrying about losing it in the freezer aisles. He started laughing. Looking back, I feel so heartbroken and embarrassed for myself sitting in that room.

I didn't like the therapist the GP referred me to. Actually, that's unfair. I had nothing against her personally—she was just very young. (At least the old lady back in my hometown had something maternal going on; this girl didn't appear much older than me.) She spent the entire time ticking boxes on a clipboard and barely looking me in the eye. It took so much for me to rationalize being in the room—let alone get to the place—but there was no flowing conversation, just multiple-choice questionnaires. The process didn't seem catered to me, the individual, just to "An Anxious Person." Our encounters seemed dictated by one question that she posed over and over: "What is your goal?"

I didn't *have* a "goal." I just wanted to stop waking up with an invisible concrete block on my chest every morning. This wasn't specific enough, she said. Too broad. Without anything focused, we simply couldn't proceed! I stopped seeing her after four weeks—I think I said I was going on holiday—because I didn't feel held in her mind as anything other than a name on a piece of paper. After what ended up being the final session, I walked out of St. Leonard's Hospital on Kingsland Road thinking: *It's just not fucking worth it. No one understands.* But even worse than the bilious, lost feeling was the growing belief that because my anxiety hadn't improved even slightly with therapy, I must be immune to treatment. Resistant, incurable.

Like my recollections of my very first steps into the mental health service, my memory of that time sparks anger. How *dare* a GP laugh at how I described my situation?

I listened then, of course, because I knew no better. The antidepressants did nothing miraculous or definitive. The side effects—an upset stomach (nothing new there), nausea, excessive yawning and very strange dreams—were uncomfortable for a couple of weeks, but over an indefinable amount of time I gradually felt able to step outside my obsessive thought webs for longer periods, and that in turn helped me to gradually expose myself to the outside world again. My appetite came back. I went to the big Tesco and bought peas. I can honestly say that out of everything I've achieved in my life, walking through those automatic doors with a bag of Birds Eye Garden Peas and some fish fingers in my hands felt seismic.

I confided in my course leader via email, who very kindly sent seminar notes for me to read at home, with a note saying: "I know how difficult you might be finding it to get here at the moment. But you should know that 'getting better' is relative. What we do is learn to cope." It didn't register then that she was saying she knew first-hand what I was going through, but I now realize through subsequent correspondence that she was.

I also told one friend! This was a huge deal, considering how I'd kept my breakdown hidden from even the people I shared a bathroom and kitchen with. My flat mates were usually too hungover to notice whether I was even there, which at the time I saw as a godsend. The friend I had told clicked into a new setting. She turned up on my doorstep to take me for walks in the park, texted me something silly in the mornings and gradually got me moving farther and farther away from the house. Her innate understanding, at twenty, of how to help someone who was struggling the way I was startles me to this day. We grew apart socially, as people do, but I feel I owe her a great debt. Lucy Luscombe, if you ever happen to read this, you helped me out of a great ditch, girl.

PADDLING

I STAYED ON THE MEDICATION FOR A COUPLE OF YEARS. The fear of having a panic attack or being "caught out" still draped the back of my mind most days, but the curtains had become less heavy. When I would have an attack—one a week, maybe, rather than every day—it'd take another few days to get back to normal, but I was all right, really. I was managing the anxiety reasonably well, and Christ, compared with how I had been, management felt like great progress.

Capitalizing on this new distance from daily fear, at twenty-one I threw myself into editorial internships left, right and centre. I made enough tea to fill the Vredefort Dome, did photocopies for anyone who'd have me and treated every tiny paragraph I was allowed to write like sacred script. Soon enough, I was employed as a junior writer. I'd *done* it. Because I had at the last minute given up a degree in medicine to do English literature—a decision affected in no small way by how I was feeling at the time (scared shitless at the prospect of seven years of study)—my being handed a contract with the word "writer" on it was really something. After a while I tapered off the pills. I was good—still living with daily anxiety, but going out a lot and generally feeling connected. I tried recreational drugs and liked them but never really drank. With alcohol I felt

I couldn't control the high as much, and losing control of my body was at the root of the whole sorry thing, obviously.

Between the ages of twenty-one and twenty-seven, I achieved a lot. I wrote for almost every broadsheet newspaper and glossy magazine I ever wanted to. I got a job as a junior editor at *Dazed & Confused* (a title I worshipped as a teenager), and over the years in subsequent positions, I travelled the world interviewing people I admired and reported on interesting things. On the surface I was buoyant, gliding through life like a swan and able to take whatever life threw at me: tense meetings, long-haul flights, tighter deadlines and more high-profile commissions. But like that proverbial swan, serene above the water, under the surface, gradually, it had become chaos again. Paddle paddle paddle.

Towards my twenty-seventh birthday, the old safety behaviours started to creep back in. My social life shrank. People were cancelled last minute when I felt funny about leaving the house. *Just in case.* The only exception was Kate, my closest friend. With her I'd have to fall to the ground and attempt to drink my own urine like water from a fountain before she'd bat an eyelid. She has an anxiety disorder too, see. She knows the language. Speaking freely and, as Kate and I have, laughing about the ridiculous things anxiety has led us to think or do is a relief like no other. We've cackled ourselves to *tears* over things like how she filled a water bottle with diluted whiskey and Bach Rescue Remedy just to get through the day in art school during a bad period of anxiety. Hearing how marooned other people have felt makes your own experience less of a skyscraper.

Around this time, my mornings would begin with the sensation that my ribs were actually being squeezed—a new symptom. I felt a strong, physical pressure in my lungs as soon as I opened my eyes, and it got worse throughout the day when I started to ruminate about how bad I felt again. One small cluster of thoughts, spurred by something as innocuous as having to vacuum the hallway, could actually change my breathing and I couldn't seem to stop it:

> *Why am I getting anxious about this? It's just vacuuming the fucking carpet. Does getting anxious about this mean I'm back to square one? Is this what my anxiety has reduced me to? A person fearing going into the basement to get the vacuum cleaner? The absolute state of me.*

Obviously, things like boarding a plane to travel somewhere for work, which did have to happen a fair bit, became less and less straightforward. Once you're hurtling through the sky in a giant bean can, there's no way out. I wasn't scared of crashing. Rather, it was a fear of not being able to leave my seat with a clear escape route to the toilet—the only place no one could see me freak out if I freaked out. Once, at the apex of a panic attack I had on a plane to New York City, I imagined myself with crystal clarity opening the doors at thirty-seven thousand feet and throwing myself out. It was a beautiful thought, and one far superior at that moment to having to deal with another second of the abject dread and nausea crashing through my body. "I'll be fine if I roll," I said to myself. Later, as the panic fell away, I laughed out loud at where my mind had gone. I imagined surviving the jump and having to explain it to reporters: "Yeah," I'd say, teeth a row of bloodied black stumps, femurs sticking out my thighs like cutlery, "I just needed some air."

Sitting at my desk at the *Observer*, where I worked on the supplements for a few years, I would agree to have lunch with colleagues over iChat, then cancel at 12:55 because I couldn't stomach sitting in the canteen, where I wouldn't have a quick escape route. *Just in case.* The anxiety was bearable when I sat at my own desk working, but walking towards a different bank of desks made me seasick. It didn't take long for the chest-crushing thing to be a daily constant. *Am I going mad? I feel like I'm going mad.*

Just locking up my bike and getting into the building every day felt like a huge achievement. Several times I thought about going back to the doctor, only I now equated going to the doctor with not being taken seriously. I knew antidepressants were an option again but had begun to find the idea of them quite foul. I saw them as the point of no return. Here are a few things that went through my mind as I worked out what the hell to do with myself:

> *Antidepressants are a marker of failure. In taking medication, surely I am entering last-resort territory. In having to take a "happy pill" every day to function normally, am I resigning to being a fuck-up? So what if people are getting tired of me can-celling on them last minute because I've had a panic attack en route to meet them and can't imagine moving any farther than whichever street corner I am on? So what if I called in sick to work more than I felt comfortable with? Why should anyone know? Can't I just cope with this? I can cope with this.*

I wasn't coping, though. I couldn't. Not alone. That's the thing, and it has always been the thing. I was pretending and I needed help. I quit my job under the guise of going freelance, but subconsciously I think I knew I was going to implode.

Incredibly, no one knew. I hid the truth as best I could from absolutely everyone, using physical illness or happenchance as a bluff for anxiety. Over the years I'd become a master of disguise and no one, but no one, could have told you I had a serious problem with anxiety. My parents had no idea I was suffering again, either. By not talking about anxiety in years, I assumed and hoped they'd forgotten about how I was before I went to university. The only people who had some insight into how I was feeling were my partner, Hanna, and my best friend, Kate. But I couldn't even bring myself to be completely honest with them, the people I trusted most in the world.

My previous partner had known I suffered with anxiety, but I never told the whole truth then, either. I spent a great deal of our relationship hiding from it in ways that must have been very frustrating to live with, slipping in and out of moods that must have appeared sulky, vacant, or daydream-y at best but were actually instances of trying to talk myself out of a meltdown. If I started to get panicky and feel unwell while we were out somewhere, I'd just make up an excuse and go home early. I'd say I had a headache or a stomach ache if I couldn't imagine myself getting on the Tube to go and meet people, because it was essential that no one knew. I couldn't just say "I feel very anxious," because I could barely accept the reality myself. Avoidance behaviour after avoidance behaviour enabled me, as they always had, to live the bones of a normal life. Then, four years ago, I had another breakdown. That word again. The only one that fits. This time the fall was much harder.

In retrospect, it had been building for a while. I'd run

out of excuses for flaking on people. My insides had never recovered from Appendix-gate and I found myself in the position of needing bowel surgery. This was a frightening prospect, which I couldn't seem to rationalize, even with the help of my new therapist. (Yes, I had found one, and got on with her initially, but now believe she held me back significantly in ways I'll go into later.)

Travelling for work became increasingly stressful, each airport departure lounge lifting the cloche on a new set of anxiety symptoms. Before going to Kenya on an assignment for the *Guardian*, I sat in a toilet in Terminal Three convinced, absolutely plain as day, that my neck vertebrae were about to snap like bits of chalk and paralyze me because the pressure in my head as my thoughts spun out of control was so strong. It was as if a separate entity to myself sat on the porcelain: *What if I have a panic attack in the middle of the Kenyan countryside and have nowhere to hide or go to the toilet? What if I freak out on the plane and am not allowed out of my seat? What if I lose it in a part of the world where I know no one and end up being locked away somewhere because no one knows what to do with me?*

What if!

It's exhausting and boring as all hell just typing those words.

Eventually, though, each panic attack I had took longer to get over than the one before. Within a few months, they joined up in a constellation of frustration, tears and despair.

A MIND ON FIRE

Depression is melancholy minus its charms.
—SUSAN SONTAG, *ILLNESS AS METAPHOR*

DEPRESSION. A MELANCHOLY NOT JUST MINUS CHARM but defined by physical pain. It was physical disease. The "break" was marked by crying, constant dizziness, all-over body aches and a completely diminished appetite. This latter, for anyone acquainted with me and my Henry VIII–like ability to gorge, would probably be the most alarming thing of all.

Hanna somehow knew exactly what to do. She didn't look at me taking an hour to eat one piece of toast and say, "Come on, finish it." Nor did she force me to try to get up and do things. She asked me what I needed every day and most days I told her just to go to work. I wanted, needed, to be alone and she understood my fear of being viewed as an invalid. I remember thinking: *Please don't leave me.* But I never said it. The only time she got frustrated was when I eventually asked, "Why are you sticking around for this? What can you possibly be getting from this relationship right now?"

It seemed that I went to bed one night and woke up the next morning a different person. The pressure at the back of my head, the cerebellum, buzzed like a fridge in the middle of the night. I recognized that buzz. Over twenty-four hours, I became someone who could hardly eat, wouldn't answer the door or the phone and couldn't run a bath without sobbing at the desolation and pathos of it all. I was supposed to be finishing a book proposal for my new literary agent, but all I could do was eat Ryvita, watch *Friends* reruns on YouTube and read *Gone Girl* (shout-out to Gillian Flynn for writing something so compelling I could have the luxury of being distracted from my thoughts). It was like looking over the edge of the Grand Canyon the entire time, like having a deep vertigo at my very core. I wasn't just experiencing physical symptoms—I'd *become* them. Anxiety had finally got me by the neck, with a claw on every finger, and said, "Time's up, mate."

DEPRESSION AND ANXIETY frequently go hand in hand. In fact, the symptoms are often indistinguishable. Every seven years, the British government's Health and Social Care Information Centre does a survey in England to measure the different types of mental health problems people experience in a year. It was last conducted in 2009 and found that 9.7 people in 100 had mixed anxiety and depression disorders, often referred to, somewhat unfortunately, as MADD. In Canada, those numbers are even higher. According to the 2014 "Survey on Living with Chronic Diseases in Canada (SLCDC)" conducted by the Canadian government, 11.6 percent of Canadians eighteen or older reported that they had a mood and/or anxiety disorder. Additionally, 27 percent of those affected reported that their disorders had impacted their life "quite a bit" or "extremely" in the preceding twelve months.

When I became depressed, my rational brain knew somewhere that such a heightened state of arousal couldn't be sustained. It makes sense to me now. I went to see Professor David Nutt, a psychiatrist, professor of neuropsychopharmacology at Imperial College in London and the chair of the UK's Advisory Council on the Misuse of Drugs until 2009, to talk about drugs and mental health for this book. He told me: "There's just nowhere for that much maladaptive arousal to go, which is how I teach my students that anxiety can become unsustainable for an individual."

Still on the crest of this new, sour terror, I couldn't accept that depression had become a symptom of my anxiety through sheer mental overload. That, to me, was failure, no matter what my partner said to the contrary and how much love and patience she bathed me in. I was repulsed more than ever by the way I had become. Angry as a forest fire.

But frustration and anger are too close to anxiety, and as the momentum of thoughts like *Why has this happened to me?* and *Why couldn't I stay in control?* gathered, the worse I felt. I'd forgotten what it was like to experience and recover from depression before, or that recovery was inevitable—because it is; it is inevitable, full stop. After enough time passes you can tuck memories of pain away so tightly that you almost forget they're there. Almost.

For three weeks I didn't go farther than the shop at the end of my road and felt, for the first time in my life, rationally suicidal. When your mental and physical pain are so acute, you're desperate for something bigger than you to vacuum it all up. Once that pain seeps into every second that you're awake, the only thing bigger than you is death.

I didn't really want to die, though. I yearned in my bones to see the ink-spot eyes of my future newborn babies. To stand at the feet of Jordan's high mountains. To huff the warm bellies of all my future dogs as the animals lay blinking in the sun. Dogs filled a lot of my thoughts then whenever I closed my eyes, as did jumping into bodies of water. I wanted a future, I did. I just didn't want to be living in fear of the next minute, and when there's no respite from the savageness of depression, you fantasize about how you could just make everything . . . stop. I don't ever want to feel like that again.

An infuriating thing I found about depression was my inability to connect with music and images I knew I loved. It was as if my synapses had become blocked like fatty arteries. Lying on the bed—not under the covers, because this was *really* giving up and something in me wasn't ready to do that—listening to music on YouTube through my headphones, I tried to "test" my emotional responses to songs I loved. Working my way up to my favourites, I hoped I'd flip a fuse somewhere that would snap me out of despair. A few songs had an effect. ELO's "Strange Magic" transported me to lying on my back with my sister, doing foot wars, Jeff Lynne's voice hanging on the same breeze that brought the smell of roast potatoes through the house. Dennis Wilson's "Lady," a short soft dream of a song, evoked memories of nice train journeys. The jackpot was Nina Simone's "Sinnerman," played so loud my earphones crackled. I *felt* her. The words barely registered, despite concerning someone going frantic on judgment day, trying to hide from divine justice behind talking rocks and in bleeding, boiling seas: the kind of imagery ripe for a depressed person to roll around in. I played it over and over for days on end because the pace and cacophony took me out of myself. These days I run to it, luxuriating in the freedom of the movement I didn't have then. I always feel a pang as the first few piano notes tinkle.

One song really fucked me up during these bed-based DJ sets, though: "Good Fortune" by PJ Harvey, which contains what might be my favourite lyrics ever. But hearing them at three in the afternoon as children laughed outside my bedroom window made me feel so wrong. Why this song over any other had such an effect I don't know, but it made me agonize: *Would I ever be somewhere like Little Italy again? Would my reflection bounce off someone's face if I found it too terrifying to go outside and be around people?*

This is the mortifying reality of depression. It turns everything inwards. You relate every sound, every vision, back to your suffering and what it means. It's selfish and bratty and desperate. But no one can see into it. Not really.

Only Hanna knew the storm I was carrying around. But even she couldn't *really* know, because no one can see into another person's brain when standing in front of them. The writer Matt Haig explains this kind of dual existence in his memoir of depression and recovery, *Reasons to Stay Alive*, when he writes about first becoming depressed while living in a villa in Ibiza:

> The weirdest thing about a mind is that you can have the most intense things going on in there but no one else can see them.

The world shrugs. Your pupils might dilate. You may sound incoherent. Your skin might shine with sweat. And there was no way anyone seeing me in that villa could have known what I was feeling, no way they could have appreciated the strange hell I was living through, or why death seemed like such a phenomenally good idea.

One morning I found myself trying to work out what might knock me out for a decent amount of time but not require my stomach to be pumped and a compulsory hold on a psychiatric ward. That was the same morning I looked online for the nearest CBT (cognitive behaviour therapy) therapist because I'd read a lot about CBT being "The Thing" for anxiety. I also rang my GP and asked for an emergency appointment. Enough was enough. I knew that I'd probably have to wait for a referral for CBT on the NHS—National Health Service, the wondrous taxpayer-funded universal health care system in Britain that's ready to catch us in its regulation-uniformed arms when we fall; free, no matter who we are or where we're from. But I didn't feel that waiting was an option, so I was pretty sure I'd be going private. Within a week I had seen both a new therapist and a GP. This was big. The GP was fantastic, except she rejected my desire for some medication that would just send me to sleep, which initially made me very upset. Instead, after taking a thorough history of my experience with anxiety, she prescribed a low dose of an SSRI called Citalopram.

On the day I went to see the new therapist, whom I'll call "S," I watched the clock until the time came to walk to his house, about six hundred metres from mine. My brain was a swarm of flies, but I tried to feel hopeful.

"I think this is peaking now, and you can regain control," he said after I'd told my story.

And despite my legs shaking against the chair with the urge to bolt from his house straight back to my bed, I listened. He was dry-humoured, incredibly kind and appeared to have a scientific understanding of why the brain behaves the way it does, which appealed to me instantly. Humour and straight-talking science were obviously the ticket, since that afternoon was my first real turning point in fifteen years.

Why? Because even though this episode of depression had made me believe for a while that I was finished, I had finally sat down and told a professional everything for the first time and felt like the person got it—and me—completely. There was genuine rapport. I cannot give descriptive justice to that relief. On the way home, to "celebrate" I bought myself a pack of those caramel wafer things you can get from the tills in Starbucks and ate four in a row.

I began doing a weekly session with S. With his encouragement, I told my parents about how I'd been feeling, and they were much more sympathetic this time around. I begged to be left alone, though, saying everything was "fine" and that I was "dealing with it," because I didn't want them to see me weak. That was a layer of stigma I wasn't ready to peel off yet. Perhaps I should have let them in, but I still don't think it would have made me feel better then to see them. Dad informed me of the research he, too, had been doing online about anxiety. He would send me quotes he'd read every so often, along with a good biweekly sarcasm bulletin. A particular favourite was a blurry photo taken on his massive red Nokia phone of an old *Viz* magazine Crap Joke depicting a man lying underneath a car in a doctor's room: "Doctor, I've been feeling a bit run down lately" read the caption. I laughed and cried at the stupid fucking joke and the unspoken love my silly old dad was expressing.

Within a month of this intensive approach, along with a commitment to S to do daily relaxation exercises and go on walks farther and farther from my house every day (perhaps the most helpful direction anyone has ever given me), my desperation for what Haig refers to as "an absence of pain" grew less powerful. I laughed, but I wasn't "happy." Not yet. The side effects of the Citalopram were making me feel quite strange, above everything else. "If you have ever believed that a depressive wants to be happy, you are wrong," Haig writes in *Reasons to Stay Alive*, in the chapter that invites us into his head in the moments before he almost jumped off a cliff. The following words are so close to how I felt, it makes my teeth ache:

> They could not care less about the luxury of happiness. They just want to feel an absence of pain. To escape a mind on fire, where thoughts blaze and smoke like old possessions lost to arson. To be normal. Or, as normal is impossible, to be empty. And the only way I could be empty was to stop living. One minus one is zero.

"A mind on fire" is exactly how it feels.

Eventually, I started telling my friends about how I'd been

feeling, because they'd started wondering where I was. As with many of these grand revelations we build up in our heads, the news wasn't a big deal, even though I felt like I was finally telling the truth after living a lie for fifteen years. With truth telling comes all sorts of emotions, and guilt was a big one for me. My friends were glad to know, and when I said, "Please don't refer to me as your mad friend," they said they couldn't pigeonhole me like that if they tried. "Relax," said Nell, one of my closest. "You're about as defined by your anxiety as I am my socks." I doubt she remembers telling me this, and she's said even better stuff since, but what a weight those words lifted.

Another interesting thing about "coming out" as someone with a mental health problem was how many people confessed to having difficulties themselves. I have friends who have been open about their troubles in the past (why this couldn't have made it easier for me is still a mystery), but there were friends and colleagues I'd never have suspected had the same issue who suddenly became more open, and our eyes truly met for the first time. I saw struggles that looked a bit like mine.

People can be magic if you're honest with them. It may be optimism (some will say I'm just naive), but I do believe that deep down most of us are capable of empathy. Some of us might have to work hard at it, but, sociopaths aside, we're all able to identify with others. In being transparent about my problems, I've also learned how crucial it is to remember that while most people *do* want to help, listen and understand, they may rely on your actually asking them to. Not everyone is perceptive enough to pick up on when you're feeling bad, but that doesn't mean the person doesn't care. The world doesn't stop turning when you're open about your mental health, nor should it. Realizing that people usually just want to get on with their lives with you in it, in whatever capacity you can manage, is important. If you need to be listened to for a while, you might have to say so.

"A TOTAL FUCKER"

I EXPERIENCE SOME KIND OF ANXIETY DAILY. HOWEVER, through therapy I've learned to manage my anxiety far better than I have since I became an adult. It does not *define* my days, for the most part. I've also continued to take medication at a low dose. I'd love to be writing this from the perspective of having truly knocked anxiety on the head, but I'm not. There's some redemption, but not total. I still have panic attacks—just fewer than I used to. I have bad days—weeks even, often in relation to my menstrual cycle—when my world gets smaller and I start thinking that I'm just one anxious twenty-four-hour stretch away from losing it again. Images whizz through my mind's eye of me collapsing, going "mad" and being taken to hospital. These images are based on no evidence whatsoever, because none of that has ever happened. But the images haunt me nonetheless.

They call this way of thinking "catastrophizing"—imagining the very worst thing that could happen. A fear of going mad is incredibly common and can be a big trigger for panic attacks. I've become better at stopping my thoughts before they get to this point, and trusting what S calls my "rational mind"—the part of me that knows from research why a total detachment from reality (psychosis) is very unlikely to happen because of being anxious. Anxiety doesn't just "become" bipolar disorder or paranoid schizophrenia. The irony, of course, is that people with those conditions aren't always "mad" and sitting rocking in locked rooms. Like any other mental health problem, if it's well treated, you may never be able to tell someone is living with it. I learned recently that an ex-colleague with a young family was schizophrenic, which made me think just how wrong my preconceptions about the illness were. I enjoy getting reality checks like this.

People with anxiety disorders often talk about their fears of mental precariousness—the sense that they're always just one slip away from falling off the tightrope. "*Am I losing my mind?*" can be a horribly persistent question. For me, the fear brings both a greater inability to be in the moment and less trust of my ability to stay in control. Such lack of trust is another classic feature of anxiety and often means I've started *looking* for things to fear in calmer moments. Which is absurd. Not feeling anxious was such a rarity for so long that it became an untrustworthy state, wrong feeling. In an anxious brain, calmness is often pierced with a voice that says, "Oi! How are you getting away with this?"

A textbook example of this was an evening I spent with a friend at a restaurant opening. There we were, sitting across from each other, eating bits off each other's plates and mucking around. When there was a momentary lull in conversation, I remember thinking: *Huh, I haven't felt anxious yet tonight.*

My friend went to the toilet and my thoughts continued: *I wonder why I don't feel anxious? What's going on? What have I done right? I really hope it doesn't creep up on me, because I'm having a great time and don't want to go home yet and really want to try that dessert.*

Clang. Like magic, I started to spiral. Of course, it's not magic at all. It's a self-fulfilling prophecy. Once I began to question why I'd been feeling not just okay but good, the whole circuit sparked into action:

Ah, here it is. The nausea. The dizziness. The sudden aware-ness of activity far down my colon. Oh, look! Now I can't concentrate on the conversation. What if I faint and fall off my chair in front of this whole restaurant? What if I can't get to the toilet quick enough? What if people can see in my face that I'm struggling? If I can't finish this mouthful of squid, will she notice? Will she ask what's wrong? What will I say if she does? I can't go home yet. What am I going to do? How can I get out of here?

I breathed deeply as imperceptibly as I could. I didn't leave. But once those wheels have started turning, it's like the present moment, my presence, is contaminated.

Trusting anxiety-free moments or days is also something I have gotten better at. I have realized in therapy that I can gently stop my brain searching for something to hang my anxiety on. It takes a lot of practice and doesn't always work, but that it works sometimes is progress.

Around eight months after my second bout of depression, I became senior editor at *VICE*. It was a demanding job at a rapidly expanding media company and required being "on" seven days a week, often twelve hours a day. Even on the weekends I was married to the Gmail app on my phone. When I took the job, I had some doubts about whether I could handle the pace, which sparked another short period of uncomfortable anxiety, but it turns out that not only could I handle the pace, I thrived on it. I was still prone to anxiety, sure, and was aware of having to "catch" it on occasions most days, but during my time at *VICE* I'd say I lived at a "normal" level of dysfunction. By that I mean my dysfunction looked like everyone else's when we sat in the pub and vented on a Thursday evening.

I left *VICE* after a year and a half to write this book, and I'm still doing okay. As I said, I have to manage my anxiety in some way every day, sometimes in very subtle ways and sometimes with more effort. I'd rather not be managing it at all, but considering how I have been, it's a reasonable deal. That noted, I will never be one of those people who say they wouldn't change anything about their lives because their experiences have made them who they are. Not a sodding chance. If at seventeen I could have been like Neo in *The Matrix* and been presented with two pills that would alter the trajectory of my life—blue for the life I've had up to now, red for a life without anxiety and episodes of depression—I'd have swallowed the red pill before you could hand me the glass of water. I wouldn't wish how I've felt at my worst on a serial killer.

If anxiety has "given" me anything, it's an increased awareness of judgment and other people's emotions, as well as a fascination with the exciting, perplexing spectrums of the human mind. I take a perverse sort of comfort in knowing that in many ways we are still scratching the surface of what makes us who we are. My experience has made me acutely aware of how fragile anyone's mental health can be if the circumstances are right—right enough to go wrong.

Where other animals differ from humans is in lacking the
sensation of selfhood. In this they are not altogether unfortunate.
Self-awareness is as much a disability as a power.
—JOHN GRAY, STRAW DOGS

Anxiety is a total fucker. It reminds us, as Scott Stossel, editor of the *Atlantic* magazine, writes in his magnificent memoir on anxiety, *My Age of Anxiety*, that we are "like animals, prisoners of our bodies, which will decline and die and cease to be." Of course, it's our ability to worry about the future, as well as recall and get stuck in the past, that makes us different from any other animal. The biggest threat of all to a person isn't a snarling beast galloping towards them out of the gloaming— it's what lies in the gloaming of their mind. The stuff sat at the back of the cupboards, sporing memories. And because anxiety is such a bodily experience when it strikes, we can easily forget who we are—forget our sense of self.

Quite early on, S told me something that made me feel like I'd been shot in the face. He said that the only real way of living with anxiety is to stop hoping for a "cure"—the very thing I'd always been searching for, asking the sky for and praying for. S knew this truth, he said, because it came as an epiphany after thirty years of anxiety and depression. It was the reason he'd trained as a therapist, to turn his suffering into something helpful. Essentially, his thesis was that I'd have to accept that anxiety is *part*—not all—of who I am, and I'd have to realize I could live a full, highly functioning, love-filled life *with* it, rather than be in a constant fight to get rid of it alto- gether. "Coming to an accommodation with it" was a well- used phrase. He also added that understanding this had been the turning point for most of his clients with anxiety, which eventually started to make sense.

I have worked very hard (conducting an intensive analysis of the way you think is hard; it's *work*) to reach a point where I am approaching acceptance, and I am doing okay a lot of the time. In fact, if you met me, I'd put serious money on you not having the faintest idea that I've struggled with anxiety so much. Unless we met in the week before my period.

I have found that the only way to lower my general levels of anxiety is to accept that anxious thoughts *will* come in and that I can't stop them coming in, because they're coming from a part of my brain so deep it's beyond my conscious reach. What I can practise is controlling my *reactions*. Saying to myself, *I CAN'T LIVE LIKE THIS ANYMORE* every single time a bad thought comes into my head only amplifies the anxiety. Doing that is what got me into this dreadful mess. Instead, I know that addressing the deep part of me that is trying to protect me when I imagine myself having a panic attack in the pub—"Oh, you again, nice to see you, thanks for your input"—is much better. It allows me to identify the thought for exactly what it is: a thought.

I *can* choose what to do with a thought. Most of the time.

And yet—*and yet*—the idea that I can one day have total acceptance of my anxiety remains an exotic island, which will take a series of long-distance flights to get anywhere near. I know that I've still got a lot more accepting to do, and that part of the journey for me is about attempting to understand anxiety itself: How did I get as bad as I did and how could I have stopped it getting so bad? How much have genetics contributed? Should there have been warning signs when I was a child? Why do some people develop anxiety disorders and others don't, particularly in relation to trauma? Were my bad experiences with therapy a reflection of people's wider experiences? How is it possible that anxiety is both the most pervasive mental health issue in the world and perhaps the most misunderstood? Where does our stigma—internal and external—about mental health problems come from? How can we change it? Why was I so afraid of telling people? Why have the treatments for anxiety, particularly medications, remained the same for so long? When will they evolve?

Maybe in tunnelling deeper, my acceptance will grow. What follows is the result of the dig.

PART II

WHAT IS ANXIETY?

A PRICE TAG ON FREEDOM

Anxiety is the dizziness of freedom.
—Søren Kierkegaard, *The Concept of Anxiety*

Anxiety itself is not a mental illness. Let's make that clear.

As part of our hardwiring as human beings, and what it means to be conscious, anxiety is a law of human nature. Natural selection gave us minds, and with them, we were released from the shackles of biological determinism. But the power of the mind is a whole new set of chains, because there's always something to be anxious about. We worry because that's what we've evolved to do.

Jean-Paul Sartre famously wrote that *"l'existence précède l'essence,"* existence precedes essence, and believed that the root of anxiety was the cheery-as-hell awareness that we are all essentially alone and have no defined purpose unlike, say, a stapler. Let's consider the stapler. It is made to fire out thin bits of metal to hold pieces of paper together. That is its *essence*—its whole point of existing. Human beings don't have that luxury. We just find ourselves here, existing, and have to wake up every day not knowing why. For some people, that thought is too much to bear. I'm not religious, but I can certainly imagine the comfort of believing in something bigger.

In fact, when I was depressed, I often thought about going to the church at the end of my road and sitting quietly among the wood and echoes. I thought about talking to a priest. Who knows what either of us would have said, but there were moments when I could imagine myself feeling cradled, briefly, by someone else's faith. To be told, when I felt most rudderless and alone, that there were plans or coordinates written for me. Because we *are* alone, all of us. Bone, plasma, heart, soul and brain—big clever brain—alone. Our animal natures don't easily find comfort in the demands of today's world.

ANXIETY ISN'T *just* the dizziness of freedom, which the great Danish philosopher Søren Kierkegaard said it was in 1844. It's our freedom's price tag. No other animals on earth can contemplate their existence, future and the passing of time the way we do. I often hold my dog Pamela's face, gaze into her teddy bear eyes and ask her if she knows she's a dog. "Do you?" I whisper, as she cocks her head.

She doesn't. She doesn't know she's a dog. She's hardwired with instinct and responds to emotion. But when I first got her, I worried all the time about her being bored. I asked the vet about it when she went in for her second lot of vaccinations.

"One thing you must realize is that dogs can't tell the time," she said, giving Pam some liver treats. She'd said this before.

"How can that be?"

"They don't know if five minutes or five hours have passed. Their brains aren't advanced enough for existential crises."

"Okay."

"Okay?"

"Sure, but what about when she just sits there and stares into the middle distance for ages? What is she *thinking*?"

"Please don't worry," the vet said, ushering me into the waiting room.

That the human condition has anxiety right at its core also suggests that our mental lives are marked by a conflict deep in our psyche. Freud, of course, believed that anxiety was a symptom of repressed impulses—boys wanting to sleep with their mums, girls envying their brothers' penises, that sort of thing. He believed that in order not to be anxious, we must delve into our subconscious in psychoanalysis and allow what we say—on purpose or by accident (the famous "slip")—to be interpreted as symbols for buried desires and feelings. Only then would we be able to stop them trying to pierce our consciousness. But even the great man himself wondered whether that was truly possible.

"There is no question that the problem of anxiety is a nodal point at which the most various and important questions converge," he said during his classic introductory lectures on psychoanalysis between 1915 and 1917, "a riddle whose solution would be bound to throw a flood of light on our whole mental existence."

A riddle indeed.

When you consider that almost every single person alive knows what being anxious feels like—even the Dalai Lama— the universal experience of anxiety makes Sartre's gloomy existentialism seem on the money. As in fact His Holiness says under the "Countering Stress and Depression" section on his website: "At a fundamental level, as human beings, we are all the same; each one of us aspires to happiness and each one of us does not wish to suffer."

No one really wants to feel fear or pain, unless orgasms depend on it in a consensual setting. We don't want to feel uncomfortable or unsafe in our own skin, and being anxious is always an apprehension of some kind of pain—be it physical or emotional. Something as simple as embarrassment is an emotional pain, even if it's momentary. We don't just think it—we *feel* it. We *feel* disappointment. We *feel* uncertainty or failure. A whole world of fear surrounds future-oriented questions like "What if?" and every single one of us experiences different levels of anxiety relating to future situations: speaking publicly, a job interview, an awkward first kiss, jumping off a rock face into the sea on holiday, a meeting with the bank manager. A whole weekend with your mother-in-law and her knack for inviting you to examine your entire life with a throwaway comment in the kitchen.

Plenty of things can make us feel threatened and wake up our old friend, the fight-or-flight response. In response to stress, the adrenal glands pump the hormones epinephrine (adrenalin) and cortisol into the bloodstream, causing the body to click into a state of high arousal. We tense up. Our muscles constrict. We sweat, shake and find our hearts are pounding. Our mouths go dry. We have trouble breathing. We might feel very sick, dizzy and like something interesting is going to happen in our trousers. But what paleolithic cavemen needed when they saw a bear approaching their cave is not what a modern person needs to attend a job interview. Without the release of quick action—running away, or charging the bear to fight it off—the hyperactivation in the body becomes an anxiety attack. Stage fright is often called "self-poisoning by adrenalin" and that's basically what it is. The fight-or-flight response serves a tremendous evolutionary function, but in our modern world it overserves us constantly. We don't need it to be as sensitive as it is. We are no longer on the savannah looking at lions in the distance, thinking: *Eat lunch or be lunch.*

In his new book *Anxious: The Modern Mind in the Age of Anxiety*, the pioneering neuroscientist Joseph LeDoux—a man who has been at the forefront of research into anxiety for decades—writes about the individual experience of anxiety. All human brains are similar in overall structure and function, he notes, but "are wired differently in subtle, microscopic ways that make us individuals." These differences come from both the combination of genes passed from our parents and from our experiences as we move through life. "Nature and nurture," he says, "are partners in shaping who we are, and that partnership is played out in each of our brains."

An important aside: if people tell you they *never* experience anxiety, they're either (a) lying or (b) sociopaths. Really. In the latest version of the American Psychiatric Association's *Diagnostic and Statistical Manual of Mental Disorders* (DSM-5), antisocial personality disorder with psychopathic features is characterized by "a lack of anxiety or fear and by a bold interpersonal style that may mask maladaptive behaviours (e.g., fraudulence)." Something to bear in mind.

Anxiety isn't always negative, either. The fight-or-flight response might be a bit simplistic, but *some* anxiety can be helpful—essential, even. It prepares the body to *do* something, to act.

Let's think about someone like Andy Murray, a very successful tennis player who, as far as we know, doesn't have an anxiety disorder. Murray has, however, talked openly in the past about his pre-match and on-court nerves—a prerequisite, you imagine, of playing sport at his level. Those nerves—a form of stage fright—may manifest themselves in ways we don't see on our television screens. Before taking to the court, Murray may pace, the weight of expectation and Judy Murray's impaled-owl stare heavy in his chest like a dumbbell. His heart may race a little, meaning he must take bigger breaths. He may mutter in that way he does, running through potential scenarios in his mind and applying the tools he's learned in his coaching to tone down the physical discomfort those thoughts bring. And then he'll be ready, his body flooded with cortisol, the stress hormone designed to enhance our speed, reflexes, heart rate and circulation so we can run—to be, quite literally, on our toes. This surge in adrenalin, if managed well, will enhance his performance.

Stage fright isn't a commonly-spoken-about anxiety among performers, maybe because they think doing so is bad luck. But we do sometimes hear about the bad cases. As Adele told British *Vogue* in an interview, "I puke quite a lot before going onstage, though never actually on the stage." Nevertheless, she appears, blazing. Smiling. "I shit myself before everything," Adele continued. "But the bigger the freak-out, the more I enjoy the show!"

Adele seems able to transcend her anxiety by the time she gets onstage, knowing somewhere that the retching will give way to excitement. Others can't get past the nerves, though. There is a big intermediate group of people whose careers haven't been finished by anxiety but *have* been changed by it. Daniel Day-Lewis famously fled a London theatre stage midway through a performance of *Hamlet* in 1989 and has only played film roles since. The anxiety of such intimate performance with no margin for error became too much. Barbra Streisand repeatedly forgot her lyrics one night during a performance in front of more than a hundred thousand people in Central Park in 1967. The night frayed her nerves so much she didn't perform live for twenty-seven years afterwards unless it was for charity.

We can also think of smaller arenas than the ones these stars play in. Operating theatres, say. Surgeons about to perform complex operations have to manage nerves differently than musicians do, because surgeons are actually responsible for lives—not just heightening lives through giving pleasurable performances. Adrenalin must feed precise concentration.

A more day-to-day performance most of us can relate to is the job interview. Experiencing at least *some* degree of anxiety before an interview is very common. Any interview I've had has been preceded by at least two or three trips to the toilet. I have a friend who, on her way to a big interview at Vogue House, got herself into such a tizzy over her lack of preparation that she ended up downing a bottle of sparkling water from the Pret a Manger next door to try to settle her "dicky tum." Of course it did nothing of the sort. Good thing she was early, because she had to spend twenty minutes before the interview sitting on a bench in Hanover Square, forcing out a series of rattling, baritone burps that probably wouldn't have endeared her to the editor of a glossy fashion magazine.

Most of these examples are what would be called "appropriate responses": reasonable reactions to situations that are in some way threatening. Usually, once the feared situation has begun or been resolved, the chemicals that were causing the anxiety are shut off. The person feels safe and the urge to flee passes.

But not always.

APPROPRIATE RESPONSES

T HE TERM "APPROPRIATE RESPONSE" IS KEY WHEN WE talk about anxiety, because it's only when our experiences of anxiety become *disproportionate* to the level of perceived threat that we can start talking about disorders. When symptoms of anxiety begin to disrupt our day-to-day functioning, we use the word—one that makes me squirm and think of glinting surgical equipment—"clinical."

"Appropriate" anxieties might include those arising from having to pay bills or to look for a job; embarrassment or self-consciousness in an awkward situation; butterflies or sweating before a big test, business presentation, stage performance or other significant event; fear of an actual dangerous object or situation; making sure that you are healthy; anxiety, sadness or difficulty sleeping immediately after a traumatic event.

Disordered, or "inappropriate," anxieties may mean constant and unsubstantiated worry that causes significant distress and interferes with daily life; avoiding social situations for fear of being judged or humiliated; seemingly out-of-the-blue panic attacks and the preoccupation with the fear of having another one; irrational worry about, and avoidance of, something or somewhere that poses little threat of harm; performing uncontrollable repetitive actions such as excessive checking or arranging; recurring nightmares, flashbacks or flash-forward relating to a traumatic event that occurred months or years earlier.

Diagnosing an anxiety disorder largely depends on a key word: "functioning." There's no blood work or finger-stick test that will give you a positive or negative result for having an anxiety disorder. Not yet, anyway. You might feel like someone has stuffed a pile of raw potatoes into your chest cavity when you wake up in the morning, but it ain't going to show up on any X-ray.

Generally, if because of anxiety you are unable to function in the way you want to or need to in your life, it is considered disordered.

A child who is not functioning well might exhibit extreme distress about going to school or engaging in any kind of social activity but not yet have the cognitive maturity to explain the feeling the way an adult can. A child's anxiety is not as easy to mask as an adult's, and although some older children can become more adept at hiding their thoughts and feelings, the presentation is usually much more obvious. For adults, it can be very different. Yes, someone with severe anxiety may end up taking a lot of sick days, be socially reclusive or avoid travelling, but a disorder can be raging in ways that might not be known to anyone except the sufferer. I am proof of that. People who don't like touching the hand rail on the Tube escalators because they're aware of the germs hanging out there but who carry on normally with their day afterwards, probably aren't disordered. However, people who won't touch the handrail, repeatedly sanitize their hands after exiting the station and can't bring themselves to touch any food for hours afterwards in case someone's poo bacteria have multiplied on the pads of their fingers may well be.

COMPUTERS IN SKIN SUITS

A NXIETY IS THE MOST PREVALENT PSYCHIATRIC problem of our time. It is also one of the biggest puzzles. Decades of research have gone into probing the mysteries of anxiety and we are still in many ways fumbling in the dark. Our findings are largely inconclusive.

Historically speaking, it's taken a hell of a long time to give sufferers across the world any kind of official language or means to be diagnosed and treated accordingly. This is amazing, really, when you consider that anxiety has been written about for thousands of years. Hippocrates, the Greek physician born in 460 BCE, is generally regarded as the founder of medicine as a rational science—the first to untie it from superstition, magic and the supernatural. He is credited with describing a patient with social anxiety for the first time. Robert Burton, in a book he wrote in 1621, *The Anatomy of Melancholy*, includes the following quote attributed to Hippocrates: "He dare not come in company for fear he should be misused, disgraced, overshoot himself in gesture or speech or be sick; he thinks every man observes him."

It was only in 1980 that anxiety disorders were introduced at all into the DSM (*Diagnostic and Statistical Manual of Mental Disorders*), the American Psychiatric Association's classification and diagnostic tool used not just across the US but across the world. In 1980! Only within the past *forty years* has the idea that clinical anxiety might not be solely due to repressed Freudian desires been eclipsed—in the literature, at least. And anxiety disorders only became recognized by the DSM *after* new drugs designed to combat anxiety had been sold into the market. It seems bizarre. As Stossel writes: "In an important sense, the treatment [of anxiety] predated the diagnosis—that is, the discovery of anti-anxiety drugs drove the creation of anxiety as a diagnostic category."

A person who suffers from anxiety might be rightfully asking what use there is in knowing all this background, but I think this is one of those rare situations where a lack of clarity is so great that it's actually helpful to know the confusion is universal. That confusion is woven into the very tapestry of modern existence. But we *still* don't have definitive knowledge of whether anxiety is a medical illness or some kind of glitch in our philosophical matrix. *Is* it genetic? *Are* we born worried? Am I, an anxious adult, *really* still reacting to a trauma that happened when I was young? Is my anxiety in part just a (mal) function of how stressful modern life is?

As I said, there are no clear answers to any of these questions. The best we can say is that anxiety is generally thought to stem from a combination of genetics, personality or psychological traits and life experiences.

ANXIETY IS EXPERIENCED on an emotional level and is scientifically measurable on a chemical one. It's psychological as much as it is sociological. Dr. Mark Salter, a consultant psychiatrist who works in acute mental health care in the NHS across East London, told me over a pint one very hot evening that anxiety is "a problem of both our hardware and our software." I love this analogy.

"If we think of ourselves as computers in skin suits," he said, "there are two significant layers to our functioning. There's the complex, hidden logic boards and minute engineering in the hard drive that is the core of the machine's functioning. And then, on top of that, there's the software that you can add or subtract from the same machine."

GENETICS VS. LIFE EXPERIENCE

What we *do* know for sure about anxiety is that there are certain chemicals involved. Though of course, we don't know exactly how. Research has shown that different neurotransmitters—dopamine, gamma-aminobutyric acid (GABA), serotonin, norepinephrine and neuropeptide Y—appearing in different quantities in the brain either increase or decrease anxiety. We know that several parts of the brain play key roles in the production of anxiety and fear. The main guy is the amygdala, an almond-shaped structure deep inside our brain's temporal lobe, which is believed to be a communications hub—a tiny switchboard—between parts of the brain that deal with incoming sensory signals and parts that interpret those signals.

Thanks to groundbreaking research by LeDoux in the 1980s, we know that the amygdala is where the fight-or-fight reflex "lives." This little thing effectively dials emergency services to alert the rest of the brain that a threat is present, then triggers an anxiety response throughout the body. The amygdala is also thought to hold our emotional memories and as such plays a key role in anxiety disorders. In a paper called "Emotional Memory," LeDoux writes:

> In a situation of danger, processing of threatening environment stimuli leads to activation of the amygdala, which in turn transmits information to networks in the hypothalamus and brainstem. Activity in these areas then leads to increases in brain arousal (due to activation of modulatory systems that lead to the release of neurochemicals such as norepinephrine and acetylcholine throughout the brain) and to the expression of behavioural, autonomic and endocrine responses.

This is how fear is "made" on a molecular level. The "expression" he's talking about is however anxiety manifests in a person. This theory goes on to suggest that a person with an anxiety disorder may have an *overactive* amygdala. My brain certainly feels like it has an overactive almond in it a lot of the time. How it became like that is up for debate, but somewhere along the way this overactivity and repeated arousal of my brain and body have made me, over time, struggle to distinguish what is a "real" threat and what isn't. Millions of people—including me—have ended up responding to our own thoughts as if they're tigers. Fearing fear itself.

Some of the major figures who have shaped our understanding of anxiety knew nothing of molecular biology. Kierkegaard, author of the groundbreaking *The Concept of Anxiety* in 1844, is generally regarded as the world's first existential philosopher, but neither he nor Freud could see inside brains the way we can now. However, both men were, in the early and later 1800s respectively, pioneers in their interest and commitment to understanding anxiety. As Stossel points out in *My Age of Anxiety*, until 1950, when the psychoanalyst Rollo May published *The Meaning of Anxiety*, they were the only people to have ever published any lengthy text about anxiety specifically. Including Sartre.

We've come a really long way in terms of both research and general awareness about anxiety. Compared with the neolithic days of trepanning people who become mentally unwell, we're in a much better position. But without any clear "truth," we have no neat panacea for anxiety. Any kind of gold-standard discovery to make anxious people's lives better might be centuries away, or it might never materialize, because when it comes to the brain, there are areas of understanding as grey as the matter itself, no matter how much we scan and prod it.

The riddle of anxiety even extends to one of the most successful treatment options: cognitive behavioural therapy. Those delivering the therapy are trying as best they can to fit a person's presentation into their general experience, but there's not a singular, guaranteed thing a therapist can do to sweep someone's anxiety away. There can't be, because no one can *really* know what is happening in someone else's brain. This can make anxiety even more frightening for the person experiencing it. It can feel as though we haven't a clue what is happening to us or why, or how the hell we can get out of it. Trusting our treatment options can be difficult.

I'VE ALLUDED TO my own experience with antidepressants already—if you recall, I was treated with them during a particularly distressing period of anxiety after my new GP took a close look at my history and surmised that antidepressants might be the right fit for me. And I'm not alone in having that kind of treatment. Anxiety disorders are often treated with antidepressants. SSRIs (selective serotonin reuptake inhibitors) are commonly prescribed to those who are struggling to function. I will explore medication in more detail later, but it feels right to touch on the subject now because—more riddles—no neuroscientist on earth can give a crystal-clear explanation of how antidepressants work. This murkiness troubled me immensely, especially when they were prescribed to me. For a while, it became an obsession. I know from plowing online forums like Reddit, one of the most revealing cultural specimens of our times, that I am not alone, either. The anxious mind is prone to fixate, and for me the fixation was directed at something that could potentially help *stop* me fixating. (There's a punchline in there somewhere.)

Antidepressants can work well in lowering anxiety levels for millions of people across the world. I am one of those people. But as I've said, no one knows exactly why. Unlike how the blood sugar of an insulin-dependent diabetic can be measured and fine-tuned with medication, there's no test that can show how an SSRI is altering our brain chemistry— despite making so many of us feel better. The website of the Royal College of Psychiatrists says: "We don't know for certain, but we think that antidepressants work by increasing the activity of certain chemicals' work in our brains called neurotransmitters. They pass signals from one brain cell to another.

The chemicals most involved in depression are thought to be serotonin and noradrenaline."

Don't know for *certain*.

We *think* that.

Are *thought* to be.

I want yes and no, for fuck's sake.

Anxiety relies on an overactive imagination, but having one can make the fogginess surrounding one of your major treatment options quite scary. Uncertainty is the enemy, because it says: *You're not in control of this*. If you're on high alert and constantly monitoring your body for the slightest change, the idea of taking pills that might alter your mental or physical state in ways you have no sway over can be challenging. You take an ibuprofen and know that it will help your headache, but you don't take an antidepressant and know, definitively, what it will do. It's like prepping for a gale that might turn into a tornado, or vice versa.

When it was suggested by my GP that I try taking antidepressants again, I fought with the idea like a sibling. Over and over until the battle ended in tears. First time around, at twenty, I was ignorant of any of the theories surrounding antidepressants. Back then I would have eaten a drainpipe full of worms if you'd told me it would make me feel better. I imagine the placebo effect of taking *something* that could help played a part in my recovery. Second time around, in my late twenties, it was a different story. I knew much more by then about mental health, treatments and drugs. Too much.

As my anxiety spiralled out of control, so did my addiction to Google and trying to log each potential reaction I could have. I was depressed, both afraid of and obsessed with what was happening to me, and thought that if I spent enough time on the Internet reading about other people's experiences, I might gain some clarity about my own. The Internet is an incredible source of communication for people in mental distress across the world and has completely changed the landscape for how we talk about mental health generally, but I was "researching" the side effects of antidepressants until I was blue in the face, looking for anything that might assuage my fears. That I'd responded well to antidepressants previously was neither here nor there.

Shame was a problem, too. I'd stirred up cauldrons of it. Just holding the packet of medication in my hand would, I thought, instantly make me a mental health statistic. Not a person, a patient.

I may as well have been walking around with a tin foil hat on. I got into such a state about taking antidepressants that it did feel like I was losing my grip on reality for a bit. No matter how many times I read about SSRIs being at the mild end of the psychiatric drug spectrum and being both generally well tolerated—even by close friends of mine!—and therapeutic, I paid much more heed to conspiracy theories about being a "Big Pharma lemming" (a phrase I read in a *New York Times* piece once).

This all sounds to me now like the musings of a different person, but my brain was blowing up then and the pills had become a symbol, I suppose, for my fear that I'd finally have to accept I was really suffering. That once I'd opened that blister pack there was no going back.

I can't control my anxiety levels without medication, I told myself over and over, as if it actually mattered at that point. *This is what I've become, someone reliant on medication to function normally. False happiness. Chemical safety.*

Walking back from the pharmacy, I tried to remember moments I'd felt the safest: Saturday mornings sitting cross-legged on the living room floor with my sister, eating Frosties and watching *The Raccoons*. Falling asleep at my grandma's house under a crunchy feather duvet while drunken-family discussions seeped through the walls. Playing with the ears of my first dog, Sniff. Stepping off a diving board at Loughton Pool and feeling my dad waiting there in the deep end for my big jump; when he pulled me up through the water, his cheers sounded metallic, like an underwater robot. I felt so far away from being held like that now.

I can't imagine I'm the only person to get worked up over what it means to be taking a psychiatric drug. Not just because of how moralized drugs are left, right and centre, but also because of the sheer number of people around the world who take them. In 2013, the *Guardian* did an investigation into antidepressant consumption in twenty-five countries around the world and found that in every single country studied, consumption had risen since 2000. In July 2015, psychiatrists at King's College London released new statistics that suggested at least one in eleven British adults now take antidepressants. Canadians are among the world's biggest antidepressant users. According to a 2013 study from the OECD (Organisation for Economic Co-operation and Development), 9 percent of the population is taking a type of antidepressant—the third high-est among twenty-three developed countries surveyed. That equates to 86 doses taken daily per 1,000 people. Australia (89 doses per 1,000 people) and Iceland (106 doses per 1,000 people) were the only countries that ranked higher.

I pored over these statistics in my obsessive episodes—of course—but they were of little comfort. It took me four days after getting the prescription to take my first dose of Citalopram and I called the doctor three times to ask if any of her patients had reported bad experiences. She was very patient and reassuring and told me, during the third call, to take it as soon as I hung up and that she was only a phone call away if anything should happen. So I did. Down it went with a glass of milk (I'd read something about making sure to line your stomach), after one last Google of "Citalopram Success Stories" on my phone. Then I wanted to bury myself in the wall.

What the hell is this going to do to me?
What. The. Fuck. Have. I. Done?

I'd spent the previous twenty-four hours reading about side effects such as projectile vomiting, vertigo and brain zaps—all sorts. But after a few hours of feeling nothing post swallow except a creeping, gluey tiredness setting in, I calmed down. As before, I had a short period (about two weeks, I think) of feeling nauseous and exhausted, but nothing truly unbearable. Some people aren't so lucky, though SSRIs like Citalopram are generally pretty well tolerated in the weaning-on period, much more so than other, older, antidepressants like SNRIs (serotonin-norepinephrine reuptake inhibitors or serotonin-noradrenaline reuptake inhibitors). Coming off them can be a slog, but the side effects at the beginning and the end *do* go away. When my brother took an SSRI for a while, he didn't experience a single side effect, and I know quite a few people who have gotten away with just feeling a bit tired.

If I can offer a key piece of advice at this point to anyone who might be reading this and wrestling with the idea of taking medication, it would be this: Do not do what I did if you can possibly help it. Google feels like your friend, but it is also your enemy. I realize that telling an anxious person not to over-think is like shouting "STOP" at a car rolling down a hill with its handbrake off, but I have a lot more perspective now. Trust me: allow yourself ten minutes of Google a day at most. Set a fucking alarm if you have to. The Internet is an incredible echo chamber for sharing our pain and uncertainty, but because of the way bad stories are so often grouped together (and easily found), we can too easily forget that no two people are the same. Flooding your head with other people's experiences of medication is about as useful as a rhubarb shoehorn. You have to accept the reality that how you react biologically will not be influenced by how a lady from Kansas called "sillymommy808" couldn't keep her oatmeal down for a couple of days.

"FLAVOUR"

THE WAY EACH PERSON EXPERIENCES ANXIETY CAN vary enormously. Not only do we each have our own, different, constellation of symptoms but we all have a unique pattern of issues that we develop anxiety about. What is stressful to one person may barely cause another to bat an eye.

Some of the "classic" symptoms of anxiety are a pounding heart; sweating; gastrointestinal upset (nausea, indigestion, diarrhea); dizziness; frequent urination; shortness of breath; tight chest; muscle tensions; headaches; fatigue; insomnia; implacable feelings of dread; trouble concentrating; feeling tense and jumpy; being irritable; feeling restless; feeling detached from your surroundings and that nothing is real, or that you're living between two layers of double glazing; numbness or tingling in the arms and hands; trembling; monitoring your body for signs of illness; feeling like your mind has gone blank; feeling like something terrible is about to happen.

However, for precisely the same reason that anxiety symptoms vary from person to person, the complexity of each individual brain means that this list is far from exhaustive in terms of what you may think or feel when you're anxious.

In 2013, the list of diagnosable anxiety disorders in the updated DSM-5 expanded to a whopping thirty-seven, split into the following categories: anxiety disorders; obsessive-compulsive and related disorders; trauma- and stressor-related disorders; depressive disorders; and somatic symptom and related disorders. While I was leafing through the manual in the medical reading room at the British Library, I diagnosed myself with at least twenty-five disorders. I headed for the canteen at lunchtime in a daze, feeling quite odd as I picked my way through a summer minestrone.

When Jon Ronson was researching his book *The Psychopath Test*, he had a similar encounter with the manual. Ronson actually met Robert Spitzer, the editor under whose charge the DSM's waist expanded most dramatically, and asked him if he thought he might have created a world in which the line between normal human behaviour and psychiatric diagnoses has become dangerously blurred. "I don't know" was Spitzer's response, one as hysterical as it is scary. Because it really is hard to be comfortable with a manual hundreds of pages long that includes nebulous-sounding conditions like "sluggish cognitive tempo disorder" (you might just be a lazy bastard).

The Psychopath Test, therefore, gently encourages us to be suspicious of the psychiatry industry and explore our grasp of the idea of sanity as a movable concept. But if we are talking about diagnosing disorders, the DSM's power dramatically eclipses the reach of Ronson's book.

The expansion of the DSM in 2013 met with a lot of controversy. Professor Peter Kinderman, head of the Institute of Psychology at the University of Liverpool, told the BBC at the time: "[DSM-5] will lower many diagnostic thresholds and increase the number of people in the general population seen as having a mental illness." He said that "normal grief" would now be classed as a major depressive disorder and childhood temper tantrums would be a "symptom of disruptive mood dysregulation disorder." There was also vast criticism of the way DSM-5 classifies conditions based on symptoms. Dr. Thomas Insel, previously the director of the US government's National Institute of Mental Health, in fact said at the time that the DSM had a "lack of validity." He posted a blog saying:

> Unlike our definitions of ischemic heart disease, lymphoma or AIDS, the DSM diagnoses are based on a consensus about clusters of clinical symptoms, not any objective laboratory measure. In the rest of medicine, this would be equivalent to creating diagnostic systems based on the nature of chest pain or the quality of fever.

Anxiety disorders are usually broken down into the following: generalized anxiety disorder (GAD), social anxiety disorder, panic disorder (incorporating agoraphobia), obsessive-compulsive disorder (OCD), specific phobias and post-traumatic stress disorder (PTSD). Of course, there is no "right" presentation for any of them. The experience of living with a particular anxiety disorder will vary from person to person. The rumination and cycles of fear may follow a similar *pattern* across all anxiety conditions, but the subject and content of those thoughts, as well as the physical symptoms they provoke, can differ wildly. When I'm anxious, I obsess over things that wouldn't even enter other people's minds.

The borders between the diagnoses themselves are fuzzy. Most clinically anxious people will likely find that they have symptoms fitting more than one set of diagnostic criteria, and as such, disorders aren't always diagnosed singularly. It's like having your own personal recipe for anxiety: a pinch of something here, a glug of something there, another element finely grated on top.

A diagnosis may read something like "panic disorder with associated agoraphobia, social anxiety and depression." But anxiety disorders also share many of the same symptoms of depression. Everyone I know who has experienced or lived with acute anxiety has also known depression to some degree. We picture anxious people as buzzing flies, hyper and flapping around, and depressed people as tired and apathetic. But depression can be understood as a reaction to a perceived threat as much as anxiety can. Anxiety and depression appear to be two nests of symptoms that in fact stem from the same neurological condition, whatever that condition is, because so many symptoms we associate with depression—anger, issues with sleep, listlessness, suicidal thoughts, loss of libido—also occur with anxiety. Many of the thought patterns are the same and can't be easily slotted under either term. Let's remember, too, that the same SSRI drugs are routinely prescribed for anxiety and depression, and are effective at lessening symptoms of both.

If every person with an anxiety disorder were represented by a marble, no two of those marbles would be identical. It's impossible. Our brains and their individual archaeologies of memory are far too complex to allow any kind of truly mirrored experience. Which is why those seeking therapy for issues with anxiety need to be listened to very carefully, because there's no one-size-fits-all approach. Or at least there shouldn't be.

Dr. Nick Grey, clinical psychologist at the Centre for Anxiety Disorders and Trauma at the South London and Maudsley Hospital, one of the largest mental health trusts in the UK and home to some of the most cutting-edge research into treatments for anxiety, used the word "flavour" to illustrate this idea of individual experience when I went to meet him at the centre.

"Everyone's flavour of anxiety is different," he tells me one afternoon in his airy treatment room. A faint rainbow spreads across his forehead as the window prisms the sunlight. When I talk about my gut upsets, nausea, the urgent need to find a toilet and the immediate visions of throwing up all over myself and everyone around me, he nods, as if he's listening to a familiar speech.

"Lots of people experience panic attacks with cardiovascular and respiratory issues like chest pain, fast heart rate and trouble breathing," he says. "But lots don't. Panic symptoms, which are often so physically alarming an individual may take themselves to Emergency over and over with them before getting psychological treatment, can be so wide-ranging."

"There're a few suspicious stains on the carpet," I say.

"Yes, people have been sick in here a few times when they've been acutely anxious," he replies, drawing a semi-circle with his toe around a stain. "It's crucial that we talk about how variable the experience of every kind of anxiety disorder can be when we're trying to learn and educate others about not just what it's like to live with it but also how to treat it."

"So there's no 'standard' cognitive behavioural therapy approach? Even though it's the type of therapy most people in the UK who present to a GP with anxiety symptoms will find themselves being referred for?"

"What we're trying to do in CBT and in any kind of treatment of anxiety is to try to take the unique presentation that any individual has and see how that might fit with some of the kind of general findings that we have from a whole range of people. We bring into play things we have learned from other people, but have to think about how they can be applied in a slightly different way to the person that we're working with. Different flavours of anxiety have different keys, if you like, to unlocking them."

At this point I think back not only on the crappy experiences I've had with therapy over the years but also on how often people have asked me, puzzled, how I can be so good at dealing with "big stuff" and then find it tricky to leave the house on days I'm feeling really anxious. It's a legitimate question because I have sailed through things like legal battles and hectic print deadlines in offices with only the faintest dapple of sweat on my upper lip. I've interviewed shirty celebrities and not felt my colon flutter. Surprisingly, too, given my history with hospitals, I've dealt with the various surgeries and invasive treatments I've needed on my insides pretty well, for the most part. I find being in hospital unpleasant but can get through the procedures without too much drama, making good use of a knack for sweet-talking anesthetists into explaining everything they're doing and every single drug they're administering.

When I *have* to keep it together because there's simply no other option or other people are depending on me, I often can. I also find it very natural to want to be there emotionally for people in a crisis. It's horrendous to watch someone you love in pain and I feel it acutely, but I'm able to click into a different state when people need support. I'm mentioning all this not to paint myself as The World's Most Brilliant Mate™ but to make a distinction. Because all that strength, resolve and compassion seem miles away on days when I wake up feeling anxious and I get stuck in a bog of fearful thinking and I really need to go Tesco's for cat food because the cats are circling my legs like hairy sharks.

This paradox in my capabilities is difficult to explain. A lack of self-compassion is something that's come up with my therapist a lot. It's been suggested that I prioritize other people's well-being over my own. This may be true. But I also agree with my friend Alice when she says that altruism is impossible. Her theory is that we are unable to help one another as human beings without feeling some benefit ourselves, even if it is just a simple warmth, and she believes that's completely fine and good if someone is genuinely benefiting. Deep down, I know that part of why I'm so ready to help others is that it stops me focusing on myself. Perhaps my "flavour" profile means being more able to contain my anxiety where other people's welfare is concerned, but less so when it comes to my own day-to-day contentment.

See what I mean about anxiety being a riddle?

MORE THAN A (GUT) FEELING

L ET ME TELL YOU ABOUT TOILETS. PUBLIC TOILETS. If, when walking around town, I am struck with a wave of that feeling Freud called "nameless dread," it will rumble through my insides incredibly quickly. Sometimes, I have to locate a toilet. As my psychic bowels start to gurgle, so, too, do my other ones. Sigmund would have *adored* me.

Using various rationalization strategies I've learned in CBT, I've gotten much better at catching that creeping feeling before it reaches the point where I need to rush to a toilet, but it still happens. I don't know which end needs to empty sometimes, either. If my body were a hurricane, its angry eye wall would be travelling midway in these moments, alternately making both my bottom and top halves feel full and livid. That is what causes me to panic: the not knowing. The need to get to a toilet, or at least somewhere out of public sight, before something happens becomes an instant obsession.

In truth, it's incredibly rare that I'll vomit at the apex of a panic attack. In fact, it's only happened *once*, years ago. Much more likely is that I will urgently need to expel whatever is in my large intestine. Sometimes, but not always, once I've done that and taken a bit of time to breathe and collect myself in private, I feel a bit better. Word to the wise: toilets for the disabled are (apart from fancy hotel toilets) the Holy Grail. There is no more comforting thing for an anxious person with an impending bowel issue than being able to close a heavy door on the world and rid the body of matter and anguish with no one hearing or pacing outside, reminding you that life would rather you didn't slow down, thank you very much.

It goes without saying that if a less able person is waiting to use the loo, I will change course. Anyone who says that it's taking liberties to wander into a posh hotel to do a poo, however, can suck a very fat one. Same to anyone who says it's not very nice or it's TMI to be reading about where a woman does bad poos. People struggle with this bathroom need every day, all over the world. Bodies are weird and leaky and stinky, and your embarrassment is your own deal. So, yeah, I don't care if I'm not a Russian oligarch's wife, face-lifted into 2067, grunting at waiting staff instead of deigning to open her mouth and say actual words. If I urgently need to use a toilet and I am near a nice hotel, I will walk through the revolving doors with purpose. I will greet the doorman, quickly scan the reception area so I can make my way to the loos without having to ask, and I will quite literally get my shit done, in my own sweet time, hopefully with one of Chopin's nocturnes tinkling through the speakers. I will wash my hands several times with the posh, woody Penhaligon's soap. I will take many moments to luxuriate in the soft towels. I *will* moisturize my hands. Then I will leave.

The relationship between anxiety and the gut can be debilitating for some. You can end up walking around feeling like a ticking time bomb and develop all manner of safety behaviours relating to being any kind of distance away from a toilet. But it's not just diarrhea that goes hand in hand with anxiety. There is a superhighway between the brain and our entire GI system that holds great sway over us. Adults have around nine metres of bowel in total. The small intestine is a long, narrow tube of about seven metres and looks like Krang, the supervillain from *Teenage Mutant Ninja Turtles*. The large intestine, so called because it's wide in diameter, is about one and a half metres long. That's a lot of organ with the potential to react. Our entire digestive system is sensitive, which means that nausea, retching, gas, stomach ache, bloating, lack of appetite, constipation, diarrhea and vomiting are all symptoms associated with anxiety and many other mental health problems. Gastric disturbances during depressive episodes are widely reported. In comedian Rob Delaney's now infamous blog post about his depression, he writes: "The first thing I did every morning was throw up."

"It's awful, but a sudden urge to evacuate your bowels actually serves an evolutionary function when our fear response is activated," says Dr. Miriam Adebibe, a surgeon of bariatrics (concerned with obesity) at London's Homerton Hospital, who is conducting ongoing research into the relationship between anxiety and the gut. I tell her I've read about the redistribution of blood during acute anxiety but can't understand the mechanics of it having that quick an effect on our bowels. She laughs. "I know. But think about it. If blood is frantically being pumped elsewhere so our reptilian selves can run away from a predator, that means the flow of blood to our guts is disturbed. It affects peristalsis [the wave-like muscle contractions that move food and poo along our digestive tracts], and if the bowel can't operate normally, it wants to empty itself," she explains. "The muscles of the gut are smooth, too, and can become extra-extra-sensitive during the fight-or-flight response, which may also be partly to blame for gastro symptoms being felt with anxiety. Our digestive system contains upwards of a hundred million neurons linking it to the brain, known as something called the 'brain-gut axis.' Many scientists actually refer to the stomach as the 'second brain'—such is the extent to which it communicates with the one inside our skulls."

There have definitely been times when I've felt more controlled by this "second brain" than the other one.

Irritable bowel syndrome (IBS), while not a psychological disorder in itself, is one closely linked with anxiety because of the brain-gut connection. It's thought to affect up to 20 percent of the population. Men and women are both affected, but it's more common in women and can afflict people of any age. Many sufferers can recall times when they've desperately needed the loo but haven't been able to get to one. I know people with IBS who have soiled themselves on public transport. Of course, once this has happened, sufferers can become anxious any time they're not within easy access to a toilet. This creates extra sensitivity in the gut, and lo, a vicious cycle begins.

My insides have never been right since the appendix saga, and while I have had a diagnosis of IBS, I'd say my bowels lean towards "livid" rather than "irritable." They're full of scar tissue and prone to obstruction; consequently, I have needed surgery numerous times.

Despite all this, and because I believe my fears around losing control of my body mostly stem from my teenage hospitalization—a period defined by a loss of control—I have never shat myself in public. I have felt close to it happening but have always managed to figure it out. Somehow. In spite of the overwhelming evidence that I can control myself, the old memories of not being able to—in a hospital bed, unable to move—have filtered into the present. My anxiety is so tied up with bodily function. It is entirely irrational. But irrationality is, as we know, anxiety's kindling.

IBS can make life very restrictive for some. During a flare-up, it can remove the unspoken trust you have in your body and make you constantly monitor your insides for any niggle or clue that they're about to detonate. The monitoring can become obsessive.

"Before I got told I had IBS, I didn't realize that how you feel mentally could affect you so much physically, and vice versa, and that really messed me up," says Jennifer Callahan, twenty-five, who works in music management in London. She has IBS and generalized anxiety disorder. "I started having panic attacks around that time, and before the diagnosis, I honestly felt like I was going crazy. I started getting stomach cramps and would think it was just because I was anxious. Then I'd get more anxious and the cramps would get worse. It was a cycle in my head I couldn't break. Even when I felt absolutely fine, I would start panicking and think I was going to shit myself, and so I just wouldn't leave the house."

She tells me that not long after she started having these attacks in 2008, she began "looking for exits and toilets everywhere" and desperately trying to avoid using public transport. "I could only get on the Tube for a couple of stops at a time, if I got on at all. I missed weeks of college because I literally couldn't get on a train. I'd walk to the train station, the train would come, and I just couldn't move my legs to get on. I would walk home for hours in the middle of the night from wherever I was because I couldn't get on a bus in case something happened."

This lack of trust in one's body is incredibly familiar to me. Like me, Jennifer says her "attacks" happen far less often thanks to some intensive CBT, which helped her recognize her thought patterns and develop strategies to "intervene" when she felt herself starting to panic. She says it wasn't easy to talk about her fear of incontinence and how disabling it was—again, very familiar. I don't think it's easy for anyone to talk about this stuff initially. British people in particular seem to have an inbuilt aversion to discussing their innards—a broad stroke I can't apply to myself, having had to talk about my colon to strangers for the past sixteen years. But having to utter the words "I'm constantly scared of shitting myself" to another person takes a lot. That IBS is as common as it is, and so inextricably linked with anxiety, means a hell of a lot of people out there are walking around with the same fear.

Even after making huge improvements with her CBT treatment, Jennifer says that when her IBS flares up, it's "easy to forget" what she's learned. Travelling isn't impossible the way it used to be but is still hard. She still wrestles with her fear of getting on public transport and can feel a lot of guilt and frustration if she finds herself unable to. This I know well, too. A flare-up of IBS can worsen anxiety and make people like Jennifer and me feel we're back to square one. It speaks to some dark, clever interplay between the bowels and the head that we just can't interrupt.

If you've ever made a "gut decision" or "followed your gut," you were likely getting signals from your enteric nervous system (ENS)—that second brain hidden within your digestive system. Research in this area is beginning to revolutionize our understanding of the links between digestion and mental well-being.

The ENS is two thin layers of more than a hundred million nerve cells lining our GI tract, from esophagus to rectum. It is not capable of imagining the future or triggering tears at a sad memory, but it is not autonomous. "Its main role is controlling digestion, from swallowing to the release of enzymes that break down food to the control of blood flow that helps with nutrient absorption to elimination," explains Dr. Jay Pasricha, director of the John Hopkins Centre for Neurogastroenterology, in an entry titled "The Brain–Gut Connection" on the centre's website. Pasricha, whose research on the ENS has gained international attention, elaborates: "The enteric nervous system doesn't seem capable of thought as we know it, but it communicates back and forth with our big brain—with profound results."

For decades, it was thought that anxiety and depression *contributed* to conditions like IBS, but Pasricha believes that irritation in the GI system may send signals to the central nervous system (CNS), *triggering* mood changes.

The way research has continued to explore the ENS–CNS connection has meant that gastroenterologists are now routinely prescribing SSRI antidepressants and cognitive behavioural therapy as treatments for bowel disorders. It makes sense. If our two brains are "talking" to each other, therapies that help with one may also help with the other. It's not because they think the physical symptoms are all in a patient's head.

Our gut microbes may have a significant connection with our state of mind, too. "Recent evidence indicates that not only is our brain 'aware' of our gut microbes, but these bacteria can influence our perception of the world and alter our behaviour," write Justin and Erica Sonnenburg—both of whom hold a PhD—in *The Good Gut: Taking Control of Your Weight, Your Mood and Your Long-Term Health.* "It is becoming clear that the influence of our [gut] microbiota reaches far beyond the gut to affect an aspect of our biology few would have predicted—our mind."

How it does this appears to have a lot to do with our happiness regulator: serotonin.

"The gut microbiota influences the body's level of the potent neurotransmitter serotonin, which regulates feelings of happiness," the Sonnenburgs continue. "Some of the most prescribed drugs in the US for treating anxiety and depression, like Prozac, Zoloft and Paxil, work by modulating levels of serotonin. And serotonin is likely just one of numerous biochemical messengers dictating our mood and behaviour that the microbiota impacts."

There has been an explosion of interest in the connections between the microbiome and the brain. Most microbiome-based brain research has been done with mice, but there have been a few studies involving humans, as a piece by David Kohn in the *Atlantic* ("When Gut Bacteria Changes Brain Function," June 2015) explored. The article cites significant research by Stephen Collins, a gastroenterology researcher at McMaster University in Hamilton, Ontario. In 2014, Collins "transferred gut bacteria from anxious humans into 'germ-free' mice—animals that had been raised (very carefully) so their guts contained no bacteria at all." Afterwards, the mice behaved "more anxiously."

Kohn's article goes on to cite the well-known study of microbiome by Emeran Mayer, a gastroenterologist based at the University of California, Los Angeles. Mayer worked with twenty-five healthy women for four weeks. Twelve of them ate a cup of widely available yoghurt twice a day. The rest didn't. Many yoghurts are, as we are assured through our TV screens daily, a probiotic, which means the yoghurt contains live bacteria. In this experiment, the yoghurt contained strains of four species: *bifidobacterium, lactococcus, streptococcus* and *lactobacillus*. All the women had their brains scanned before and after their yoghurt consumption to examine their responses to several facial expressions. The results were published in a journal called *Gastroenterology* in 2013 and showed considerable differences among the women. Those who ate the yoghurt had much calmer reactions to the images than those who didn't. The subjects' gut microbes had, it seemed, modified their brain chemistry.

It seems *ridiculous* to think that at some point "eat more yoghurt and you'll feel better" might be something that's said seriously to an anxious or depressed person. Yoghurt! When we think about the complex world of pharmaceuticals and all the talking therapies out there, the fact that some natural yoghurt might also contribute to a happier, steadier mindset feels like something Chris Morris would have written into a *The Day Today* script. But it's not. As scientists learn more about how our microbiomes work within the brain–gut axis, such organisms could in theory be isolated and manipulated to treat mental illness. "These bacteria could eventually be used the way we now use Prozac or Valium," Mayer told the *Atlantic*. These microbes are likely to be subtler than the pharmacology we currently have, which would hopefully mean fewer side effects. "I think these microbes will have a real effect on how we treat these disorders. This is a whole new way to modulate brain function."

Maybe we all should have listened to Gillian McKeith. The shamed TV quack's "beneficial bacteria" monologues seem to have reasonable standing if you ignore the rest of her nonsense. But before the microbiota can be hacked to some therapeutic end for the masses, millions of us will carry on feeling the sting of emotion in our gut. That said, in cognitive behaviour therapy we learn that if we lower our *general* levels of anxiety through daily maintenance with things like exercise, mindfulness, eating and sleeping well, among other things, our physical responses to anxiety will become less intense. We also learn that we can develop strategies and new thought intervention techniques to address our anxiety levels while they're at a three or four out of ten (a bit of a sore stomach) rather than letting them get to a seven, eight or nine (painful cramps, nausea, urgent need to find a toilet, blind panic), when we start to feel very unwell.

But it doesn't *always* work.

My general anxiety levels are—at this writing, at least—the lowest they have been for some time. The urgent, excruciating bowel discomfort I've been talking about happens less. But even with my arsenal of CBT techniques and commitment to keeping myself well, I have runs of bad days when it feels like they all go out the window and I have to re-teach myself. During these times, I can find myself feeling constantly nauseated, bloated, without appetite and generally *no bueno* inside for days. I feel like my skin is a translucent green, my guts full of pond scum. I'm convinced people must be able to see my malaise, that my eyes have gone full Garfield. Pulling back from these "blips," as they're often called, can be hard. Sometimes I feel back at square one, locked in a vicious cycle of physical pain and churning negative thought, each exacerbating the other.

Throughout *My Age of Anxiety* Scott Stossel describes how profound his gastric symptoms are with anxiety. I spoke to him about various things in this book, but beforehand we discussed how much a period of feeling bad (an IBS flare-up, a few days of bad anxiety) can set a person back.

"It's like, how competent and capable can I really be if, at this age, this is what I'm reduced to? Being totally at the mercy of my hyper-reactive physiology that puts me into this horrible state," he says. "If I've gone a long while without having a set-back, it's this feeling of, *god*, I felt like I was doing much better and here I am, thrown back to living in a state of quivering in my boots or my bed."

We both laugh—awkwardly. Because there's not much laughing when you're at the mercy of your physiology. "This is the kind of state that can send you into depression," he says. "So I'm usually very determined to get out of it."

Being at the mercy of our physiology doesn't always mean long stretches of profound mental unhappiness. All of us are in the clutches of our body's needs every day, and ignoring them can make us feel very odd. Hunger is something each of us feels acutely in our bellies and our heads, and is a great example of how much the gut and brain "talk" to each other.

I am an anxious person, so I often find myself struck by strange moods: waves of dread, uneasiness or sadness. But these moods are particularly bad when I'm hungry. "Hangry"—a staggeringly clever portmanteau of hungry and angry—is now defined in the Collins Dictionary as "irritable as a result of feeling hungry." I reckon the Collins people should also include "hangxiety."

The *Guardian*'s Oliver Burkeman did a good "This Column

Will Change Your Life" piece about how quickly a hangry mood can escalate; how you can teeter on the brink of dizzying existential crisis, when in truth what you need is a bloody sandwich:

> I think of myself as generally happy, but every so often I'm struck by a fleeting mood of unhappiness or anxiety. On a really bad day, I may spend hours stuck in angst-ridden maundering, wondering if I need to make major changes in my life. It's usually then that I realize I've forgotten to eat lunch . . . One tuna sandwich later, the mood is gone. And yet, "Am I hungry?" is never my first response to feeling bad: my brain, apparently, would prefer to distress itself with reflections on the ultimate meaninglessness of human existence than to direct my body to a nearby branch of Pret a Manger.

These transient moods have extraordinary power over our state of mind. Being hungry can, as Burkeman points out, condition how you feel about everything. I know people who become absolute shits when they're hungry, and others who become mute, nervous wrecks incapable of either talking or making eye contact. I wrote a piece about all this when I was at *VICE* and it seemed to strike a chord—the brilliant US podcast *The Dinner Party Download* even asked me to do a short show about it.

Susie Orbach, a psychotherapist and author who's been writing about the human appetite for over forty years, concludes that being out of sync with hunger like this is "a very modern phenomenon." But how does hunger so radically alter our moods, turning the most serene people into trembling wrecks? I spoke to Paul Currie, a professor of psychology at Reed College in Portland who has conducted a lot of research in the area. He told me it's largely down to one hormone: ghrelin.

"When we're hungry, there's an increased release of ghrelin from the stomach, which increases our motivation to consume food," he explains. "Elevated levels of ghrelin might also activate the hypothalamic-pituitary-adrenal axis, otherwise known as the stress axis." Ghrelin receptors are also present elsewhere in the body, namely in the spaghetti junction of our metabolism, the hypothalamus. The more this hormone circulates, the more churned up the brain gets.

"Animal studies show that direct ghrelin injections into the hypothalamus increase anxiety-like behaviour, suggesting there's overlapping brain circuits mediating food intake and emotional behaviour," says Currie. Our senses go into overdrive when we're hungry: noises seem louder, lights brighter, smells smellier. It could be why someone in the flat below you blasting a trance remix of Adele's "Hello" on repeat might be more nerve-shredding when you're hungry than when you're not. But while being hungry may not stand up in court as justification for you smashing a hole through your neighbour's ceiling with a broom, it might ease your conscience to know that somewhere, somehow, the cause is chemical—that it kind of isn't your fault.

Courthouses are a good example of hunger's power. In 2011, a paper appearing in the *Proceedings of the National Academy of Sciences* examined one thousand rulings by Israeli judges conducting parole hearings. Over ten months, more lenient verdicts were given in the mornings and immediately after scheduled breaks (for instance, lunch). The authors found that favourable rulings peaked in the morning, then declined over the day from a likelihood of around 65 percent for a positive outcome to nearly zero. After a meal break, probability rose again to around 65 percent. Hunger was proven with empirical regularity to have effect on judgment. The old saying that "Justice is what the judge had for breakfast" clearly has some credence.

Hunger is, along with the need to shit and sleep, a base impulse. It's one of the first experiences of fear and satisfaction we ever encounter as human beings. But while a baby can scream its tiny pink throat raw until a nipple or bottle is put in its mouth, as grown-ups we don't *generally* have the same luxury. We rely on physical prompts: the sad, squelchy sounds of our empty gut wrestling with itself. So when hunger tips over into mental discomfort, is our body trying to get our attention a different way?

"This is exactly what we think might be going on," says Currie. "The increases in arousal [anxiety, for example] elicit the appropriate behavioural response—to satisfy our need for food or energy. The brain circuits mediating intake, motivation, arousal and emotion are overlapping."

Would these overlapping circuits explain why eating can provide such an immediate calming effect after feeling hangry?

"Yes," says Currie. "Once you actually start to eat, ghrelin levels in the brain decline rapidly, reducing the arousal and continued signalling associated with seeking out food."

This information makes the popularity of certain diets and the explosion of the "wellness" trend a bit worrying. Juice fasting—or, as its advocates would have it, "cleansing"—scares the shit out of me. Because eating disturbances like this, in which hanger and some degree of mental upset are pretty much guaranteed, can "compromise our physical, emotional and cognitive function," Currie says.

Fasting is as old as time and still practised, carefully, in certain religions, but the juice boom in the Western world has something sad and complex at its heart. Any doctor will tell you that (a) any weight lost will return with normal eating, and (b) the "cleansing" part of it is bollocks. Our bodies are stuffed with organs whose sole purpose is cleansing.

However, smart, high-functioning people still keep falling for the Gwyneth Paltrow approach to sustenance. Why? "We're in placebo territory," says nutritionist Claudia Louch, who runs the Harley Street Nutrition Clinic. "The human body is the perfect machine. Our liver, kidneys, digestive system and skin remove toxins very effectively. Anyone with a sound understanding of the body will know that it isn't the healthy option people are duped into believing it is."

Does the popularity of this kind of dieting suggest that not only do certain people have an otherworldly resistance to hunger but some actually thrive on hanger? On hanging in a perpetual state of anxiety? Significantly, juice cleanses are more popular with women, a fact that psychotherapist and social critic Susie Orbach suggests is a symptom of our addiction to "the idea of a quick fix" and could be due to "our constant bombardment with weight consciousness."

Nearly forty years after breaking ground with her book *Fat Is a Feminist Issue*, which urged women to return to eating within the rhythm of their appetites, Orbach believes that "appetite, and therefore satisfaction, is tainted with fear." So it seems that feeling hangry, for some people, means feeling in control—of desire, impulses and, most of all, weight. Being thin. Occupying a small space.

If we're constantly stuck in a cycle of dieting, it's a given that we'll be more hungry. Lisa Sasson, a professor in New York University's Department of Nutrition and Food Studies, told the *New York Times* that weight consciousness may explain why women report "hunger-related moodiness" or anxiety more often than men do. "Women sometimes feel that if they are satiated—if their bellies bulge the tiniest bit beyond flatness—then they may have overeaten."

This makes me want to drown my sorrow in a pint of chip fat, but there must be an alternative answer. Obviously, it's impossible to shut out all the noise surrounding weight loss and food, but Orbach says we should "really dare to learn to eat with our hunger." It takes practice, she says, "but being aware of our different levels of fullness is a start." For example, on one day we might be hungrier than the next, and that's fine. "Follow the hunger urge like you would the urge to pee."

Sometimes hanger is unavoidable. We can't always eat exactly when we need to. But pre-empting where and when we might get hungry is probably a good thing, because unlike hunger—which is a good thing—hanger is intolerable. I generally try to be prepared with a bag of cashews in my bag at all times. There's always a fine nut sand at the bottom of my rucksack. In desperate moments, I have scooped up this sand and eaten it from my palm like a pony.

DIAGNOSIS: SHAME

NXIETY PLAYS A ROLE IN MOST PSYCHIATRIC
conditions. I had never really thought about this, but
Dr. Mark Salter, a consultant psychiatrist at Homerton University
Hospital, told me that fear and anxiety are major symptoms of
paranoid schizophrenia, bipolar disorder, borderline personality
disorder, dissociative disorder, addiction and eating disorders.
Feeling very anxious and unable to control all the physical symptoms that come with it can, he said, be the most frightening part
of a wide spectrum of unpleasantness.

"Symptoms of anxiety are often what prompts people to
seek help for their mental health, whatever their condition is,"
he explains. "Schizophrenia doesn't necessarily trump anxiety,
in the sense that an awful lot of people with it are stable, functioning and no longer hallucinating."

Learning this amplified for me just how devastating anxiety
can be, above or alongside all the other manifestations of mental distress. Severe anxiety isn't just "feeling a bit nervous"—it's
feeling so ravaged you have no idea what to do with yourself.
However, living with this kind of anxiety does not mean you
are going to suddenly "become" schizophrenic, for example. I
have had those thoughts. Believe me. I've thought: *I'm one step
away from losing grip on reality.* But this fear of "true" madness
is a common symptom of anxiety. In reality it cannot happen.

Anxiety cannot turn into schizophrenia or bipolar disorder. I have now been told this by enough experts that I believe it.

Being diagnosed with an anxiety disorder after living in such torment can be a great turning point for many people—particularly those who have lived with it for a long time. To sit in front of someone who can say, "You're not dying or losing your mind. I think you have X, millions of others have X and this is how we can treat X so you will feel a lot better going forward" can be a huge relief. Giving the beast a name helps you tame it.

A young ex-colleague of mine confided in me once that she'd been having "intrusive thoughts"—a clinical term for involuntary negative and menacing thoughts that creep into our minds, often to the point that they become an obsession—for years. Over iChat, she said she thought that I might understand (she'd recently published a piece about anxiety, which I'd advised her on) and that she felt she needed some guidance because the intrusive thoughts had become a lot worse and she was struggling to get through the day at work. I'd noticed she'd been looking quite tired. She told me that the thoughts were highly graphic and involved the self-mutilation of a very delicate area. She'd had intrusive thoughts before, she said, but nothing like this, and she'd never sought help. The new focus of her obsessive thinking had made her feel, in her own words, "fucking insane" and was making her want to drink heavily to "knock herself out" so she "couldn't think."

"What is wrong with me?" she typed.

I told her to go to her GP the next morning and she did. She didn't come to work but texted me to say that he'd said it sounded like obsessive-compulsive disorder. A week or so later, after her first cognitive behavioural therapy appointment (the waiting list on the NHS was too long so she borrowed some money and saw someone privately), she said with a visible lightness on her face that OCD had never once entered her mind as a possible cause but made perfect sense when it was explained.

"I literally thought OCD was about flicking light switches," she said. "But it can mean having intrusive thoughts of any kind." Having a diagnosis made her feel "so much more human," she tells me now, "because I'd started to feel totally out of control and was having all these weird physical things happen to me, like vertigo and feeling sick all the time. It was a catalyst for me to take action not just over my own treatment and well-being but also to expand my knowledge of this thing that had made me feel bewildered and angry for a long time."

I haven't rejected the idea of a diagnosis per se, but haven't found the terms suggested at various points by both my GP and S—"panic disorder," "generalized anxiety disorder," "post-traumatic stress disorder" and "emetophobia" (fear of vomiting)—helpful in the way others might.

I have long resisted labels of any kind. It's not so much the case that I now know more, but in the past I have found terms like "disorder" and even "mental health problem" hard to stomach. How could they apply to *me*—the person who looks and ostensibly acts completely normal on the outside? My irrational brain has told me, even though I know that I am far, far more than An Anxious Person, that those words are certificates of madness: Bonkers Eleanor Morgan with her anxiety!

I *know* this is absurd. I have *never* thought this about anyone who has gone through something similar and never, ever would. And yet ... oh, and yet. When it comes to myself, every-thing changes.

I've been told by experts that when the brain's arbitrarily defined limit of anxiety has been reached, its natural defence mechanism can often be depression, and yet, despite experien-cing a period of depression in the past five years that felt like free fall, I still secretly can't believe the word applies to me. Why is that? It goes against every single one of my own beliefs and all the knowledge I have about mental distress, but I still, some-times, feel quietly ashamed of how my mind falters. Sometimes the anxiety rabbit hole feels never ending, and enduring shame or self-hatred about being anxious or depressed adds another level of frustration and sadness, which makes it all so much worse. Reaching the point of being ashamed of your own shame is a meta shit sandwich.

The inability to shake off ideas of what I should and shouldn't be is, I know now, part of what has taken me so long to really dive into my anxiety and work out how to make the next chapter of my life better. Among other things, shame held me back from truly living. It made me divide the world into two: Me and Everyone Else. At my most anxious peaks, I've thought: *I'm not like every else. Down here chewing the carpet, I've slipped off the Everyone Else axis.* Today, though, I'm able to ask: What exactly does "everyone else" mean? Mental distress doesn't just affect the "other"—the statistics unequivocally tell us otherwise.

Shame is a very real, very uncomfortable thing to live with, but it's *entirely* at odds with the reality of modern existence. *Everyone's* mental health exists on a spectrum. When we break it down, there's no "everyone else" to compare ourselves with when we become mentally unwell, because we all know someone who has been there, if not us ourselves. Any mental health problem can easily fray our sense of self, but this idea that we are somehow an anomaly or a smudge on the clean canvas of humanity is absurd and wrong. I am wrong about my own faltering and I am working hard on being able to realize this more easily. The more I talk to people, the more I see that it all stems from one rotten seed: stigma.

Stigma (which I'll explore in greater depth later) prevents the right care from reaching so many people who need it; often with fatal consequences. Millions of people across the world live secretly with anxiety disorders because they're either too frightened, awkward or ashamed to seek help. They also may not actually realize that for years they've been what a professional would call disordered.

As Dr. Grey tells me, "People with serious anxiety issues can effectively disappear. They can live inside their houses, eating, drinking, sleeping, communicating and functioning on a micro level. They come to believe that's how their life has become and will stay."

Dr. Bruce Clark, who is both an OCD specialist and consultant child and adolescent psychiatrist at Maudsley Hospital, tells me that it can often take "between six to seven years" of someone living in misery with anxiety before the person comes forward and says, "I can't live like this anymore—please help me."

In *Anxiety*, LeDoux argues that having a better understanding of the nature of these conditions would be "extremely helpful to just about everyone," particularly given how many people out there are "impaired by uncontrollable fear or anxiety." Even though the symptoms of anxiety permeate just about every corner of our society, so many people are left lacking the clinical language they need to describe the anxiety itself.

I agree with this emphatically. I wish so much that, as a kid, I'd had *some* understanding of mental distress beyond the term "nervous breakdown" whispered around school about teachers and friends' parents. At seventeen, if I'd had even a whiff of knowledge that what I was experiencing in that toilet was a panic attack, or had an idea of how to recognize one, I might never have gotten as bad as I did.

Of course, we can parrot the "just let kids be bloody kids!" argument ad infinitum, endlessly wringing our hands over what children should or should not be taught in a classroom, but is that good enough? It was so exciting when forward-thinking political parties were lobbying for the introduction of compulsory same-sex sex education in schools around the last general election—even among the deafening brays of the "don't put ideas into their heads" brigade—because the proposal spoke to a genuine desire to give kids as broad an introduction to, you know, *life*, as possible. I am, of course, not aligning homosexuality with mental illness (the DSM-II did until 1974, though—only some forty years ago!), because we are not in the twelfth century. If anyone in 2015 had told me sincerely that my queerness was a pathology, I would have pulled my bottom lip up over my head and swallowed myself.

My point is that, both from my own experience and the experiences of many others, it seems very clear that an overhaul of PSHE (personal, social, health and economic education) in schools, which incorporates age-specific education about mental illness, is an absolute imperative for adults being healthy and aware. Why? Because how can we *begin* to talk about parity between physical and mental health when government statistics tell us that *at least* one in four people in Britain have a mental health issue during a year? Without education, we flounder.

Knowledge isn't just important for the person living with anxiety, either. It's crucial for those trying to live with it by proxy: partners, parents, siblings, friends, colleagues and bosses. Shit, even those who consider themselves pretty stable will suffer bouts of excessive worry and fear sometimes and have no words for describing them other than "I feel like I'm losing the plot"—a thought that can bulldoze a tunnel of uncertainty and dread in even the strongest of minds.

Anxiety is the most common mental health issue *in the world*. If it's not affecting you, it's likely affecting someone you know. So let's not look the other way; let's look into the different anxiety disorders and what the experience of them might be like. We hear the terms "OCD" and "panic attack" all the time, but what is their human reality? Trivializing the experience by asking someone struggling with anxiety, "What have you got to be anxious about?" will break that person's heart. If this book helps even one person from having to hear that question, I'd be, to borrow from my three-year-old neighbour's arsenal of joyful phrasing, "over the top of the moon."

GIVING THE BEAST A NAME

THERE ARE SIX MAJOR TYPES OF ANXIETY DISORDERS, each with its own symptom profile. In this chapter I explore what these disorders "look" like and how they often present themselves. The obvious caveat, it bears repeating, is that no one person's experience of anxiety is identical to another's. Even with the same diagnosis, there will be differences.

Generalized anxiety disorder (GAD) is what most people have in mind when they use the term "anxiety," and is thought to be the most common type of anxiety disorder, so it seems reasonable to start with it. GAD involves excessive, unrealistic worry and avoidance behaviours and thoughts. Sufferers will likely feel unable to stop them or attribute them to a specific cause. Common symptoms are fatigue and low energy levels, tense muscles (especially in the neck and back, and across the shoulders), bad guts (exacerbation of conditions like IBS is incredibly common—anxiety is the worst shit stirrer), constant restlessness, irritation, trouble concentrating on tasks or being present at social events and feeling detached or "not quite there."

Intrusive thoughts are a big part of GAD and all anxiety disorders. Let me tell you about intrusive thoughts. They're like having schools of barracuda darting through your cerebrum, nibbling on your sanity. When anxiety dominates your life, you can have intrusive thoughts about all kinds of things. At the sharp end, they may be about going mad, becoming gravely ill (health anxiety is very common) or even dying. Lena Dunham, all-round Good Thing and creator of the series *Girls*, wrote a piece called "Difficult Girl: Growing Up, with Help" for the *New Yorker* magazine, which describes the formative stages of her anxiety disorder. She really struggled as a kid and has spoken openly in interviews and on her social media accounts about how she still struggles with anxiety now. In the *New Yorker* piece she paints a brilliant, sad picture of how high levels of anxiety can make us constantly monitor our health and potential contaminations.

"An assistant teacher comes to school with a cold sore. I am convinced he's infected with MRSA, a skin-eating staph infection. I wait for my own flesh to erode," she writes. "In school, we are learning about Hiroshima, so I read *Sadako and the Thousand Paper Cranes*, and I know instantly that I have leukemia. A symptom of leukemia is dizziness, and I have that when I sit up too fast or spin around in circles. So I quietly prepare to die in the next year or so, depending on how fast the disease progresses."

An anxious mind overestimates the degree of danger to itself or others. It thinks of all the worst possible things that could happen. As we've seen, this is called "catastrophizing"— worrying about how to either solve non-existent problems or furiously making plans to address problems that don't arise (worrying that a spell of dizziness is leukemia, for example). In anxiety, we fear that we'll suffer. But we're already suffering what we fear.

I am an old man and have known a great many troubles,
but most of them never happened.
—MARK TWAIN

Catastrophizing isn't always about ourselves. Loved ones are often subjects, too. Journalist, author and filmmaker Jon Ronson has spoken openly about his anxiety and propensity to catastrophize about his family. He tells me about it over Skype from his Manhattan apartment:

"I think I'm definitely more anxious than most people on an every-minute-of-the-day level, but not in a way that makes it impossible for me to function generally. I wouldn't say I have GAD necessarily, but there are two things that stop me from being able to function: not being able to get my son, Joel, on the phone; or making a mistake in my work. I cannot function until those things resolve."

Although he's never had a formal diagnosis, he says the term "disorder" fits with his experiences because he "goes into complete panic" and really is "totally unable to function" when his anxiety is triggered.

"I'll give you an example," he says. "I remember this story really well, because it was particularly extreme. It was when Joel had just been born and I was in Washington, D.C., writing my first book and trying to investigate the Bilderberg Group [a private conference of political elite]. I was in a hotel room and I always had a deal with my wife, because she knows how panicky I get if I can't reach her on the phone. She would always call at 8:30 p.m. London time to tell me everything was okay or leave a message, but she hadn't. I completely lost it. I started phoning everyone, my family, the police, neighbours, and then finally Ian Katz, previously of the *Guardian* and now the editor of *Newsnight*. I begged him to go round to our house. Then Elaine phoned me and said there had been a power cut and she had gone to a friend's house. She said she was sorry. I was literally at the hotel for one night and it was before mobile phones. When I got my phone bill the next morning at checkout, it was $900. That's how frenzied I become now when I can't get hold of Joel. I hyperventilate, my heart rate goes through the roof and I become convinced that he's dead. Then I start to experience symptoms of grief. It's very irrational and completely horrible," he says with a laugh.

Just as Ronson has strategies in place with his family to ensure they can always be contacted—technically called "safety behaviours"—the natural desire for any anxious person is to avoid situations that provoke these kinds of horrendous feelings. Of course it is. But here is where everything gets tangled up. In a highly anxious brain, thoughts become fused with past experiences and are accepted as absolute fact in the present moment. Because Ronson feared his son was dead when he couldn't get hold of him once before, he now automatically clicks into believing that he's dead every time he's unavailable. Disordered, anxious thought patterns are based on what has made us anxious in the past—not on fact. Ronson, like Mark Twain, has known a great many troubles. Only, they were all in his head.

SARAH GOT IN TOUCH with me on Facebook, saying her sister had suggested she do so after I put a call out for people living with anxiety who might be willing to share their stories for this book. "It's like a relay race of anxious thoughts," noted the thirty-five-year-old English literature lecturer, the sister of an old school friend. Sarah told me she had been living with "bad anxiety" for years and had waited a very long time before going to see her GP. We agreed to meet in Soho one lunchtime, and I realized as I was leaving that I hadn't seen this girl—woman— since I was about fourteen.

Sarah was four years above me at our all-girls school. When I was in year seven, she was in sixth form and was just . . . That Girl. She turned younger girls' heads like a puppeteer. Shiny and lithe, giggly but composed, she was every *Bliss* magazine beauty tip made manifest. Vaseline on the eyebrows. Thick, mothy eye-lashes crumbly with Collection 2000 mascara. Beneath her uni-form dress shirts she would always have the neck of a black T-shirt peeking out. I always wondered what was on that T-shirt. Everyone knew this girl's laugh and sniffed the air as she walked past. Dewberry spray from the Body Shop, and Tiger Balm from Creations, the hippie shop in town. Heaven.

If I'd had to pick anyone from my cache of school mem-ories who suffered from an anxiety disorder, it wouldn't have been Sarah. But here she was, my first crush and probably many others', telling me, over a shitty cappuccino in the Caffè Nero on Old Compton Street, about how anxiety had taken hold of her life.

My surprise at that initial message was ridiculous, of course, because there is no off-the-peg "look" for mental distress. That one-in-four statistic I mentioned earlier forbids stereotyping. Here are some of the types of people who might be living with an anxiety disorder: judges, politicians, teachers, maga-zine editors, doctors, stockbrokers, fashion designers, models,

landscape gardeners, chefs, taxi drivers, fishermen, police offi-
cers, women with luxurious muffs, women with nay a pube to
their name, full-time mums, full-time dads, artists, musicians,
tree surgeons, social workers, bin men, zookeepers, glass blow-
ers, microbiologists, bricklayers, bramble pickers, babysitters,
black, white, trans, gay, tops, bottoms, bisexual, pansexual, cis-
gender, gender fluid, thin, fat, large-breasted, small-breasted,
bearded, clean-shaven, people with pierced eyebrows, people
with no piercings, people with tattoos, people without tattoos,
blue-eyed, brown-eyed, small-lipped, full-lipped, people who
like licorice, people who don't.

You get the idea.

Back to Sarah. "I find that each anxious thought sprints
on its own for a bit, then catches up with another one," she
says. "Then the new thought will find another one to hand the
baton to, while still running in the background, and it just goes
round and round and round."

The more insistent the anxious thoughts become, she says,
the worse the physical symptoms get. "I've worked out with
my therapist that the whole anxious cycle can start with just
one thought. This could be anything, although my triggers
usually centre on my health or the slightest whiff of being in
trouble with someone—my boss, a friend or my boyfriend,
doesn't matter. Being late for anything, too," she adds with a
laugh. We swap stories about going loco in train stations and
turning up for things ridiculously early, to "settle in" to a new
environment. She was at the café twenty minutes before we
needed to be, and I'd travelled into town with at least half an
hour to spare.

"Once I've been triggered, I'll feel the physical symptoms

start. My chest will tighten, my head will go fluttery, my insides will churn, I'll be aware of my heartbeat and whatever it's doing," she explains. "Then I start focusing on what's happening in my body *as well as* my mind, and the vicious cycle starts. I'm vibrating with anxiety about the very fact that I'm feeling anxious and *how* I'm feeling anxious. In the past I've actually found myself trembling. Once I've reached that point, the idea of being calm ever again feels impossible. I can't escape the feeling that something terrible is going to happen. I couldn't tell you what that terrible thing is, although I suspect, in my subconscious, that it's a fear of dying."

"Do you ever feel like you get stuck in a loop of thinking about thinking about thinking?" I ask.

"God yeah," she says with a laugh that is close to a sigh. "That's exactly it."

"And how often do you get stuck in those loops?" I inquire.

"I'm taking a low dose of an SSRI and having regular therapy now, which keeps my anxiety within manageable levels most of the time, but I lived pretty much constantly like that for years, getting worse and worse until the point where I just couldn't make or keep any commitments. I would get home from work and just sit in my bed, holding my chest, feeling like I was unravelling and couldn't catch the thread."

The unravelling-thread image is one that pops up time and time again in literature, probably because that really is how it feels. Franz Kafka, a writer whose name is frequently used to convey despair and upside down-ness, described his own paralyzing anxiety as "the feeling of having in the middle of my body a ball of wool that quickly winds itself up, its innumerable threads pulling from the surface of my body to itself."

PANIC DISORDER IS very different from GAD, although it can, over time, have similar aspects. Everyone is prone to panicking now and then, but panic disorder is defined by episodes of mental and physical turmoil so severe that people will often call ambulances for themselves. That's how bad a panic attack can feel. I've never called emergency services at the peak of one but have thought about it.

This delight of a disorder is characterized not just by having recurring panic attacks but by living in near-constant fear of having one. "Everyone experiences feelings of anxiety and panic at certain times during their lifetime. It's a natural response to stressful or dangerous situations," says NHS Choices. "However, for someone with a panic disorder, feelings of anxiety, stress and panic occur regularly and at any time."

The living in fear of having an attack is where GAD-like symptoms come in, and, very often, agoraphobia. In fact, agoraphobia, per the NHS website, "usually develops as a complication of panic disorder," with only "a minority of people with no history of panic attacks" affected. The website defines agoraphobia as "a fear of being in situations where escape might be difficult, or help wouldn't be available if things go wrong." Much more complex than just a fear of open spaces, then.

People with agoraphobia might be scared of specific spaces, like public transport or shopping centres, in case something terrible happened there, rather than fearing leaving home in general—although over time the latter might become a dull, background fear. They will do their best to avoid situations that cause anxiety (as I did with the Tube) and, in severe cases, may only leave the house with a friend or a partner. Safety behaviours.

Panic attacks can be triggered by many things. Stress, an oversensitivity to bodily sensations, or seemingly nothing at all. I've had panic attacks lying on the sofa, reading a book; watching television; in the bath; in the pub; cleaning the kitchen. During sex. The "happening when you're actually feeling relaxed" thing is part of what makes them so frightening.

Panic attacks involve profound mental distress but are most known for their physical symptoms: rapid heartbeat (palpitations or irregular/fast-paced heart rhythms); sweating and hot or cold flashes; tingling sensations, numbness or weakness in the body (I get a hot, prickling sensation up and down my arms and all over my torso); trouble breathing; headaches; ear pressure; trembling (in the past I've shaken so hard my teeth chattered like one of those wind-up toys); dizziness; chest pain; digestive problems (anything from nausea and indigestion to diarrhea and vomiting); depersonalization (feeling like you're "outside yourself" or like nothing is physically real).

Psychologically, feelings of doom, helplessness and despair tend to get stronger as the physical symptoms get worse, until they're raging like a bull: *I'm going to die, my heart's about to give out, I'm going to explode, this is never going to end, I'm trapped, I'm going to shit myself, I'm going to lose my mind, I'm going to pass out, please make this stop, please, help, I can't take it, I can't take it.*

During some of my worst panic attacks, to escape I have fantasized about being knocked over by a truck or having a builder's scaffolding pipe drop on my head. I had one on my bike once and thought about how easy it'd be to swerve into oncoming traffic. To flatten the swollen carton. I'm confident I would never do this, but those who have experienced panic attacks will know what that desperation for an "off" switch feels like.

We hear and see the term "panic" or "anxiety attack" used quite freely, but I wonder how many people who say things like "I feel I'm going to have a panic attack over this" when their stress levels are peaking really *know*.

They say panic attacks can last anywhere from ten minutes to half an hour, but I've definitely had long buildups to preposterous peaks of discomfort that have lasted longer. Then there's the crash afterwards. These days, perhaps because I have them far less, a panic attack will take me a day or two to get over. It feels like I've been bulldozed. If all this sounds terrible, it's because it is. There's little point softening the truth: having a panic attack can make you feel like you've been poisoned and are about to die. I know I can deal with them now much better than I ever have, but I'd offer my toes to a guillotine one by one if it meant never experiencing a panic attack again.

Obsessive-compulsive disorder, like agoraphobia, is widely misunderstood. I had been completely off the mark for years until I met people who actually live with it. Images of excessive hand washing until the skin cracks and bleeds, light switches being flicked on and off, pavement cracks not being stepped on formed the basis of my "knowledge" of this frequently debilitating disorder, often called "the doubting disease." But obsessive-compulsive disorder is far more than superstition and worrying about germs.

OCD often *does* take the form of being obsessed with

germs and contamination, but it is defined by having recurrent intrusive thoughts that invade one's consciousness. These thoughts, which can take infinite forms, are accompanied by repetitive urges and actions aimed at reducing the fear these ideas bring (e.g., excessive hand washing to "remove" germs). These are safety behaviours, which ultimately allow the condition to keep mushrooming.

According to the website OCD-UK, the illness affects as many as 12 in every 1,000 people (1.2 percent of the population) from young children to adults, regardless of gender or social or cultural background. "In fact," the website says, "it can be so debilitating and disabling that the World Health Organization (WHO) has ranked OCD in the top ten of the most disabling illnesses of any kind, in terms of lost earnings and diminished quality of life. Based on current estimates for the UK population, there are potentially 741,504 people living with OCD at any one time. But it is worth noting that a disproportionately high number, 50 percent of all these cases, will fall into the severe category, with less than a quarter being classed as mild cases." Per the Canadian Psychological Association, approximately 1 to 2 percent of the Canadian population will have an episode of OCD. In the US the figure is around 1 percent, says the Anxiety and Depression Association of America (ADAA).

OCD presents itself in many guises, and while sufferers often realize that their obsessive thoughts (O) are irrational, they believe that the only way to relieve the resulting anxiety is to perform compulsive behaviours (C) to prevent perceived harm to themselves or someone they love.

OCD-type symptoms are probably experienced by most of us during times of stress, when we find ourselves succumbing to some strange, nonsensical need to perform unrelated behaviour patterns. (Maybe I'm not the best example, but when I have a big deadline, I often tell myself that I will be "unable" to concentrate properly until the entire flat has reached the hygiene standards of an intensive care unit. Even with an hour to spare I might still have a toothbrush in my hand, scrubbing the grout.) However, OCD can devastate a sufferer's education, work, social life and personal relationships.

The key thing that segregates those people who take a strange pride in saying they are "a bit OCD" when they line up their DVDs by colour is that *f*-word again. Not *f* for "fucking annoying"—although it is, I think—but *f* for "functioning." The upsetting, unwanted experience of obsessions and compulsions that interferes with someone's ability to live his or her life is the key component in the clinical diagnosis of OCD.

Delays in diagnosis and treatment are incredibly common. Per OCD-UK, the average person with OCD waits for ten to fifteen years from the onset of symptoms to seeking treatment. This is because the content of their intrusive thoughts can be shocking and deeply shameful.

My ex-colleague, for example. Telling someone you have driven yourself mad by thinking about slicing off your own clitoris isn't like going to your GP with a cough. Which is why OCD is also often called the "secret illness" and is particularly difficult for young people experiencing it to talk about.

"Children often can't make sense of their symptoms," says Dr. Bruce Clarke, the OCD specialist at the Maudsley, "and they vary enormously. We aren't just talking about the visible symptoms that may make a parent aware of their child's discomfort— washing hands, ritualistic arrangement and de-arrangement of things—because they are the tip of the iceberg. A child or teen-ager having sexual or violent thoughts is going to be incredibly frightened and ashamed of them."

Someone who knows a lot about secrets and shame is Rose Bretécher, a writer whose book, *Pure*, came out in 2015. Bretécher has a type of OCD called "pure O." People with it experience repetitive thoughts, doubts and mental images about things like sex, blasphemy and murder. "Unthinkable" things that are never acted upon—only obsessed over. We meet in a pub in Dalston. Bretécher sits waiting, tall, cheekbone-y, dusty blond and Slavic-supermodel looking.

"Waking up every day with crystalline thoughts of anuses doesn't actually make you feel that pure." She smiles—the kind of smile, high and wide, that makes you see exactly what some-one looked like as a kid.

Pure is the story of Bretécher's life, tracking what the back cover describes as "her farcical decade-long path to redemption," from the time, as a teenager, that she was first seized by graphic mental images of a naked child, to her eventual recovery through therapy, self-acceptance and love. It is an urgent, unflinchingly honest and very funny book. I've rarely met someone who's lived the desperation of anxiety and doesn't have a black, puerile sense of humour, and I knew I'd get on with her while I was reading her book.

Now twenty-nine and living what she describes as a "full, pretty liberated" life, Bretécher has reached a point after "finally having therapy with an OCD specialist" where she can accept that the thoughts might always be there but that she can allow them to roll gently in and out without causing despairing loops of fear and compulsion.

Among the many laughs Bretécher weaves into her story ("I met Jake Gyllenhaal on a music video shoot and watched his face melt into a chubby vagina"), there is a crushing sadness. A huge chunk of her life has been spent obsessing herself into incapacity over two main questions: "Am I a pedophile?" and "Am I gay?" She has lived this torment mostly in secret. Her description of her first intrusive thoughts and subsequent panic attack, although different from my own, made me freeze:

> The more I tried to stop thinking about the image—a little boy naked—the quicker it flickered. It flickered and flickered and flickered, and something like lint was invading my lungs. I pulled my thighs up to my chest and felt my cheeks flush hot as I pressed my eye sockets against my knees, breathing hard. When the dog licked my ankle I raised my head and gasped as if breaking from water. Fuzzy green circles trembled in my vision for a couple of seconds before twirling off left and right, and then a stillness came over me. I mouthed the words slowly to the dark, slamming my hands against my mouth, "What if I'm a paedo—" And with that question I was sucked inside my head, where I spent the next decade fretting at the unanswerable like a fly on a lamp; all the while telling no one, all the while playing a role in life—a role to belie my secret.

OCD is an eminently treatable disorder, but when it explodes, Bretécher says, life becomes "life." After the initial images of naked children, her intrusive thoughts took the form of naked women. She'd see the backs of women's necks and imagine licking them, the detailed shape of their labia through their swimming suits, triangulating the elastic. She obsessed and obsessed over whether these images meant she was gay and that her heterosexual relationships were founded on lies. Her life became defined by ritualistic "checking" (for example, buying gay magazines like *Diva* and comparing the cover woman to the man on the cover of *Men's Health* and "testing" her reactions) and a sense of detachment wherever she was.

"How can you be truly present at a festival," she asks me, "when you're imagining everyone's genitals flapping around and then can't stop thinking about how you can't stop imagining it? It makes you want to run away from yourself"—something she attempted several times. She tells me about thinking herself into such a state at a festival that she ran to its perimeter and violently threw up. Eventually, she says, "my life grew inverted commas and flew away."

I know exactly what she means.

SPECIFIC PHOBIAS DON'T just take the form of jumping up onto a stool and clutching your knickerbockers, *Looney Toons*–style, every time a spider runs across the kitchen. New places, high bridges, old lifts, rodents, needles, insects may make many of us feel uneasy or frightened. We might try to avoid things that make us uncomfortable—my mum will rarely get into a lift if she doesn't have to, muttering things about cables, Keanu Reeves and *Speed*—but many of us are able to control our fears and carry out daily activities without too much hassle.

For people with specific phobias, though, life can be a constant battle. The fear may not make any sense, and although they know this, they feel powerless to stop it. People who experience excessive and unreasonable fear in anticipation of a specific place, object or situation can find their daily routine, work efficiency, relationships, friendships and self-esteem greatly affected by their need to avoid the often terrifying feelings of phobic anxiety.

The Anxiety and Depression Association of America (ADAA) reinforces how important it is to distinguish between everyday anxiety and phobic anxiety. "An everyday anxiety may include feeling queasy while climbing a tall ladder," it says on its website, whereas a phobia of heights may mean "refusing to attend your best friend's wedding because it's on the twenty-fifth floor of a hotel." The organizaton cites a further example: an everyday anxiety is the fear of taking off in a plane during a lightning storm; phobic anxiety is "turning down a big job promotion because it involves air travel."

For people with a specific phobia, being exposed to the object of their fear can provoke the whole spectrum of wretched anxiety symptoms. For many, though, it's not about exposure, because that will rarely happen. Through safety behaviours and avoidances, sufferers whittle their lives down to a series of familiar patterns *just in case* they are exposed to their fear—no matter how irrational it is—which leaves them in a constant state of anxiety.

I mentioned emetophobia (fear of vomiting) earlier on, but it warrants further exploration. It is a phobia that's still shrouded in taboo, despite being pretty common (it's thought to affect one million people in the UK), and when severe, it's very disabling. A handful of famous people have talked about having it—Joan Baez, Denise Richards, Cameron Diaz, Kate Beckinsale—but it remains one of those manifestations of anxiety whose all-consuming nature is difficult to articulate. Fear of flying is something most people can understand and empathize with, even if they're not remotely afraid themselves; but fear of being sick isn't really the same. People with emetophobia may find it embarrassing to say that they're not just afraid of being sick but *obsessed* with it (phobias and obsessive-compulsive disorder have much crossover in terms of ritualistic thinking patterns). Obsessed all the time. It's not very sexy, is it?

When I was at *VICE*, I produced a week-long project on mental health in association with the charity Mind, featuring thirty articles and one short film. Of all the pieces I commissioned, one really stood out to me. It was by a young woman with a fear of vomiting that controlled her life to the point where she was unable to hold down a job. From morning to night, she'd ask herself the same question: *Am I going to vomit?* To which the answer surely was: *Yes. Yes, I am.* Eventually, she had a breakdown that involved acute depersonalization—again, mostly lived in secret.

In our email correspondence she told me that she wanted to remain anonymous—one of the only contributors who did throughout the whole project—because she'd never told her family the truth about the anxiety that had made her so ill. She thought they'd find it hard to believe. "My life," she said, "is spent secretly monitoring my body for the slightest twinge of discomfort that will mean imminent vomit, and hardly anyone knows."

In addition to the celebrities mentioned earlier, other notable figures have spoken out. Emetophobia's biggest "voice"—in the UK, at least—is the writer and broadcaster Charlie Brooker, who has written about his phobia a few times. A piece in the *Guardian* springs to mind, which he wrote in 2008 during Norovirus season—the apocalypse for emetophobes.

"The media have had a field day," he notes, "and to an emetophobe like me (someone with an uncontrollable, inbuilt fear of puking), this merely amplifies the terror. A headline such as "Vomiting bug spreads across nation" sets my pulse racing twice as effectively as 'Mad axeman on loose.'"

He goes on to talk about his public toilet rituals: "You have to turn the tap with your elbow, wash for fifteen seconds (time it: it's longer than you think), then turn the tap off with the other elbow. Then you'll need two paper towels: one to dry yourself, and the other to open the door with on your way out. Unless you do all of this, you're doomed."

Eating at restaurants is a minefield, he continues: "Even if your chef is hygienic in the first place, unless he's devoutly following the paper-towel hand-washing routine outlined above to the letter he may as well wipe his bum on your plate." Brooker's tiredness is palpable: "I've become an obsessive-compulsive disorder case study, repeatedly washing my hands like Lady Macbeth on fast-forward, acutely aware of where my hands are at all times, what I've just touched, and where they're heading next. It's exhausting, like consciously counting every blink."

Underneath the piece, in the comments section, are many variations of "I know exactly how you feel." One woman even confessed to burning her son's copy of *The Very Hungry Caterpillar* after her son vomited on it. That all the comments were under Internet aliases seemed telling: with anonymity, you can spill all kinds of truths.

Browsing Twitter one evening not long after we'd published the *VICE* series, I saw Marie Phillips, author of the very successful book *Gods Behaving Badly*, tweeting about mindfulness and anxiety. "How does mindfulness help with anxiety?

When I try to do it I just get *really* aware that I'm anxious,"
she wrote. I replied, saying it takes quite a while to get used
to "allowing" the thoughts and physical symptoms to do their
thing, and she said, "I have vomiting phobia, and anxiety makes
me nauseous, so it's a real vicious cycle!" We went back and
forth a bit and agreed to chat on the phone. She recounted how
her fear of vomiting eventually led her to being hospitalized:

"I've been scared of being sick for as long as I can remember," she tells me down the line from Amsterdam, where she
lives with her partner. "I'm thirty-nine now and haven't been
sick since I was ten, but it doesn't matter—I'm convinced I will
vomit everywhere I go."

Phillips has experienced panic attacks from the age of eight
but says that no one used the term "emetophobia" until she
was twenty. "I had no idea what was going on with me," she
says. "I just felt nauseous and panicked all the time, very out
of control. Wherever I went, I would spend the whole time
planning my 'vomit route'—how I would get to the toilet in
time, or how I could be sick without people noticing. Just the
other day I was at a gig and I'd had a beer. I thought: *I won't
put this cup down because if I'm sick I want to do it in there.* Over
the years I have let people believe I'm scared of flying when,
in fact, my fear is that I'll get airsick and not be allowed to get
out of my seat if there is turbulence." It got so bad five years
ago that she had herself admitted to a psychiatric hospital—a
period that, when she looks back, "feels as though it happened
to someone else."

I have never been hospitalized, but I identify with Phillips's
difficulty in recognizing that it was the highly functioning person talking to me on the phone who became unwell. I sug-

gest that when we hear the term "mentally ill" we still, even if
we have experienced it and despite our better judgment, tend
to think of straitjackets and *Girl, Interrupted.* "Absolutely." She
laughs. "But it's people like me, people you'd never 'suspect.' "

I look at all the Google Images of her face—dark hair, dark
eyes, gorgeous—and have to check myself when I think for a
split second: *She doesn't look like someone who'd be emetophobic.*

"I didn't realize how bad it was getting. My first novel did
very well but my panic attacks were getting worse," she says.
"All my friends were getting married and having babies and I
think I felt isolated. There was a window where I could have
gotten help sooner, but I didn't have a lot of resources. My GP
just wanted to put me on Prozac. Eventually, the panic attacks
joined up, and I tipped one day after taking a tablet and choking on it. I retched, and because I was already panicking and
nauseous all the time, that tipped me into a cycle of not eating
for fear of choking and being sick. I stopped leaving the house.
I was in a battle to the death and was losing an incredible
amount of weight. You *can* not leave the house but you can't
not eat, and I just forced myself to manage tiny things."

Hearing her talk about this felt familiar because I had done
a similar thing at seventeen. I was just at the beginning of the
anxiety I would come to know, and at that stage was convinced
something was physically wrong with me. I had the same fear
of eating in case it made me choke or feel even more ill. I'd get
painful pangs of hunger after picking like a sparrow throughout
the day, and end up frantically making rounds of toast, to find
that as soon as I bit into a piece, my throat would feel like it was
swelling up. It was strange and scary.

"It all came to a head when I went to meet my mum in

Oxford Circus," says Phillips. "I couldn't walk down the street without reading a book, so was weaving through the crowds with it in front of my face like a shield, a talisman. I walked into John Lewis [a UK department store] reading the book to meet her and fudged my way through a coffee. When I got home, she rang me and said, "I think you might need to go into hospital," and I said, "I think so, too." My parents paid for me to go to a private psychiatric hospital. I just packed a suitcase full of books."

I ask her what it felt like once she got there.

"Honestly, I always knew somewhere that I'd end up there. It was a relief to not have to deal with my life anymore. But one of the nurses recognized my name and started asking me about *Gods Behaving Badly* and I had to be, like, 'Not now, sorry. I can't chat,' as she settled me into my suicide-proofed room."

It's been five years since Phillips's hospitalization, a period she describes as "incredibly eye opening" because it completely shattered her ideas of what kind of people end up in a mental hospital. "It was people like me: creative, intelligent people I'd want to talk to in the pub," she says. I tell her that when I met Dr. Salter, he said being hospitalized for a mental health problem is a comma in a sentence rather than a full stop, and often a great turning point for getting better. "That's definitely the case for me. These days I am well-functioning. I feel far more in control of managing my phobia and how it can cause an unpleasant backdrop of fear in day-to-day life. I've come to terms with the idea that I'll probably always be managing it and how it doesn't mean that if I become anxious somewhere, I'm not enjoying [myself]. Jesus, I even eat sushi now."

THE TERM "POST-TRAUMATIC STRESS DISORDER" was coined in the late 1970s, in large part due to diagnoses of US military veterans of the Vietnam War. The disorder has been noted since at least the nineteenth century—variously called "shell shock," "battle fatigue" and "soldier's heart." But it's not just the trauma of war that can cause PTSD—a wide range of traumatic events can lead to the development of symptoms.

Events that trigger PTSD include violent personal assaults (sexual assault, robbery or mugging); prolonged sexual abuse, violence or neglect; military combat; being held hostage; natural disasters like earthquakes, floods and tsunamis; a diagnosis of a life-threatening condition or the unexpected severe injury or death of someone close to you; witnessing violent deaths or severe injuries. Paramedics, for example, see burnt flesh, death and blood daily and are highly susceptible to PTSD at some point in their career. In fact, figures are steadily increasing. The findings of freedom of information requests submitted to NHS regional ambulance services in England, published in 2015, showed that both the number of paramedics on stress-related leave and the amount of time they take off have increased dramatically in the past three years. Paramedics took a total of 41,243 days off in 2014—up 28 percent since 2012.

PTSD isn't usually related to situations like failing an exam or botching a job interview. According to the NHS, the condition develops in around one in three people who experience a severe trauma; it's not fully understood why some people develop the condition and others don't, although having previously experienced depression or anxiety, or having a family member with a history of mental illness, is thought to make a person more susceptible.

When I spoke to Dr. Andreas Danese, consultant child and adolescent psychiatrist at the Maudsley, he said that one in ten people (significantly fewer than the figure on the NHS website) who experience a severe trauma will develop PTSD, and he described the condition as "practically the only anxiety disorder, along with phobic disorder, in which we can go some way to identifying a specific cause." Yet even extreme traumas, like those experienced by Holocaust survivors, aren't a guarantee of someone developing a post-traumatic disorder. "A percentage of people who walked out of Auschwitz were happy three, six months later," he remarked. "It's extraordinary."

PTSD can be very frightening. The World Health Organization's ICD-10 Classification of Mental and Behavioural Disorders summarizes the diagnostic criteria as "exposure to a stressful event or situation (either short or long-lasting) of exceptionally threatening or catastrophic nature which is likely to cause pervasive distress in almost anyone."

Symptoms may include persistent remembering or "reliving" the stressor by intrusive flashbacks that can feel like hallucinations, vivid memories, recurring dreams or experiencing distress when exposed to any circumstances resembling the trauma, and avoidance of circumstances associated with the trauma that weren't traumatic prior to the incident, which might mean something as simple as walking down the road near a house where abuse took place.

In the National Comorbidity Survey, the first large-scale field survey of mental health in the United States (initially conducted in 1990–92 but revisited in 2001–02 with the same subjects), the traumatic events most frequently reported by men were rape, combat and childhood neglect or physical abuse. If you have read concert pianist James Rhodes's memoir, *Instrumental: A Memoir of Madness, Medication and Music*, you will have a vivid insight into the ramifications of an unfathomable childhood trauma like rape.

Rhodes jokily apologizes for his privileged upbringing throughout the book, but of course privilege is no barrier against child molesters. A man named Peter Lee, a gym teacher at the London prep school Rhodes went to from the age of five, took a shine to him as a six-year-old. The first time Lee asked Rhodes to stay behind after class to "clear up," he gave him a box of matches—more dangerous omen than gift. More presents followed, then an invitation to join the after-school boxing club. Initially over the moon, Rhodes became withdrawn.

"Little Rhodes needs to toughen up," teachers said.

But it wasn't the boxing he didn't like; it was the "clearing up," which meant being held down on a gym mat and raped by Lee—an excruciating trauma that changed Rhodes in an instant. "I went, literally overnight, from a dancing, spinning, gigglingly alive kid who was enjoying the safety and adventure of a new school, to a walled-off, cement-shoed, lights-out automaton," he writes. "It was immediate and shocking, like happily walking down a sunny path and suddenly having a trapdoor open and dump you into a freezing cold lake." Reading the book, I felt it truly remarkable that no adult had an inkling what was happening, particularly when Rhodes was found crying, begging to be let off gym class, with blood on the backs of his legs.

Those who have followed Rhodes's story will know it's a miracle the book was published. In May 2015, the Supreme Court lifted the temporary injunction brought against it by

Rhodes's ex-wife, whose case was that their son would be distressed should he ever read it. Judges ruled that Rhodes's right to tell his story was paramount. But it's not just legalities that make this book a miracle. At several points in his life, Rhodes was so set on self-destruction after years and years of reckoning with his past that he never thought he'd see forty.

Rock bottom was a spell in a psychiatric hospital, where he successfully outwitted the guard watching over him 24-7 and snuck a TV aerial cable into his bathroom. He fashioned a noose ("not too different from tying a double Windsor") and tried to hang himself by jumping off the toilet seat. He didn't break his neck but was dangling there, choking to death, when the guard walked in.

Rhodes writes in his book that he is now "happier and more content" than he has ever been, even though he must manage his anxiety daily. He is proof that even if your journey towards self-acceptance runs into the deepest potholes, with strong self-compassion you can keep trauma from defining your life.

SOCIAL ANXIETY DISORDER is a whole lot more than shyness. Shyness is to social anxiety what a Dairylea Triangle is to a box of Vacherin cheese. The texture might be similar, but the two are *not* the same thing.

Like agoraphobia, social anxiety disorder is a type of complex phobia that often starts in childhood or adolescence and tends to be more common in women. Children with social anxiety disorder might cry more than usual, have tantrums or freeze. They might be fearful of school and taking part in group activities and school performances. In adults, the disorder translates into an overwhelming fear of social situations and can mean having intense anxiety over everyday things many of us take for granted, like shopping or talking on the phone.

However, people are unique about the social situations that make them anxious. For one person, socializing in a big group or at a busy party may be nightmarish. This is definitely something I can identify with. Social anxiety is not my main problem, but going to parties or socializing in large groups is difficult sometimes. Not impossible, but difficult. My mind tends to invert when I think about how many people could witness me having a panic attack, were I to have one. Naturally, this leads to a constant monitoring of my anxiety levels that stops me being fully present. For another person, eating and drinking in front of other people causes panic.

Everyone worries about certain social situations sometimes, but people with social anxiety disorder will worry excessively, not just before and during the event but also afterwards. They fear doing or saying weird stuff that will be embarrassing or make people judge them, stuff like blushing, sweating or stumbling over words. Cruelly, these are all common ways in which anxiety can show itself, and in the case of social anxiety, the fear of blushing can become a self-fulfilling prophecy. Just as Phillips's phobia of vomiting manifests as feeling sick a lot of the time, people with a fear of blushing in social situations may find themselves blushing even at the *thought* of socializing. Or if they feel anxiety in their gut, they may find they need to poo a lot in the run-up to going out, or even during the social event.

I exchanged a few emails with a man called George, who

I found while browsing the No More Panic website message forums—a place I visited a lot, without ever actually posting, when I felt most unwell with anxiety. If you find yourself Googling anything about the experience of anxiety, chances are a No More Panic link will come up. It's an incredibly popular site that allows people with anxiety disorders to talk freely with one another. George is thirty-four and told me he has had social anxiety for as long as he can remember.

"When I was at school, I used to get these dizzy spells. My mum took me to the doctor and they did some tests and found nothing physically wrong with me, but I always seemed to get them when I was sat around with everyone at lunch or in the playground. I started to get worried about getting dizzy in 'inappropriate' places, where people would have to watch me putting my head between my legs or sitting and closing my eyes. Eventually, over a number of years, I became so frightened of my 'performance' in front of other people—whether that was going to work or just to the shops—that I'd be on edge from the minute my eyes opened in the morning. There was only a small handful of people I felt comfortable being around. Strangers were uncharted waters."

I asked him if it ever became debilitating.

"Yes. When I was twenty-nine, I found myself beginning to fear any social plans or work meetings—not just days but weeks in advance. I remember having a date in the diary to go to friends of mine to meet their new baby and having such bad insomnia as the date approached: imagining getting dizzy or slurring my words (something that's never happened!) at their place that I started to feel really ill. I had a few days off work with exhaustion and paced the house like a dog, eating my way through the tins of beans in the cupboard so I didn't have to go to the shop and talk to anyone. That was when I finally sought help. I'd had some counselling as a teenager, but knew I needed something more intensive."

George is now doing a lot better after seeing his doctor and being referred for CBT but still finds it hard to explain to people how what he has isn't just shyness. "I'm not shy!" he says. "I actually love meeting and learning about new people. It sometimes just takes me a bit longer to do that."

IF WE THINK about the hardware versus software theory, people with any of these anxiety disorders—or a blend of them—are running a bugged program in their hard drive that's making them think in an irrational way—a way they struggle to control. But our software isn't static. It's an ever-expanding helix of our experiences and environment, which can be infinitely influenced. It's life, basically: what happens to us, what we do. But so many people living with anxiety, like me, cannot believe that they're not somehow "wired" badly. There *must* be something biologically wrong to make my experience with life so difficult, right? If every thought is an electrical, *physical* thing happening in our brains, then in what way have the components of those brains been shaped by genetics? More to the point: Who in my family can I blame for this tendency towards self-lacerating anguish?

PART III

WHY DOES ANXIETY HAPPEN?

BLAME, TIME AND PLACE

BLAME IS A FUNNY THING. APPORTIONING IT CAN help shrink pain, but for some people blame is less of a crutch and more of a compass to navigate the wilderness of existence. It can become a faith of sorts. By believing that our actions are ultimately influenced by something or someone else and that's that, the sharp edges of life are planed back. Some people, I think, would rather spend their lives explaining away their actions and behaviour with blame rather than accepting that they have autonomy. It's tough to accept that fucking up sometimes is all right. Some people are better at it than others. If we have something to blame, it takes the spotlight off us. We think people will be more forgiving. At its heart, though, I think blame makes it easier to forgive ourselves.

These are broad brushstrokes, of course, but in asking myself who I can blame in my family for passing on this wretched thing, I'm looking for comfort. I'm looking for something to make my anxiety feel like less of a weakness. It can be very disorientating when we feel as though our thoughts have been hijacked. We want to know *why*, how, who we pissed off in a past life. What we did to deserve it.

Why is this happening to me? That's a question I've asked myself thousands of times. I've spent so long looking for things to blame so as not to feel so adrift in my own mind. But the *exact* cause of any mental health problem is, as we know, uncertain. From anxiety disorders to paranoid schizophrenia, current scientific opinion holds that mental illness comes from a variety of factors. Even PTSD, where a specific trauma can be identified as the tipping point for a collection of symptoms, isn't always as black-and-white as it seems.

It's hard to know why some people experience anxiety and others don't. There are thought to be many contributing factors, including difficult childhood experiences; stressors in our environment like money or housing; problems at work or not being able to find work; problems at school or university; recent or unexpected bereavement; diet; the psychological toll of physical illness; the side effects of certain medications; alcohol or substance abuse; drug withdrawal; trauma of any kind and, of course, brain chemistry. Our genes, our hard codes. But although research has found chemical sources of stress resilience (neuropeptide Y is one, and those with a lot of it seem immune to PTSD), an absence of anxiety is not the same as grit.

When we consider how all these things affect people in different ways, it feels like there *has* be some underlying vulnerability that tips the scales for people who do have less resilience or develop acute anxiety. Genetics *are* understood to be part of the picture when someone develops acute anxiety, which is a disorder that can send the sufferer one of two ways. Blaming our "chemistry"—i.e., something we can't change—can be bleakly soothing if you think: *I am* wired *for anxiety, not weak.* Or it can be the opposite: *I can't help it. I can't help it, so I can't stop it.* Two sides of a rotten coin that ultimately have the same outcome: hopelessness.

People like me who suffer with anxiety are obsessed with time. We mourn its passing, and if anxiety is something we've only struggled with as an adult, we mourn the old versions of ourselves that never used to be this way. We can so easily live in regret for the things that anxiety has stopped us doing and look back guiltily on lovely moments that weren't experienced "properly" because our senses were dumbed by anxiety and not able to take everything in. When we feel terrible, we desperately will time-forward, asking when the feelings will end. As such, anxiety is so often categorized as struggling to be present or "in the moment."

By its very nature anxiety is a barrier to being in the moment—there are always symptoms to check, escape routes to make a note of, social cues to keep on top of. How do we actually quantify being in the moment, though? What do those three hallowed words *mean*? Because I do try to practise mindfulness, I know that it hinges on momentarily losing (or focusing) your sense of self, allowing your thoughts and environment to just *be*; to wash over you, rather than be fought or judged. But do we immediately click ourselves out of The Moment the second we acknowledge that we're in it? Is it possible to ever truly hover in real time?

Patti Smith has explored this idea beautifully in her new memoir, *M Train*. In a passage called "A Clock with No Hands," she reflects on how she and her late husband, Fred "Sonic" Smith, lived their lives without any specific time frame, staying up until dawn talking, waking up at nightfall. Everything got done. Clothes were washed, the house stayed clean; they just did these things in whatever order they liked. Cereal for dinner, pasta for breakfast.

I closed my notebook and sat in the cafe thinking about real time. Is it time uninterrupted? Only the present comprehended? Are our thoughts nothing but passing trains, no stops, devoid of dimension, whizzing by massive posters with repeating images? Catching a fragment from a window seat, yet another fragment from an identical frame? If I write in the present yet digress, is it still real time? Real time, I reasoned, cannot be divided into sections like numbers on the face of a clock. If I write about the past as I simultaneously dwell in the present, am I still in real time?

I've thought about this passage so much since I first read it, in the bath, oiling the pages. Smith isn't writing about mental health specifically, but anyone who has felt locked in their own universe at times, I think, particularly with anxiety, will have had a tricky relationship with the passing of time; the elasticity of it, how it can snap and sting.

"Perhaps all anxiety might derive from a fixation on moments—an inability to accept life as ongoing," writes the American poet, essayist and diarist Sarah Manguso, in *Ongoingness: The End of a Diary*. Ostensibly a memoir, the book looks back on the eight hundred thousand—*800,000!*—words she's written in her journals over the past twenty-five years. "I wrote so I could say I was truly paying attention," she notes early on. "Experience in itself wasn't enough. The diary was my defence against waking up at the end of my life and realizing I'd missed it."

That last line puts into words a gently pulsing fear I've had for a very long time: that every day spent suffering with, or managing anxiety, is a day stripped of experience, written off. With S, I have worked towards resisting the temptation to get to the end of a day and think it somehow wasted because of anxiety, because I've felt anxious somewhere I "shouldn't" have. Instead, I am to talk kindly to myself (writing stuff down if need be) and remind myself that the entire day in fact wasn't taken up by acute anxiety, that I saw and heard and took in a lot of other stuff, that I am not putting stretches of time in the bin. It's one of my hardest tasks, this. Not looking back on past experiences and thinking of them as soiled by anxiety—or half real—is tough.

I remember saying something to my therapist early on about when I went to Marfa, Texas, for a *Guardian* piece. It's such a magical place. I adored the dry heat and the way the Donald Judd sculptures circling the town both rupture the desert landscape and breathe with it. The night is so clear that you can easily see the Andromeda Galaxy, a phosphorescent bruise across the sky. I loved the reverence the wildlife demands; the wild horses, scorpions, coyotes, skunks, tarantulas. (The first night, the lady who owned the guest house I was staying in blithely told me to always shake down the duvet and pillows before getting into bed in case of "critters." I woke up on my first morning there to find a rattlesnake curled up on the patio outside.)

I talk about this trip because it's one that stands out as being so marred by feeling anxious. I was literally in the middle of nowhere—from London you fly to Houston, then to El Paso, then do a three-hour drive—and the nearest big town is an hour away. I got stuck in all sorts of loops while I was there, planning how I would exit dinners eight hours in advance, stuff like that. Because I was so in awe of the landscape and everything in it, perhaps more so than any other place I've been, I've always looked at my photographs of Marfa with a heavy heart and thought: *Did my fizzing mind really let all that beauty in? Was it wasted on me?*

I'd wager that people who have lived with anxiety will have their own version of this kind of thing. It all comes back to this tension with the passing of time and worrying we've not done it—or ourselves—justice, which is why *Ongoingness* was such a staggering book for me. I imagine I'll revisit it over years to come because there are so many human truths inside. It is, as the *New Yorker* said in its review, almost psychedelic; as much an insight into one person's thoughts as a collection of sharp meditations on memory, our concept of self and the Western fear of not filling each waking moment with MAXIMUM LIFE. Like Patti Smith, Manguso is not explicitly writing on mental distress, but between the lines she explores the human mind's fight with the present and grief for time past—a fight so common with anxiety.

Our memory is a source of tyranny over our minds and our ability to be present, and I've often wondered what full immersion in the present might look like. Manguso suggests that memory makes it impossible:

> The least contaminated memory might exist in the brain of a patient with amnesia—in the brain of something who cannot contaminate it by remembering it. With each recollection, the memory of it further degrades. The memory and maybe the fact of every kiss start disappearing the moment the two mouths part.

Manguso's relationship with time changes as she gets older. Specifically, when she becomes a mother. "I began to inhabit time differently," she writes. "Nursing an infant creates so much lost, empty time. The mother becomes the background against which the baby lives, becomes time." As her baby grows in front of her eyes, a marker of a whole new time scale, she dreams of her son's teeth "beating time in months, in years, his full jaws a pink-and-white timepiece." Her body became the landscape of her son's life. She herself a world. His world. "Time kept reminding me that I merely inhabit it, but it began reminding me more gently." I am not yet a mother but long to be. When it happens, I wonder if I'll have a similar kind of shift. I hope so.

OVER THE YEARS, my fight-or-flight reflex has become so sensitive that my past can be whisked into my present in the blink of an eye. This makes fearing my immediate future very common. Which is why I'm not good on the Tube. Throughout the journey (if it's unavoidable and I can't cycle to wherever I'm going) the conditioned part of my brain says: *You've had a panic attack on the Tube before, so I'm going to try to keep you safe by making you frightened enough to get off and run up the escalators and out onto the street.* Places become tainted and "red-flagged" by memory.

It's only through learning to rationalize my symptoms as best I can in the present that the situations I fear—the Tube, busy social events, lengthy travel, spontaneity—become less frightening. I'm learning that I *can* deal with my thoughts, because that's all they are: thoughts. I am learning that practising not reacting to them like I have for the past fifteen years won't just help me in the present but will tone down my general levels of anxiety about everything. The less I react, the less frightening the thoughts will be next time they pass through. That's the ongoing process, anyway.

We know that in anxious brains, memories and associations can become as much of a trigger as a speeding car. There is science that now suggests our memories can effectively be overwritten through time if we learn to associate our recalling of them with feeling calm, which is a technique taught in CBT. The memories aren't "erased"—we are not living in a real-life *Eternal Sunshine of the Spotless Mind* script—but we *can* learn to change what we do when they pop up. For a long while, during the buildup to every panic attack, regardless of my surroundings I would flash back to being disabled and incontinent in my hospital bed.

This is all knowledge gleaned through having therapy. Learning how anxiety works is how I began to accept my propensity for it. This ongoing process will probably always be ongoing. It's hard. I am nowhere near getting over my anxiety—whatever "getting over" looks like. However, I am much better at dealing with life, being spontaneous and learning to live with anxiety in the background.

And this raises another quandary: If I'm getting better at dealing with the present, what about the past? How much could examining it make me even better at dealing with the present, recognizing patterns of thoughts and behaviours, and gaining more autonomy over them?

I'VE ALWAYS BEEN so desperate to be able to live better *right now* that I've never thought examining my past in forensic detail would be therapeutic for me until I'd finally gotten hold of my symptoms—again, process ongoing. This was particularly true in the lead-up to the breakdown I wrote about earlier.

In 2011, I started to see a new therapist, who I'll call "K." If I remember rightly, she was trained in psychodynamic therapy but today appears to have disappeared from the Internet. I had no idea then what disciplines of therapy, if any, would be most effective for my anxiety—I just knew I needed some help. She was local and I liked her face and vibe on her website. I look back now and think about how naive I was, but initially the relief of just talking to *someone* was great, because I had not shared the truth with a single person of how I felt so often. Although she was a nice, gentle woman, my relief soon gave way to a still unnamable frustration at having to turn over the earth of my childhood so much when I was feeling bad *right then*.

There were agonizing silences when she asked me about being dropped off at school or how things my mum said or did when I was eleven made me feel. When I didn't say much, she'd look at me in this "I've got your number" way, nodding. It felt like she was always rooting around for proof of her hunches about what I couldn't face in myself. Whenever I pushed back and said I didn't think something was significant, it felt like in her mind I was holding a giant neon sign above my head that trumpeted: "MY MUM HAS FUCKED ME UP AND I WANT TO KILL HER" (I don't), or something. Everything she said or thought seemed unfalsifiable; her hypotheses strengthened with every noise or movement I made.

Inside, I'd be silently screaming for some pointers to, you know, get on top of the panic attacks I was having every other day and my inability to fall asleep at night. The more we stuck with the past, the more I thought I was beyond help; that the therapy wasn't working because I was too far gone. This made me more determined to keep going back, even though I actually started to feel worse, because I just couldn't bear the idea that I wasn't trying on top of everything else.

After about ten months I found myself leaving her place each week taking a deep breath and feeling more churned up than when I'd arrived an hour before. One evening I felt so frustrated with myself and the whole situation that I squeaked as she closed the door behind me and yanked a big bit of her lavender bush out of the ground—one of those things you do in a fit of frustration and feel like a complete dick about afterwards. I wonder if she noticed.

With some obvious exceptions, I am mostly in the "whatever works" camp when it comes to living with a mental health problem. If self-help books, exercise and meditation apps keep you on an even keel—brilliant. If talking to a psychoanalyst about your relationship with your mother helps you identify and navigate your behavioural patterns and live more calmly—fantastic. My experience is singular. All I can say is what's worked for me and what I've learned directly from other people. Through all my conversations for this book and beyond, though, I've come to believe that when someone is presenting at the sharp end of anxiety and feeling at a crisis point the way I was, that person initially needs a plaster.

In an ideal world, that person would leave a therapy setting with at least one new strategy for dealing with symptoms and thoughts; an invisible Allen key to start retightening the bolts immediately. Because that's what it feels like when you're on your knees with anxiety: like everything has come loose.

Reflection is an important part of understanding and recalibrating ourselves, however, and I would never in a million years claim to have the authority to recommend one therapy over another. Happiness and peace of mind are highly subjective. We all look at our lives through the portholes of our earliest relationships, even if we don't realize we're doing it. We know that although neuroscience throws up new discoveries about the brain every day, the brain is still pocked with mystery; that our conscious minds are the tiny iceberg tips poking out of the inky ocean of our subconscious. All I know is that when I felt at my worst, lengthy contemplation of the past seemed impossible. I didn't know how to stop my thoughts, and they were responsible for provoking my symptoms and making me feel so awful.

I would contemplate getting to sixty, seventy, and think: *Jesus Christ, is it going to be like this forever? Will I even last that long if I stay like this?* Living with anxiety—or any other mental health problem—can make the rest of your life feel like a very, very long time. So when K would ask me about how my mum helped me do my homework, it barely registered as a conversation while my control over my symptoms continued to fray. My brain was too on fire. As she talked, I'd be imagining myself climbing into the cupboard under her stairs.

Now that that period of acute distress is behind me, I can say that looking at the bigger picture of my life and place in the world *has* been helpful. This has meant looking at my genetics a bit more, my family, my early years. Since then, I have not had anything resembling psychoanalysis or psychodynamic therapy. However, through my own research and the therapy I have had with S over three years, I have gained a better understanding of how the brain functions and develops, which gives me insight into what I can and can't change, and how to better work on my responses to those things.

OUR MINDS ARE NOT blank slates at birth. Nor are many of our sensory systems. In autumn 2015, *National Geographic* ran a long feature by David Owen on the science of taste. He explored how a child's palate is stamped by evolution with "inborn preferences and aversions and influences by the mother's diet during pregnancy." A baby can be born with an aversion to broccoli, for example. Of course, every *part* of us is stamped by evolution and the influences of our genes. However, when it comes to the mind and the way it is imprinted, research measuring the precise influence of certain genes is currently at a very early stage.

Without yet being able to see any biological marker of specifically who or what may have imprinted my genes in terms of anxiety, any theory is just that: a theory. The trajectory of some of these genes in my family is obvious—my maternal grandmother had debilitating anxiety, which was "passed on" to my mum in different ways that I'll get to later—but when it comes to the mental health of my older ancestors, there aren't many people I could take pointers from. Most of them are gone. Also: Where the hell do you draw the line? Should I be looking at the great-grandparents of my great-grandparents for clues? All my ancestors in Wales, Scotland and France? When do you stop time travelling? What would I, the sufferer, be looking for? All those genes, all that information, to what end? It makes me a bit seasick.

I planned to do all sorts of digging: public records, medical records if I could get them. But I started by signing up on Ancestry, a website that lets you (for about £100/C$175, if you forget the time limit on the free trial like I did) study any official documentation associated with your ancestors. I hoped I'd find something—anything—in the way of psychiatry, but found nothing. I went back and back, through the centuries, looking for even the tiniest nugget that might point to mental distress. After a while I started to wonder how anything I found would help my ongoing process and help me live better today, tomorrow, in a year's time. I am not a scientist on a quest for gold: I am a person living with anxiety who has gotten much better at the living part but still wants to improve.

Many gene strands have contributed to the way I am and the patterns of my behaviour, including my anxiety. I stopped looking for historical peepholes into that biology because I couldn't see how I could capitalize on it or discover anything new with the information. In terms of immediate family, my dad spoke to me about the anxiety that his dad, Dick, my late grandpa, experienced when he served in the Royal Navy during World War II. The years before, after and during his service, which included being part of the 1944 Normandy landings, were defined by imminent threat and fear.

"They didn't have a name for it then," he says, "but he was never the same after."

PTSD?

"I don't know. The war was long over by the time I was born and he never talked about that kind of thing in detail. No one did, really."

The last bit doesn't surprise me. We thought about the trauma my grandpa had experienced during the war—not just bloody death and decay and the mortification of humanity, but also being constantly on the verge of attack or being attacked—and pondered the possibility of that trauma trickling through the Morgan gene pool.

The idea that environmental factors can affect genes is a theory called "epigenetic inheritance." What began as broad research combining development biology and genetics in the mid-twentieth century has evolved into a very focused study of how influences from the environment—diet, smoking and stress—can affect the genes of someone's children and maybe even grandchildren. It's a pretty controversial idea and goes against scientific convention that says genes are the only way to pass on biological information through generations. Epigenetics refers to inherited changes in gene expression that *don't* change the underlying DNA sequence.

Our genes are restyled by our environment all the time, through chemical "tags" that grab onto our DNA and switch genes on and off. My brother has some of the same facial tics that my dad has, but my sister and I don't. Hanna has hated strawberries in any capacity since she was a baby and only found out recently that when her mum was pregnant with her, she developed an acute aversion to them. Even the smell of jam would make her heave.

These are things learned through environment. A famous study of epigenetics and in utero imprinting is the Dutch

Famine Birth Cohort Study. The subjects, 2,414 people born between 1943 and 1947, were selected because their mothers had been pregnant during the severe famine at the end of World War II. These children were studied to investigate the effects of prenatal exposure on later health, and because, among other issues, they had an above-average risk of developing schizophrenia. Epigenetics has led to many new findings about the relationship between these environmental changes to genes and a whole host of disorders: various cancers, immune disorders, pediatric illness and, of course, psychiatric disorders.

The effect of trauma on future generations is a big topic in modern science, and findings in 2016 from a research team led by Rachel Yehuda at New York's Mount Sinai Hospital provide one of the clearest links in humans yet; previously, transmission of stress effects had been demonstrated only in animals. Yehuda and her team studied thirty-two Jewish men and women who were either in a Nazi concentration camp, had experienced or witnessed torture or had been forced to hide during World War II. They also looked at the genes of the participants' children, who, because of the genetic component in mental health issues, had an increased likelihood of stress disorders. Their results were compared with those for Jewish families not living in Europe during the war. Holocaust exposure proved to have had a clear effect on a gene protein called FK506 in parents and their children. "The gene changes in the children could only be attributed to Holocaust exposure in the parents," said Yehuda. Further genetic analysis allowed the team to rule out epigenetic changes resulting from trauma the children themselves had experienced.

The ripple effect of Holocaust survival on future generations has been researched for years. The psychological impact of growing up in families where elders retold stories of horrific events has even prompted Jewish activists to start campaigns in support of the grandchildren of Holocaust survivors across the world.

Dan Glass, twenty-nine, from London told the *Guardian* in the summer of 2015 how he had constantly heard tales of the Holocaust while he was growing up—tales that have deeply affected him in adulthood. "All four of my grandparents narrowly avoided the gas chambers in Auschwitz and countless of their friends met with this fate. For my father, it was a daily conversation in my teens and early twenties, and even though I very profoundly understood his pain, one day I had to say to him, 'Dad, I can't talk about this anymore.'" He also noted, "My father had a whole wall of books on the subject of the Holocaust—it was all he wanted to talk about, but it was so harrowing for me."

Glass started talking to other children and grandchildren of survivors for an academic thesis, and went on to found a group called Never Again Ever!—a reference to the 1948 Universal Declaration of Human Rights and its pledge. Of course he found he was far from alone in being affected by the trauma his family had experienced.

Yehuda's research is groundbreaking. It shows the tentative beginnings of a new understanding of how one generation biologically responds to the experiences of its predecessors. It's a lot for scientists to wrap their heads around, and while this fine tuning of our genes and how they respond to the world is not quite turning evolutionary theory on its head, it could have a massive impact on revealing more about how we deal with stress. "It is," Yehuda said, "an opportunity to learn a lot of important things about how we adapt to our environment and how we might pass on environmental resilience."

My grandma Dolores is still very much alive—not far off ninety now. I would have liked to sit down with her to talk about the trauma my grandpa might have experienced and see what I could do with that information, but I should have done it earlier. As time goes on, she finds it more and more upsetting to talk about him in any way that might tarnish his memory. Dick, who died when I was young, was a brilliant, beautiful man with a capacity for kindness that transcended the roles of husband, father and grandfather. His passing left my grandma hollow. She now lives not only in the shadow of his death but also in that of her daughter's.

A FEW YEARS AGO, when she was in her mid-fifties, my auntie Jackey died suddenly of pancreatic cancer. I cannot overstate the impact this magical woman had on my life and the way I see the world. Her death is still felt acutely by all of us, but for my grandma it is the ultimate tragedy. The shattering of every timepiece. She wears her memories like overcoats now, shedding them for anyone who'll listen. But happy, idyllic memories are the only ones she lives in.

It can be trying, this endless and selective recalling of the past, but it's the groove she's slipped into in response to unimaginable pain; it helps her cope, and that demands patience and respect. Grandma spends a lot of time staring at the photo collages she has made of Jackey on her various travels, and those of grandpa on his beloved fishing trips, where he's cradling massive pikes, laughing his big head off.

The pictures of Jackey are still rich with the colours of her trips to the continent, but the ones of grandpa have, through years of sunlight and nicotine, faded to a milky sepia. We fear the same is happening to grandma's memory now. She's being tested for Alzheimer's, which aside from anything else is a major reason for me not sitting down with her to talk about mental health. She deserves to take only the safest, warmest memories with her on her journey, for as long as she can.

My favourite picture of grandpa is the one of him holding me as a toddler. I'm wriggling on his lap and we're both laughing, exposing the same thin gaps between our front teeth I have his green eyes. For generations upon generations of Morgans, only he and I don't have eyes the colour of Cadbury's Bournville chocolate. Funny who genes pick for what.

BETTY

I ALWAYS KNEW MY GRANDMOTHER WAS NERVOUS.
It was a family joke how tightly she'd grab my sister's wrists and mine when we'd cross the roads. If she took us on the 145 bus from my grandparents' Wanstead home to go shopping in Ilford, all circulation wrist-bone down would be lost the minute we stepped out the front door. As we crossed the street, our fingertips would turn a gentle blue. We'd recreate this squeeze with each other in private, shrieking with laughter when the grip became too much to bear.

"You don't need to hold my hand, Nanny!"

"Shhh. I dinnae care."

"It hurts!"

". . ."

We cackled, too, when she'd insist on suspending us over the toilet bowl to do a wee in a public toilet, even when we were far too heavy to lift and her little body would tremble under the weight. She'd flush the chain with a big wad of toilet paper over her hand. A different wad would be used to open the lock on the door. How we *laughed*!

All she ever said by way of clarification was "It's dirty," and when you're a kid, you don't question it. God but was she struggling.

Elisabeth Waugh Pearce (née Syme) was handsome and formidable: five feet two inches of working class, Scottish mining town piss and vinegar. I was in my first year of university when she died, about eighteen months before my granddad. She was a difficult woman. Really difficult. But I have so many brilliant memories of her. Her collection of Clinique make-up—a drawer of immaculate pistachio compacts that my sister and I would bolt to as soon as we got in the house. Her tight, two-piece blue velour track suit that she'd wear with pristine white Reebok tennis shoes—the kind now popular again—that made the most of her stonking tits and somehow lifted the flat arse my mum inherited and my sister and I didn't.

I think of her filling up cool bags with food from the freezer for my struggling parents to take home with us on a Sunday, every single week. Of how she'd bring out a massive jar full of coppers and silvers, count them out for me, Kate and James on the kitchen table and put them into money bags. If we were lucky, we'd get about £2.43—about C$4—each.

"There's at least a few quid in there," she'd rasp. "Be careful wae it, ya maniacs."

Her wit. Jesus Christ, her wit. Sharp as a dart, she was. Her thing was acting like she wasn't listening, sucking on her fag until the ash burnt long and red, then chiming in as soon as the conversation lulled with a line that made everyone's jaw fall onto their plate.

We all remember her farts. How she'd stand at the kitchen worktop and just start rumbling with a majestic length and timbre my ears have never been blessed with since.

"Fuckin*eel*, what was that?" she'd say, carrying on wiping or chopping.

"Nanny! It was you!"

"It wasnae. Set the table, please."

I loved her laugh, a rattling cackle that only surfaced when you'd really tickled her. Her pride. The way she refused to be patronized by anyone. An encounter with a member of staff who once corrected her in my presence in her local Somerfield lingers in my mind.

"Hiya, miss, where can I find balsmatic vinegar?"

"Er, it's bal*samic*, madam, not 'balsmatic.' "

"Alreet hen, I'm nae here for a language lesson. Where's the bloody vinegar?"

She put two fingers up and blew a raspberry behind the lady's back. If you could distill her humour to its purest elements, it would be two "up yours" fingers and a fart noise.

Her face was a picture. Constellations of bronze freckles covered every centimetre of her, just as they do my mum and sister. I remember the time Kate and I absolutely lost it one afternoon when we were staying there and somehow got to thinking of any possible insult that wasn't a swear word to whisper at her round the kitchen door. We got more and more giddy, reaching that point kids do when they're so hopped up that they turn pink and just start squeaking. *Bladder* was for some reason the final straw, and she chased us into the bedroom with a wooden spoon in her hand, eyes bulging. The freckles flushed red then—the last time I remember fully wetting myself laughing.

My favourite Betty image of all is of her late on a Sunday afternoon in her living room, wearing that velour track suit, with a roast-dinner-flecked apron overtop. She's swaying on her own in a backlit fog of smoke from the Superking Gold in her hand to Patsy Cline's "Crazy," and winks at me as I walk past the door.

That image of her lost in a smokey reverie is precious, because among all the good memories are very sad ones: vignettes of a woman in constant fight with herself. The wrist gripping and the general obsession with our mortality as soon as we stepped out the front door was one thing, but there were so many others. She feared us drowning in the bath and so would only run the water as deep as our ankles.

Cleanliness and an obsession with contamination was the big one. She was an insomniac and every single day would wake up before the birds to clean all the kitchen and bathroom surfaces with neat bleach. When I smell it now, I'm instantly transported to her kitchen: winking silver taps, and gleaming linoleum like buffed elephant's skin. People would joke about how you could "eat your dinner off Betty's floor." She'd laugh along, but it wasn't really a joke, this obsession with contamin-ation. If we ate out somewhere with her and Granddad, she'd spend five minutes polishing our cutlery, holding it up to the light to check if it was clean. She'd cut the meat open to make sure it was hot all the way through, put the tip of her knife in the middle and then rest it on her bottom lip (something my mum must have picked up as a kid, because she did the same thing with us).

She'd insist that we wash our hands when we woke up in the morning because "people scratch themselves in the night and get dirty." She'd tell us not to touch the railings on buses and Tube trains on days out to the *Cutty Sark* and the Natural History Museum, because they were "absolutely plastered" in germs. A whole seam of these apparently protective acts opens in my mind. It's heartbreaking, because of course she wasn't just trying to protect us. She was trying to calm her own obsessive thoughts.

Betty genuinely seemed to worry about everything, 24-7. As if she was just waiting for the earth to crack at her feet and swallow her up. She would sit in her recliner and watch television, literally wringing her hands, remembering things that needed doing, or overreacting to something in the news. If we were staying with her and my mum or dad were late picking us up, she'd pace the house thinking they'd died.

"They've got in a fuckin'' accident, haven't they, Paul?"

My granddad would shake his head silently.

"Why is she late? Why hasn't she called?"

My mum has many anecdotes about how Betty's anxiety manifested throughout her childhood. A standout one for me was how, if there was a storm, she'd make the kids sit in a line in the hallway with all the doors closed until it had passed, in case the lightning came through the windows. They could be there like that for hours. My mum says it got worse as Grandma got older, particularly when her grandchildren came along and around her menopause. At some point in her early fifties, when her hands were always shaking, Betty started drinking. More than a regular Scottish person's amount, anyway. It began slowly, imperceptibly. An extra Scotch, a couple of huge brandies after dinner. Over time she switched from Scotch to vodka—opaque for clear.

Never an archetypal "drunk," though, was Betty. No wild anger or slurring, save her tendency for the odd late-night phone call to my mum to tell her how disappointing my granddad was—theirs wasn't a marriage of visible affection.

In the mornings she'd sit at the head of the table with a heavy crystal tumbler of clear liquid as we ripped open the Kellogg's selection boxes she'd always have lined up for us when we got up. We brawled over the Golden Nuggets, as we did the car's front seat, and it wasn't water in the glass, but she was calm.

Betty died far too early. Her tiny body couldn't cope with the drink, but her mind couldn't manage without it. From the outside, to use one of those hackneyed tropes that so rarely reflect reality, life was okay. She and my granddad worked bloody hard to make and save money, as a school dinner cook and Redbridge County Council officer respectively. They had a lovely home, albeit one that must have needed to be fumigated with a jet engine when they moved out—the walls were basically blowing their own smoke rings. They were comfortable in their retirement and had a young family who were obsessed with them and visited all the time. They had a lively circle of friends. But as we know, none of this matters if you're living with anxiety all day every day.

The serenity of the swan gliding across a lake belies the paddle of ugly feet under the surface.

My mum and her brother both firmly believe Betty's alcoholism was self-medicating; that the shots of whiskey she'd have for her "nerves," one day became a steady Smirnoff-ing of profound inner torment. They tried to make her go to the doctor many times, but she wouldn't, couldn't, admit to having a problem. She didn't hide it, but she didn't know what to say. She knew she worried a lot, but the language to explain the force of that worry wasn't within her grasp. Terms like "anxiety disorder" and "OCD" weren't in her vocabulary. Life was just life, however difficult it was. You lived it, played the cards you'd been dealt and that was that: "It's just the way I am."

My uncle has a line now about how people of Betty's generation from tiny working-class towns didn't talk about mental illness, and although it's a generalization, I think he has a point. Maybe, if she'd known more about these things, if a twenty-ton press hadn't been placed on her emotional language at some point in her early life, she could have been helped. Instead, she chose the thing that could help her symptoms. That helped her exist quietly, in smaller and smaller spaces.

I've come to believe that the greater the pain of life, the smaller the space it is lived out in. When I was depressed, that space was bedroom sized. When my friend was having treatment for breast cancer, that space was a wipe-clean armchair in a "room" cordoned off by NHS regulation blue curtains. In the end, Betty's space was one chair in the kitchen of the home she and my granddad moved to back in Scotland after selling up in East London. It was a home she rarely took outings from with her shiny new Scottish Older and Disabled People bus pass— and my god was there green mineral beauty to see up there at the foot of the Clackmannanshire Mountains.

The outside didn't really concern her anymore, though. She joked that she liked staying at home because of the Jacuzzi (why in god's name there was a state-of-the-art silver Jacuzzi in an old folks' bungalow in a sleepy Scottish town is anyone's guess), but by that point the cancer was tearing through her gastrointestinal tract. She was weak and in pain.

That bus pass blazed in my memory after she died. Thinking of the picture inside it, imagining her standing in a photo booth in Tesco while my granddad spun that stupid seat around so it was high enough for her face to fit inside the circle, is too much. She was smiling but looked so small. Transparent, almost.

Eventually, her living space became a hospital bed. A child-sized coffin.

I wish she'd known it could be better. That the many people she represents—who have gone before, and suffered without a name for what they felt, and been labelled for the way they tried to cope (alkies, junkies, pill poppers)—knew it could have been better.

GREY MATTERS

BETTY WAS PART OF MY NATURE AND MY NURTURE. I spent every day with her from the age of six weeks until the age of two. My parents were barely in their twenties, living in a tiny flat in Walthamstow and trying to run a clothes shop. They had no choice but to work and relied on her and my granddad's proximity. Obviously, I can't remember any of it, but there are hordes of pictures of me flopping about on her bed, gummy stingray mouth, gleefully arranging plastic phones and Care Bear teddies. Betty is laughing in the background in a lot of these pictures, catching the flash with her gold tooth. My mum said she was fantastic with me and I don't doubt it. But I do wonder what kind of influence she had on my brain in those highly impressionable years of cognitive development.

Then, of course, there's Mum: Betty Version II. When I was a kid, many of the things that Betty used to do, my mum did, too—although to be fair, she was not as visibly fraught with the shaking hands and rigid shoulders. Nonetheless, germs, contamination and illness were themes that defined my early childhood and were behind all sorts of irrational, controlling behaviours on her part. While I wasn't an anxious child in terms of being avoidant, I did use to fixate on the things my mum said, and think very strange stuff that would, when I went over it in private, make me rigid with frustration.

For a short time—a few weeks, I think—I started pulling out my hair. I had a wall chart for a while, which awarded me a gold star and twenty pence to buy some penny sweets if I went a day without twiddling and yanking a piece of hair out. My dad became quite the deft hand at French-plaiting my hair over the bald spots, and the chart soon found its way into the bin.

My childhood fixations were *all* about contamination. If I walked past a dog turd and realized I had my mouth open, I'd start panicking that I'd inhaled some of the bacteria in the turd's force field and that I'd be gravely ill later on. I'd imagine literally puking myself inside out until I was a puddle of offal and bone on the bathroom floor. I'd take special care not to ingest anything that my mum said didn't "go" together—milk and orange juice, for example—because they might curdle in my belly and cause me to throw up buckets of scrambled stuff.

The fear of bacterial invasion and uncontrollable, forceful illness was at the root of it all. When I started ruminating, I'd do this thing with my hands where I'd repeatedly tap my fingertips into my palm. My mum would laugh when I did this and tell me not to be so stupid, and so, too, would my sister. Years later the whole family would laugh about it, using words like "weird." My mum's laugh was the same half-angry, stop-messing-about one she'd have when I first started experiencing panic attacks and would struggle through dinner, expecting every mouthful to choke me. So, I'd save up all the finger smashing and do it on my own in bed, in the dark, until I was exhausted and could read my books in a Garfield-eyed state of relaxation.

I don't want to go on about this stuff, because I know my mum will be reading this and I don't want to upset her. There's nothing to be gained from that at this point in my life, and my mother didn't understand what was going on inside her mum, herself or me. But if we're talking about genetic predispositions to anxiety and the shame that comes with the anxiety, I don't have to look very far. I knew what anxiety and shame were from an early age—I just didn't have the words.

"Predisposition" is the right word to use with anxiety. A family history of anxiety is less likely to be a guarantee of inheriting it in the way that we might inherit a genetic condition like Crohn's disease or hemophilia. Instead, our specific blend of genes puts us *at risk* for reacting to the world in different ways. What we inherit, really, is a vulnerability to anxiety. The type of anxiety suffered may differ from that of relatives, too. Neither my mum nor Betty, to my knowledge, had panic attacks; whereas panic attacks have defined my anxious years.

There are studies cropping up all the time that try to better our understanding of the genetic component of anxiety. Freud believed that all anxious personalities are shaped in childhood; and between the two world wars, when his theories were dominant, an adult's moods and behaviours would have probably been attributed solely to childhood and infant experiences. Psychoanalytic theory has moved on now, but even when neuroscience exploded in the 1980s and Joseph LeDoux's theories on anxiety and the amygdala were proven, psychotherapists were still over the moon because this biology also pointed to the influential role of childhood experiences.

I went to discuss development with a London-based child psychotherapist I'll call Clare. She is a lecturer at the Tavistock Centre and has over thirty years' experience in both acute and community care. "Learning that the amygdala is where we make sense of and respond to our memories was incredibly validating," she tells me. "It showed that our theories about formative experience had real biological underpinnings." Clare is a psychoanalytic therapist but "doesn't care so much" about Freud. She believes our capacity to become anxious has something to do with the neural pathways that start forming when we are inside the womb. She spent many years working in neonatal units and has a special interest in how infant experience can shape a child's emotions. She talks about how, "back then" (in the late eighties and early nineties), doctors were often very dismissive of a baby's ability to absorb its surroundings and, ergo, very dismissive of her.

The frustration was acute. "Some are still like that in many ways," she says, "but we have evidence now that clearly proves a baby's emotional intelligence. We're not just talking after they've been born, either. Even in utero, there is tremendous ability to learn and respond. Tremendous."

For a long time—up until writing this book, really—I poopooed the idea of how significant the stuff that had happened around me as a baby was. I've been quite close-minded, which is something I strive not to be. I want to be wide open, which is why I was so keen to talk to someone like Clare. After all, the very notion of "remembering" means so much more than what my conscious mind can recall today as I'm sitting at my computer.

Scientists talk about the "old" and "new" brain in terms of how we store and process memory, but a different organ wasn't lifted from a jar of formaldehyde and plopped into my head when I started to develop anxiety, however much it felt that way. My brain has become bigger and cleverer and more mixed up during my life, but it's still the same thing that bobbed under my squidgy baby fontanelle, commanding the gentlest of touch.

Talking to Clare, a woman of piercing intellect and with some of the kindest eyes I've ever seen, did away with any of the preconceptions I had stewed over on my bike ride to her house. I worried she might tut at me or suggest that I hadn't examined my childhood enough; that I still had a great big psychic basement to sift through. Assuming I'll be judged is, evidently, a habit I can't seem to shake. I couldn't have been more wrong in her case, though. She spoke of multicausality, the idea that a number of individual, community and/or environmental factors may interact to give rise to a particular condition, and shared very few ideas that many would consider "psychobabble." She also posed a lot of questions.

"What was your birth like?" she asks between sips of tea.

"I don't remember it all that well!" I laugh, knowing instantly how unfunny I sound. My hackles *just* begin to bristle. *All these anecdotal claims about people being able to remember their births and the bright lights and muffled voices make me want to blow a fat raspberry*, I say to myself, but tell her, "I've never thought too much about how my birth could have imprinted my psyche."

"That's fine, of course," she replies. "But do you know if it was traumatic?"

Actually, I do. Thirty-six hours was how long it took for me to make my way out of my mum's vagina. I was three weeks early, small and still covered in loads of that Dairylea stuff, vernix. My cord was wrapped tightly around my neck, my head as blue as a bruise. My mum was frightened and exhausted, poor woman. There were pictures, apparently, which were not kept.

All this, Clare says, can affect a young mind. She talks about a British psychoanalyst named Wilfred Bion, who presented a theory of trauma similar to Freud's idea of how we all suffer it by virtue of being born. We all experience the violent physical and psychic separation from our mothers. "In the womb," she says, "a baby can feel the edge of its world. When it reaches out, there is a wall. Being born takes that edge away. It forces the baby into a cold, wide-open space. You only have to look at the Moro reflex to see the effect of that physical adjustment to a new environment."

Also known as the startle reaction, the Moro reflex is a primitive thing that babies display very quickly after leaving their mother's body. It occurs when a baby's head suddenly shifts position, or if the temperature changes abruptly, or in the event of a loud noise. The arms jerk upwards and out-wards, palms up and thumbs flexed. The legs and head extend. Afterwards, the baby brings its arms together, makes tight little fists and screams blue murder. When I first saw my friend's brand new baby do it, I found myself gasping for breath. It was like watching the velociraptor being born in *Jurassic Park*, more reptilian than I could comprehend.

But what *is* this display? Can it, in such infancy, really be terror? Anxiety?

Bion wrote that babies are born into a state of chaos because their formative feelings aren't feelings. They are "states" that the brain experiences before proper thinking comes into being. The sheer force of those new states is unbearable to a baby.

But according to Frederick Woolverton (who holds a PhD and is director of the Village Institute for Psychotherapy in New York), in an article in *Psychology Today*, the level of trauma we experience is "determined by the nurturing we receive that helps us define, understand and exist well with, and not be haunted by, our early or "birth" trauma. [. . .] as adults, many of us continue to cope and co-exist with trauma."

"I have worked with countless families after a traumatic birth, and while there are a myriad factors that come into the equation with any anxious child, a traumatic birth is often part of the picture," Clare explains. "I believe it's part of what creates a *vulnerability* to anxiety."

I ask her to share some of her experiences with me.

"One individual really stands out in my mind," she says, taking her glasses off. "He was a boy of six or seven. He was referred to me because he was incredibly hyperactive, busy, busy, busy, couldn't concentrate at all, thought he was Buzz Lightyear. He'd run about the place getting himself in a state and found having to sit down with anything very anxious making. He just wanted to be on the move. When he was in my treatment room, he'd run around as he was talking but would stop every now and again to do this [she slowly stroked the side of her face a couple of times] before starting up again. Whenever I meet a highly anxious child, I always ask the parents about the child's history, and this includes their birth experience. When I spoke with his parents, they told me he was born very prematurely and spent weeks in a neonatal unit. We discussed what their contact was like with him while he was in the incubator and they told me how they couldn't hold him. All they could do was alternately put their hands through the hole in the glass and stroke his face."

Her eyes brim. "This lovely little chap was comforting himself when he felt overwhelmed in exactly the same way—the only way—his parents could comfort him while he was fighting for his brand new life."

This makes me cry. It's quite embarrassing.

"Remarkable, isn't it?"

Clare saw, in neonatal units, many things she'll never forget. "I worked in them a long time ago now, but I've never forgotten the parents of a very unwell baby. They were there all hours, as parents usually are, and one day the father brought in a harp to play to the child. His job was fixing them, I think, and he'd played them throughout his partner's pregnancy. There was a point where the baby's monitors started to reflect a simmering distress, and as he began playing the harp, we all watched in disbelief as the monitors began to settle."

I spent hours with Clare and she really did open my mind. I've always loved the imagery of a mind being "opened," as if our brains are infinitely expanding Narnia wardrobes we can endlessly stuff things into. And it's always interested me to read about specialists in a certain field having their minds opened by something so big it makes them U-turn on their beliefs.

Allowing our minds to be influenced and changed is crucial to the development of our knowledge of just about everything. High-tech brain scanning brought about widespread change in how scientists talked about anxiety and other mental health problems, but some psychologists changed their minds even before such advances. After decades of study committed to the sole influence of early experience, Dr. Jerome Kagan, a professor of psychology at Harvard University, began to lean more towards the idea that anxiety wasn't just learned but that it could also be part of a person's constitution.

In his 2011 book, *The Temperamental Thread: How Genes,*

Culture, Time and Luck Make Us Who We Are, Kagan lists a number of studies that shook his "inflexible commitment" to Freudian thinking. In the sixties, he was looking at evidence gathered on a group of "normal adults, born in the 1930s," who were part of a longitudinal study. Around 15 percent of these adults, who had been timid and scared in their first three years of life, told him how they "were shy, often felt unsure, avoided risky activities and were reluctant to take on difficult challenges." When Kagan and another scientist, Howard Moss, wrote a book in 1983 summarizing the project—*Birth to Maturity: A Study in Psychological Development*—they suggested that the anxious adults had, as children, "inherited a constitutional disposition." Their temperament was relevant, "where temperament refers to a set of biological properties affecting brain chemistry that are usually, but not always, due to the presence of specific genes." In layman's terms: we *can* be born worried.

More recently, Kagan followed a large group of Caucasian children "born healthy to intact, middle-class families in the Boston metropolitan area in 1989 or 1990," from four months of age until 2007–08, when they were eighteen years old. They arrived at several conclusions. Around 20 percent of the infants were "unusually responsive to events that were unexpected or unfamiliar." When brightly coloured toys they'd never seen before were put in front of them, the four-month-olds would "begin to thrash their limbs, arch their backs, and cry, as if this experience was too arousing for their brains." These infants, who Kagan calls "high-reactive" were also shy with strangers or when they entered unfamiliar rooms. At four-and-a-half years of age, most were shy when around unfamiliar adults or other kids. At seven, many needed a night light to sleep, were afraid to stay over at friends' houses and were "generally quiet in the school setting." As teenagers, many told Kagan and his colleagues that they "worried excessively about the future" and were anxious about things other teenagers weren't, like going to parties where they didn't know many people. Many of this group were also "reluctant to take the subway from their sub-urb home to central Boston," and one high-reactive adolescent even said she didn't like springtime because "the weather was unpredictable."

At the root of all these teenagers' fears was a fear of not knowing what might happen in the immediate future—the next hour, day or week—and as a result, their friends saw them as cautious and reflective. Scaredy-cats.

The next part of the study was where it got really interesting. To Kagan's "pleasant surprise," their anatomy was "in theoretical accord with their behavior"—i.e., the high-reactive teenagers' brains were found to be *physically* different from the others.

The amygdala, as we now know, detects changes in the outside world and within our bodies. It is our personal antenna that reacts to new experiences or the anticipation of those experiences by sending impulses throughout the body, causing all the lovely symptoms we get with anxiety.

A psychiatrist named Carl Schwartz viewed the brains of these eighteen-year-olds in an MRI scanner and found that the brains of the high-reactives looked different. The part of the brain that communicates with the amygdala, a small section of the frontal lobe called the medial prefrontal cortex (snappy, these names) was thicker than those not high-reactive. Their amygdalae carried on reacting for a considerably longer time to "unfamiliar pictures," such as a person's head on an animal's body, which, Kagan suggests, shows that this part of their brain resisted regulation.

To get a better grasp of what having a high-reactive brain means—or looks like—I visit Dr. Kate Jeffery, a Wellcome Trust Senior Investigator and a professor of Behavioural Neuroscience at University College London. She's there waiting for me as the lift doors open on the fifth floor of the UCL building over-looking Tavistock Square.

Images of the 2005 London terror attacks, one of which involved the detonation of a bomb atop a bus in the square, flash into my mind. What if something else happened here, today? How would I get home? What if I had a panic attack and couldn't help anyone? *For fuck's sake, stop it—*

"Eleanor? Hi." She shakes my hand, a sleek, smiley fig-ure with fine blond-grey hair. She's immaculately dressed all in black. I am a radioactive bog monster in my cycling gear. She leads me into her office and the first thing I notice, aside from the massive phrenology head by her computer screen, are three bumper boxes of Cup-a-Soup on a shelf.

"Big fan?"

"Yes," she says with a sigh, turning pink. "It's hard to get out of here sometimes."

It comforts me to think of a leading neuroscientist sipping hot mushroom water while she leads important research on human memory.

If an overactive amygdala is synonymous with anxiety, I wonder aloud, what might mine look like under a scanner. A bouncing bean in a curly grey sausage casserole?

"Uh, not quite." She smiles. "There are many types of scans we can do on the brain. A structural scan is just like an X-ray, but functional scans are where we're looking at things like oxy-gen consumption in specific parts of the brain. If some of the neurons in your brain start firing more than normal, they use up masses of energy. To supply that energy, the local blood ves-sels dilate slightly to increase blood flow and you can measure the oxygen in little bits of brain tissue. So that's what an fMRI [functional magnetic resonance imaging] scan does: it measures blood oxygen, which is a proxy for 'activity' in the context of, say, anxiety-provoking stimuli."

"If I were to become very anxious in an fMRI scan, what might show up?" I ask.

"Well, when the amygdala becomes more active, you are just getting more blood going to it. The computer turns it, or any other highly active part of the brain, into a kind of 'hot spot' on screen, so it's depicted as a bright orange blob. It's beautiful, actually."

"Not that I or any anxious person walks around with little burning suns in our brains when we're feeling bad?" I inquire.

"No, the orange is an artificial marker. But there is absolutely a physical change in the brain when someone becomes anxious."

"Which gives credence to the idea that if anxiety is one biochemical thing happening, there must be another biochem-ical thing we can do to calm it down," I note.

"Exactly," she says. "Actually, a neuroscientist friend of mine gave me a good tip for panic, because I get occasional panic attacks. They're something that has come and gone in my life and are defined by a feeling that I have to get out of wherever I am. A very strong need for escape. It's usually in airplanes or in some social situations. Even on planes I'm sure it's a social thing rather than a fear of falling out of the sky. I'm trapped in a social situation where it would be really embarrassing to freak out, and, consequently, I obsess over freaking out and then freak out."

Yep, know that one well.

"My friend said that for reasons that aren't fully clear, hyperventilation will often abort a panic attack. He said it's something to do with lactic acid. In research, lactate is often used to trigger panic for diagnostic purposes, and hyperventilation decreases lactic acid and seems to stop panic developing."

"And it works?" I ask.

"I've tried it quite a few times and it definitely helps."

"Presumably you're not propping yourself up against the wall and panting like a woman in labour," I tell her.

"No, no. You can quietly hyperventilate without people noticing. It's easier on a plane because there's all the roaring noise. So yes, this also suggests that there are biochemical switches we can sometimes trigger when we become anxious."

Many of Kagan's high-reactive group eventually grew out of their shyness and nervousness. "The consequences of their temperamental bias were now primarily on the inside," Kagan writes, "and reflected in private worries."

While the majority of the high-reactives did not go on to develop any kind of psychiatric disorder, 20 percent did. That 20 percent found themselves, as adults, unable to cope with their temperament and have been diagnosed with anxiety disorders and depression or both. One of the original group of high-reactive infants committed suicide. So what does this tell us? Kagan's sample is, of course, just one sample. It cannot be taken as a reflection of society as a whole. However, research has since produced many similar samples. If infants are high-reactive from four months onwards, an age where almost every interaction and reaction come from a place of nature and as yet still very early nurture, and the children continue to be high-reactive throughout their childhood but wind up as relatively well-adjusted adults, what has happened to the 20 percent who have found life much harder to deal with, who have developed anxiety or depressive disorders? To me, this gives weight to the idea that biology—genes—can *predispose* us to being highly sensitive as infants and then, depending on what happens in our lives, that sensitivity might become something else. Or it might not.

"Predicting the exact location where a rock will land after rolling down a mountain provides an analogy," writes Kagan. "Knowledge of the location, size, and shape of the rock, analogous to a temperament, permits an observer to eliminate many places where it will not rest, but it is impossible to know its final location because one cannot know the gullies and obstacles it will strike on its way down."

My sister, brother and I were all exposed to many of the same gullies and obstacles, yet I'm the only one who has an anxiety disorder. Both my siblings have experienced episodes of mild depression, but anxiety has never been a periodic obstacle in their lives in the way it has mine. The three of us have a similar mix of genes, but they clearly haven't made anxiety inevitable for us all.

My brother can be so laissez-faire about things that sometimes he might as well be walking at a backwards forty-five-degree angle. Interestingly, his appendix also burst around the same age mine did, when he was on holiday with my mum and her partner in Menorca. My mum found him in their villa bathroom, hair matted with sweat, being violently sick into the bathtub. Luckily, the doctors there got to the problem promptly and James recovered very quickly. These days he seems to forget it happened to him. "Oh yeah," he grunts. "That was weird."

People like him don't seem to have *any* nerves, at least on the outside. When I walk around the supermarket, apparently the epicentre of a lot of my nervous thinking, I look at people—*really* look at them, for longer than I should. I watch them puttering around the aisles, dropping heads of broccoli into their wheelie baskets, fingering bottles of special offer Radox Muscle Soak and think: *They look so calm. Do they suffer?* I mean, of course they suffer. Everyone suffers. But I wonder: *Do you get locked inside your head like I do? Do you ever feel like you're living in a bubble inside "real life" that you can't burst? Do you, Nice-Looking Suit Man buying two-for-one tortellini, know what it's like to wake up with an implacable sense of doom?*

I look at the checkout ladies cackling with each other, apparently locked into the present like mortise and tenon joints, and think: *Are we made differently, you lot and me?*

These are mini crises based on utterly irrational and superficial snap judgments of strangers in a small supermarket. I know this. I know there is absolutely no basis for staring at a jolly woman and thinking she hasn't got a care in the world. I'm doing that grand introspection thing that anxious people do, assuming everything from nothing. But over time, particularly with what I've learned about genes and how the brain can be influenced, I feel I'm able to look at the kind of people I've sometimes felt a million miles away from and say: *Yeah, we actually might be made differently. And that's all right. Genetics are a component of me, not my destiny.*

FEMALE HORMONES:
A BLOODY MESS

Our bodies and minds are such wonderful things,
even if they do act like bleeding cunts sometimes.
—Nell Frizzell, my dear friend, mid-cigarette, 2015

A NUGGET OF PENETRATING WISDOM, THAT. NELL was talking about the female body, of course, because from puberty to menopause, a woman's mind is so often at the mercy of that body and the chemicals making it tick. Gloria Steinem argued in her famous essay "If Men Could Menstruate" that should men have to work their way through a bumper box of Lil-Lets Super Plus tampons in less than a week, "doctors would research little about heart attacks, from which men would be hormonally protected, but everything about cramps." An ex-colleague of mine (male) used to create imaginary conversations between men in offices, one-upping one another with stories about their flows:

"Aw, mate, couldn't get on top of it this month. Soaked the bedsheets twice right down to the mattress. Missus flipped her lid, didn't she."

"That's nothing, mate, I have to use Super Plus Ultra with an Always Extra night pad for when it breaches, mate . . . yeah,

yeah, heavy flow my arse . . . more like Lake Superior, amiright?"

It is thought that anxiety is more common in women than in men, and it makes sense that our sex hormones might be the thing tipping the scales. Women: if you have the sheer *brass neck* to be biological, then your mind may suffer, too. Not *all* women struggle with their menstrual cycle, because, shit, not all women are the same.

I want to talk about the impact my biological cycle can have on my mental health, but I don't especially want to wear my biology as a badge of honour. It's tricky. Women have been fighting for decades to shake their image as frenzied, chocolate-stuffing slaves to their moon cycles, so it makes me feel a bit funny admitting that premenstrual syndrome (PMS) is as much a part of my anxiety as public transport and rooms full of strangers. Being open about struggling with something so inextricably laced into my biology comes with the fear of being seen as the dreaded hysterical woman; the breathing embodiment of a "she must be on the blob" joke. What a phrase that is. What semantics. If the "blob" part is the blood itself, can "she" actually be "on" it? Can she ride the blob around like a wobbly albumen Segway?

As time goes on I find it easier to talk about my anxiety, but the way PMS floors me some months isn't always part of those conversations. I try to only dissolve in private. Not because I'm prudish (I should work on being more prudish, really: it's been said that the core DNA of my humour is the phrase "up your arse"). I just don't want to be the woman who falters *because* she's a woman. As I've learned, though, not talking about things does no good. I falter in the same way millions of other women do across the world and get a lot of comfort when I hear other women talking about these things, because, to put a finer point on it, it makes me feel less mad. Less . . . hysterical.

Along with all the physical symptoms—upset guts, gas (oh boy), sweating, headaches, fatigue, dizziness, bloating, pain—being a person with a womb also means that things like aggression, sleep disturbance, reduced cognitive ability, mood swings, depression and anxiety are all considered par for the course at certain times of the month.

Without fail, my anxiety gets worse between ovulation and the first day of my period, settles throughout, then flares up again for a few days afterwards. It is literally like bloody clockwork. All the strategies and techniques I've learned in order to deal with my anxiety feel less reachable during this time. This is where female friends who know the drill are a godsend.

Poor Nell often has so much nervous energy when she has PMS that she has been known to run obscene distances, do strange things to her hair and become utterly convinced that everyone around her thinks she's an awful person, poor woman. One day she popped up in a Google chat window and informed me: "I just ran to Broxbourne [she lives in Hackney, so that's about twenty-three kilometres], got back and cut all my hair off." So we've developed a three-tier question system if one of us approaches the other with a feeling of unplaceable madness. First: "Are you about to get your period?" Second: "Do you need to eat?" Third: "Do you need a poo?" Great clarity can come with the answers.

Ever since my periods started on holiday in Cromer with my dad (I asked for money for "supplies," said I needed a tenner and spent most of it on the ten-pence machines in the amusements), I've imagined what it might be like to not have to experience this weary metamorphosis every month. I remember the few days leading up to period number one and feeling so . . . *off*. Withdrawn, conversation-less, homesick for no place or person in particular. We were playing crazy golf when I first experienced the heavy grind of period pain. I sat on the grass, between my attempts at putting a small ball into a giant, gnashing clown mouth, saying I was tired. I bled through my shorts. My poor dad.

Although I often struggle with this part of being a woman, I remain in awe of my body and the cycle itself. It's a feeling of reverential respect, wonder and fear, because really, it's black magic. If you've ever seen a picture of a womb inside a body, you'll know it looks unremarkable: a pink, glistening blob like the rest of our innards. But wombs are magic cauldrons. They grow *life*. New people, from microscopic raspberry clusters of cells. Tiny brains, skeletons, hearts, lungs, penises and tiny new wombs grow inside wombs. It's animal nature itself.

The big question is: *Why* do female hormones affect our mental health so much?

Menstruation itself doesn't kill, even when you're growling in bed with pain that is so unlike any other: an assault rifle through the sacrum and down the thighs. Even in poverty-stricken parts of the world where women are forced to use things like sand, old rags and dirty newspapers to absorb their blood because they can't afford towels or tampons—a serious world health issue and great remover of dignity that is only just being given the humanitarian effort it deserves—it's not the bleeding itself that is fatal but the way the hormones involved with menstruation affect our minds can be.

Premenstrual conditions are, in 2016, poorly understood

and in so many cases poorly managed. These things are still all too easily dismissed as "women's problems," and not being on the agenda is part of the problem. Sadly, though, it's also down to our imprecise knowledge of which chemicals do what exactly inside the brain.

I would love to be able to present a thrilling intellectual chase through the world of hormones, but despite there being over 150 different symptoms of premenstrual syndrome, the exact etiology (cause) of it is unknown. Just like any other mental health problem.

Yep, we're there again.

Research into the overlap between reproductive and mental health is ongoing, but still largely inconclusive. The brain areas responsible for regulating emotion and behaviour are studded, like a Christmas orange, with receptors for sex hormones—estrogen, progesterone and others—that affect the functioning of neurotransmitter systems. These systems can change our mood and way of thinking. So if they're functioning differently, we feel differently. However, it's not clear why some women are more sensitive than others.

Being predisposed to anxiety and depression appears to influence how hormones affect us each month, and a rule of thumb is often applied: If you already have a mental health problem, it *may* get worse between ovulation and your period. There is also a link between our genes and our vulnerability to being oversensitive to bodily changes, which would include changes brought about by hormones. The sum of any or all of these parts is symptoms. And when those symptoms are so severe that they interfere with work, relationships and day-to-day functioning, it may be premenstrual dysphoric disorder, or PMDD.

I didn't know of this acronym or even that there was a different term for severe PMS until a couple of years ago. If you'd looked in the DSM for a definition of PMDD before 2013, the explanation was "depressive disorder not otherwise specified." Staggering insight there. It has since been expanded, but NHS guidelines state that while most women with PMS find their symptoms uncomfortable, a small percentage have symptoms that are "severe enough to stop them living their normal lives." The symptoms of PMDD affect 5 to 8 percent of women in the world per the National Association for Premenstrual Syndrome, with the caveat that the syndrome is likely to be underreported, especially by women from ethnic minorities.

The symptoms of PMDD are like those of PMS, but are "more exaggerated" and often far more psychological than physical, including feelings of hopelessness; depression; very low self-esteem; high levels of tension and irritability; sleeping more or less than usual; decreased interest in usual activities; and, of course, extreme anxiety. Suicidal thoughts are also common.

Because of the way these things present, women are frequently diagnosed with conditions like bipolar disorder and medicated with the wrong kind of drugs. The crucial difference between PMDD and bipolar disorder is that the symptoms of PMDD are cyclical and subside once bleeding starts. I don't have PMDD, but this relief is something I feel most months: a wave of calm once the floodgates open. I'd happily trade a week of soaring anxiety and mini existential crises for one of pain, sheet washing and exhaustion.

Despite PMDD now being recognized as a disabling and potentially life-threatening condition, it still feels like conversations about it are too often happening in private. We have a terrible tendency in modern society to not engage with subjects we don't know much about or that don't affect us directly. We're quick to dismiss struggle we don't recognize; to think: *Surely it can't be that bad.*

It *is* that bad for some women, though, and by default, for those around them—their partners, families and friends.

Online forums teem with people desperately trying to work out together what's wrong. The exchanges ring with the frustration of sufferers feeling they can't discuss the problem openly with friends and family, in case no one will understand or they'll be thought "crazy." The desperation is palpable, particularly when they talk about even their doctors being dismissive. Women share stories of being suicidal, being unable to control their thoughts, self-medicating with all sorts of drugs. Some want hysterectomies in their twenties and thirties because they just can't fathom another month of such mental distress.

Hormones aren't "just" hormones. They can be chemical warfare.

CALMING THE TIDE

PMS AND PMDD CAN BE FRIGHTENING FOR THE sufferer and those around her, but they are eminently treatable conditions. There will always be a certain doctors (usually male, perhaps of retirement-on-the-horizon age) who roll their eyes at a woman who comes to them and says, "My hormones are destroying me"; and there is without question a gulf between what some women experience and the understanding of that experience across the medical field. However, it is wrong to suggest that women will be left to flounder if they present with symptoms of PMS or PMDD.

We have made significant progress in getting premenstrual syndromes validated. But in 2013, when PMDD first appeared as its own listing in the DSM-5 (that evocative "depressive disorder otherwise specified"), some feminists were understandably aghast. Women suffering in the run-up to their periods aren't mentally ill, they said. They're just women.

I can understand why a diagnosis of PMDD might make a woman feel like her body's natural rhythms were being pathologized. The writer Diana Spechler put this brilliantly in a column ("This Is My Brain on PMS") in the *New York Times*:

> Upon receiving my diagnosis, I, too, objected to affixing to myself yet another label—Depressed Diana, Anxious Diana,

Diana the Insomniac, Diana who turns into a raging maniac each month before her period. This was not a verdict I wished to advertise. I was not going to sport an awareness ribbon on a pin. I felt ashamed that I'd been deemed out of control of my emotions; I felt like a cartoon character woman wielding an ax, surrounded by heating pads and Advil and wadded-up Kleenex.

PMDD was also surrounded with conspiracy for a while. I read an interesting interview about this, also in the *New York Times*, with Dr. Kimberly A. Yonkers, an associate professor in psychiatry and obstetrics, gynecology and reproductive sciences who heads the PMS, perinatal and postpartum research program at Yale University School of Medicine. She tells a story about a student she met at Yale who had written her thesis on PMDD and then rang her for an interview. At the core of her thesis was the idea that PMDD was a diagnosis generated by physicians and pharmaceutical companies. Yonkers advised her to change it (which she eventually did) because she couldn't have gotten it more "backwards" if she tried.

"In point of fact," she says, "in the late eighties and early nineties when we first started treating people with severe PMS, we didn't have any medications that worked." She says women were "begging for help" and that pharmaceutical companies wouldn't support people like her in "mounting clinical trials of drugs for women with PMDD because they didn't have the patents on the medicines." The National Institute of Mental Health wouldn't support very much, either, because PMDD wasn't yet in the DSM. Essentially, the pharmaceutical companies didn't think they'd make a buck from PMDD so didn't want to acknowledge or fund it. It wasn't until companies were able to obtain patents for some of their compounds that they were "willing to loosen up and study this," and people like Yonkers had to force them, saying, "Look, people are suffering. You have to help us out." By now you might be getting an idea of the DSM's power and how it monetizes mental illness in the US.

I spoke to a lady called Kim, thirty-one, from Cornwall, who I found on a PMDD subreddit. ("Now we can all feel crazy together, aroooooo" is the tagline, its logo a paintbrush drawing of a wolf and a blood moon, of course.) Over email, she tells me about that suffering and how having her period is the only mental respite she gets every month.

"My anxiety levels build so dramatically before I get my period that I often can't sleep. I've gone for days with about two hours sleep a night because I am lying in bed sweating, feeling like my entire life is collapsing." She says she gets a couple of days after her period has finished of feeling reasonable, but knows when the hormones are "kicking in" again because she feels constantly on the verge of a panic attack. Despite having been put on the combined contraceptive pill to try to help things, "I can't think straight, have no appetite and feel constantly sick and dizzy," she says. "As I approach my period I find it difficult to leave the house, start crying in the street and feel genuinely out of control of my emotions. I call in sick to work at least three days a month because I'm such a wreck."

PMDD has made her feel suicidal on several occasions and the last episode was so "out-of-body feeling" that she got an emergency appointment with her GP, who, thankfully, acted on it swiftly. She is now taking an SSRI and "slowly starting to feel less like I only get a week of sunlight in a month."

It's hard hearing about women being on their knees like this, feeling as though no one understands or can help them. Again, no expert can say exactly what's going on in the brains of women like Kim. As Yonkers said, "We don't know how it happens. It's probably the case that it is not simply a deficit of a certain hormone or gonadal steroid; meaning, it is not that some women have a relative lack of an amount of estrogen or progesterone, or that they have an excess of either hormone."

We cannot yet isolate any one thing and blame it entirely. I have read articles about how there is a lack of research on PMDD, but I suspect it's the same deal with all mental health research: lots of science, lots of broad proof, but not enough specifics.

This brings us back to multicausality again. Premenstrual disorders are just one type of mental health issue that can arise from a confluence of biological and environmental triggers. As a woman who has an "underlying condition" (an anxiety disorder) and who finds that PMS makes it worse, do I just have to accept that there's currently no solid theory about why that happens? Right now, yes. Do I have to accept that I must live in misery because of it? No.

There *are* interventions that can make things a hell of a lot better for women with PMS and PMDD. It's key to keep a diary for two or three cycles to plot where your moods and anxiety levels change relative to where you are in your cycle, because you'll be told to do it, and it's always better to get a head start. I resisted for ages, mostly because I'd forget until I was feeling shit and then lose hope and be all *Bleerrrruuuuururughghhh, what's the point?*

Eventually, I downloaded an app (the idea of keeping a

handwritten menses journal was a bit much for me) called Clue. It gives you a nice spherical graphic that, once you've put the first day of your period in, plots when you'll be ovulating and when you might start experiencing PMS, which is displayed as little storm clouds. You can also add notes on days you're having symptoms. I have found this so helpful. If I wake up feeling odd, with a familiar sense of foreboding that doesn't disperse throughout the morning the way it usually does, I look at my app, and nine times out of ten I am either about to ovulate, ovulating or on that cloudy path to my period. These are the points in the cycle when hormone levels fluctuate most, and for me I get some comfort being able to think *Oh yeah, that explains it* when I get anxious, even if my techniques for managing it don't change.

When I recently found myself in the company of gynecologists a lot (I'll come to this), I told them about the app, and they said, all buzzing, that they would recommend it, or something similar, to their patients.

Once you have "evidence" of the pattern of your symptoms, you can go to your GP and say, "Hello, this is happening to me. Here's the proof. I can't deal with it. Help." Your doctor will invariably suggest making committed changes to your lifestyle like eating well, exercising and getting enough sleep—these things are boring, but for all a body's durability, it is still a fleshy factory that needs maintenance—as well as recommend other treatments.

Drugs-wise, the combined pill (estrogen and a progestogen) was routinely dished out as a first-line treatment for PMS for a long time. GPs are also starting to prescribe the progestogen-only "mini pill," because the combined pill *can* cause mood swings as a side effect—which is exactly what you don't want when you're seeking help for mood swings.

This is a recent shift, though, and not all GPs will be up-to-date. So, do your own research. Ask questions. Don't ever be afraid of telling your GP what you have read or what you are worried about. Don't ever, *ever* let someone say, "It's just hormones." You are not letting womankind down to say you can't cope.

If your symptoms are very disruptive, you might be recommended an SSRI, thought to be successful because the reuptake of serotonin plays some role in PMS and PMDD. The fluctuation in my anxiety levels throughout the month became less dramatic when I started taking one. Your GP should also suggest—particularly if your symptoms fit with PMDD—that you see a CBT therapist to learn new ways of managing anxiety and depressive rumination when they arise.

The tools you acquire in CBT can be applied to changes in mood or anxiety from any trigger, and if you become more confident about how you rationalize your anxiety generally, it can feel less frightening when symptoms start appearing throughout the month. Other treatments include estrogen-only patches or implants and, in severe cases when all other treatments have failed, gonadotropin-releasing hormone (GnRH) analogues that create a temporary menopause.

The most radical treatment for PMS or PMDD would be a total hysterectomy with removal of the ovaries (oophorectomy)—those innocent-looking hanging fruits that secrete our sex hormones. This elective operation is done on the NHS, and by doctors in North America and Canada, but is viewed as an absolute last resort, and because future fertility is removed with those organs, even if a woman suffers such debilitating distress each month she feels suicidal and has concluded that she prioritizes sanity over hypothetical pregnancy, she will have to do a lot of convincing.

I do wonder if we'll ever get to the point where a woman being certain she doesn't ever want to get pregnant (or, more pointedly, where a woman is willing to forsake future pregnancy for the sake of her sanity) won't be so alarming. There isn't a lot of independent information available about this operation for PMDD, but there are very popular threads on sites like pmsforum.co.uk and several blogs by women who have described their experiences, intending to create the independent, straight-talking resource about hysterectomy for PMDD that they wished they'd had access to.

There are also very good, open-minded doctors out there who are not only sympathetic to the psychological agony these syndromes can cause but are also interested in developing treatment for them. It's far from ideal in the face of such suffering, but sometimes we just have to use those gonads to find the doctors who will listen.

NEEDLES, EGGS AND FREEZERS

EARING I'M NOT BEING LISTENED TO OR NOT BEING told everything is one of the saddest, most infuriating feelings I know. And, as I've learned, frustration shares a lot of the same "qualities" as anxiety. One of the situations I find most frustrating—and therefore anxiety provoking—is someone dismissing concerns I have about my own body. Last autumn, as had been planned for a while, I had my eggs harvested to create embryos (with donor sperm) for a much-wanted future pregnancy. The process triggered one of the worst anxiety flare-ups I've had in years.

Due to the appendix lark and the surgeries I have needed since, my fallopian tubes have become blocked with scar tissue. For years I suspected that this did not bode well for future conception but found out for certain in 2014 when, before an operation, my surgeon offered to do a fertility test "while they were there." He said this with the same inflection as someone offering a cup of tea since the kettle had just boiled.

Dye was injected through my womb to see if it emerged in both tubes. No dice. I'd have to consider IVF if I wanted to become pregnant in the future. So, after a year on the waiting list at my local hospital, I began my treatment.

As I was starting my hormone cocktail, the British Fertility Society made headlines by suggesting that every twenty-five-year-old woman should be offered a "fertility MoT"—like a car service test, poking under the hood (pun thoroughly intended) to see what was working and what was not. The BFS's chairman, Professor Adam Balen, said: "There is a lack of understanding of the dramatic decline in fertility and, of course, there are pressures to develop careers. Every week in our clinics I see couples who express surprise because they didn't realize the degree to which fertility goes down in your thirties."

There is no agreement yet on what such a "fertility MoT" might include (though there have been some suggestions), but the option of egg freezing will almost certainly come into it. It was interesting to be going through the process while egg freezing became even more of a prevailing conversation topic than ever.

Women in their twenties and early thirties are always talking about egg freezing as we work out how the "best by" dates on our ovaries might fit in with our plans—a biological clock we are reminded about nearly every waking minute. We're forced to imagine future versions of ourselves, holograms of life not yet lived. It's strange being in a bind with your own biology. But while it might be great, in theory, to discover our options earlier, perhaps the reason Balen's message resonated with so many women was not that it joined the never-ending stream of diktats about pregnancy but that it pointed a big red arrow towards the stuff that isn't discussed when we talk about fertility.

Though there are endless public discussions about making babies, the complexities of fertility itself are not aired unless they're part of the omnipresent, anxious-making DON'T LEAVE IT TOO LATE warnings. What *actually* happens when you freeze your eggs is rarely touched on.

As I injected my belly daily with hormones, I thought about this MoT thing and wondered how many twenty-five-year-old women truly know what they have to put their body through in order to freeze their eggs. Who is explaining the uncertainty, pain and anxiety they might feel? It strikes me that if we're going to expand discussions about fertility, we need to be clear about what these things involve. It isn't scaremongering to be realistic. How is misinformation or the omission of the facts protecting us?

The way the term "egg freezing" is casually thrown around belies not just how hard the process can be for a woman but also that it comes with no guarantees. Right now it feels like this giant crash mat we all think we'll have to fall back on.

In 2014, Silicon Valley companies announced they were offering egg freezing as an employee perk. It was a move that, despite purporting to give women choice, also smacked of hustling them into working to an age where it becomes a lot harder to have kids. It packaged pregnancy as a rival to work that must be fenced off for corporate use. Also, there was little information about the process itself—what, as I said earlier, a woman has to put her body through in order to freezer her eggs, with no guarantees of success. The reality is that egg freezing is an experience that can make a woman feel like a stranger in her own body and mind.

Egg freezing—or embryo freezing, if you're planning for the future with your partner and/or are using donor sperm as I did—means doing a round of IVF without the embryo transfer at the end. It can be expensive as well as gruelling—self-funded egg freezing at King's College Hospital in London costs £2,500, then an additional £250 annual storage past twenty-four months. In Canada, the cost of egg freezing can be considerable. You're looking at between $3,000 and $6,000 for the retrieval of the eggs, plus the cost of the fertility drugs needed (around $3,500), egg storage ($1,000 for five years) and the IVF when the time comes to fertilize and implant the eggs (between $3,000 and $4,000 per cycle, based on which province you live in).

Depending on variables such as your natural egg reserves (if they're low, so are your chances) and FSH (follicle-stimulating hormone) levels, you will be given a bespoke cocktail of hormones to ingest and inject over a number of weeks to achieve the following: stabilize your womb lining, stimulate your ovaries into producing several massive follicles, stop them releasing eggs (ovulating) and then, finally, with an ovulation trigger injection, "mature" the eggs to be collected under deep sedation or general anesthetic.

It's important to state that many women get along with the hormone medication fine and can carry on their day-to-day lives. My experience was just that: mine. I was one woman out of hundreds using the same fertility centre at the same time. We've all heard horror stories about IVF, but there are things I wish I'd been more prepared for, especially how it might affect my mental health.

I mentioned to the hospital at the beginning of the treatment that I struggle with anxiety. As a compulsory part of the IVF process you must agree to see a counsellor, which I did. She was sweet. I told her how helpful it would be for me to receive as much information as possible about my potential responses to the drugs. I was given many printouts, which stated that the drugs can produce symptoms "similar to" PMS. This was, er, an understatement.

Some of the pills they put you on to maintain your womb lining contain huge amounts of estrogen, which when elevated in early pregnancy is thought to be responsible for morning sickness. That is what the nurse told me on the phone when I called to say that I'd been on the verge of vomiting for two weeks and was a bit concerned. "Oh yes," she said. "We should have mentioned that they can make you feel quite sick."

It was a twenty-four-hour hangover-sick feeling that put me constantly on edge: Do I dare leave the house? Do I go to that meeting if I might puke? This line of internal chatter merged with the business-as-usual one and pumped my anxiety levels up like a car jack. The only respite was the odd spike of intense, sugar-specific hunger. All I wanted to eat was cake and melon.

IVF can be lonely, especially considering how significant it feels when you're doing it. People don't want to ask you about it too much. It's probably one of those things you can't empathize with unless you've done it, which is understandable, but I think people also assume you want it to be private because it's babies, ovaries, vaginas and all that. This is a shame, when you'd actually love it if someone came round and asked questions while your gut ballooned like a gout-riddled, Tudor-dynasty drunk.

Those few weeks when I was undergoing hormone treatment made me realize how strange it is that we rely on other people's intuition so much when we're feeling vulnerable. Or, how hard it can be to say to a friend: "I'm struggling a bit, mate. Do you mind coming over for an hour?" It's a frustration that brings me to tears sometimes, this desire for company when things are tough and my inability to ask for it because I just don't know what to say. The very idea of asking makes me wince, because even though I have never considered anyone who's asked *me* for help weak—ever—that's where my thoughts go. My frustration is even greater because I *know* people would come if I asked.

My friends are wonderful people, but they're not mind readers. No one is. We all have our own stuff going on. Maybe I spent so long hiding and papering over my anxiety—my biggest vulnerability—that the groove grew too deep. I've had people fall apart on me many times over the years, but when I think about it, I don't think I've ever really fallen apart on anyone except the people I've been in relationships with. No friends, no family members. I don't suppose that's a very healthy thing, especially given how close my friendships are.

It can be interesting who your wingmen are when life coughs up a doozy. Sometimes they're unlikely figures. When I went through my last breakup, a torturous severance that knocked the wind right out of me, I was of course helped and supported by close friends. I stayed with Kate for nearly two months, sleeping on her sofa while I found somewhere new to live. She was going through a particularly bad "off" period with her on-off boyfriend of fifteen years and we would sit up every night, eating beans on toast and frozen tubs of Greek yoghurt in front of the television, propping each other up like pillows.

We ran each other baths and, by the end of the seven weeks, could have written a timetable for each other's bowels. But I also found wonderful support in a friend I'd not seen for years, who got in touch out the blue. He messaged me every day: no greeting card platitudes, only little acknowledgements of the mortification of it all. For a couple of weeks he was the first person I spoke to in the morning and the last person I spoke to at night. He shared his own experiences and generally provided a buffer between me and the world when I was walking along the sidewalk crying.

A similar thing happened with the IVF. A relatively new friend I'd met via Twitter had recently been through the same thing and was incredibly supportive. We didn't know each other that well, but she checked in with me every day and we began a real, raw dialogue that has led to great friendship. Shared experience stirs empathy like nothing else—particularly with this sort of "icky" thing.

When I saw that the artist Polly Morgan had written a piece for the *Spectator* about the loneliness of IVF (she, too, is infertile because of a burst appendix), I felt compelled to write to her. A friend passed on her email and we met the next day, quickly bonding over a garlicky Turkish meal in Hackney Wick. We've become good friends since. A special relief arose with discussing how morbidly obsessed we had both become with the world of fertility forums, where women communicate through infantile acronyms about their DHs (dear husbands), exchange "baby dust" and refer to embryos as "embies."

We laughed about how many times throughout the process you have to have the dildo-cam pushed between your legs in a room full of people, and watch earnest doctors militantly rolling a heavily lubed-up condom over it. How all the terminology surrounding fertility is so farmyard-y—"harvest," "fertilize," "egg collection"—but no one really tells you how bovine you might actually feel. The soaring anxiety that comes with the hormonal cocktails they have you on, even for women like Morgan who haven't struggled with anxiety much in the past. The druggy, cartoonish tiredness. The tears.

The harvest itself can be incredibly painful and take a while to get over. You're knocked out while they "introduce" (I love the polite words they use) a thick needle through your vaginal wall and drain the pumped-up follicles of their liquid, which hopefully contains mature eggs. But when the drugs wear off, you might not just experience "some cramping," like the nurse warns—you might have pain that makes you look like you're trying to hold an aubergine inside your arse as you walk around.

I wish I'd been told before beginning the treatment about the risk of ovarian hyperstimulation syndrome (OHSS). This condition occurs when a woman's body is very sensitive to the fertility drugs taken to increase egg production, causing too many eggs to mature in the ovaries; the ovaries then become very large and painful, inciting abdominal swelling, intense pain, nausea and vomiting. OHSS is rare, but I still wish I'd been told, because I ended up being admitted to hospital one weekend because of it.

Above all the physical stuff, though, I wish the worsening of my anxiety throughout the treatment cycle had been met with a response other than "Most women find . . ." and other parroted platitudes. I am *a* woman, not most women. If I hear the phrase "Most women find" in a hospital again, I think my tits might invert.

I understand that doctors need to fit your individual presentation with those they've seen throughout their years of practice, and I knew that there was probably nothing they could do for the increase in anxiety triggered by a potent, drawn-out cocktail of pregnancy hormones, along with a lot of time spent in an environment I find highly unsettling, but I wanted to tell someone—anyone—who was treating me to just take the pressure level down a bit.

It was one of the worst flare-ups, or "blips," of anxiety I'd had in years, which I conveyed to the doctor. His response was "Well, what would you like me to do about it?" I surprised myself in being able to reply, "Nothing, I suppose," realizing that he just didn't get it and that I was lucky to have the strategies to talk myself around. What made me angry was imagining other women receiving this response after saying they felt anxious or depressed by an ordeal as psychological as it is biological. Because if you're prone to either anxiety or depression and have a tough experience with IVF, it can really take its toll.

The following should go without saying, but I'll say it anyway: I cannot overstate my gratitude and wonder for a system like the NHS, which provides this dazzlingly sophisticated and potentially life-changing treatment free, particularly when I speak to my friends in the US who have had to remortgage their homes or move back in with their parents to afford it. In Canada, provincial and private health insurance companies have been slow to recognize infertility as a legitimate medical issue. Provinces often pay for investigative procedures, including surgeries such as repairing blocked fallopian tubes or removing endometriosis, and some also cover a portion of the cost of ovulation induction and insemination. However, only Ontario and Quebec pay for IVF.

Throughout the process I was reminded of how talking about feeling mentally vulnerable so often plays second fiddle to physical symptoms. When I talked about pain, second opinions were dialed in. When I talked about my anxiety and how I was feeling just a notch away from really not coping, no one was called. The counsellor I'd seen previously wasn't available because I'd not given enough notice. Sadly, I didn't anticipate becoming as anxious as I did.

Another disclaimer: I knew it wasn't going to be easy, contrary to the beliefs of some commenters on a piece I wrote for the *Guardian* about the procedure. "Surely you should be getting yourself informed beforehand on things you are about to do. Why complain about it afterwards?" said someone called "Oomph." I wonder if Oomph's thesis should apply to anyone doing anything vaguely medical ever. An actual pregnant lady, for instance. "Now, come *on*, silly cow," he'd say. "You knew what you were getting yourself into when you opened your legs, so for the love of god, stop your wittering about indigestion and incontinence. Get a grip!"

WE CAN LOAD UP on information that's available until we're blue in the face. I did plenty of research—of course I did—but a million web pages and photocopied leaflets have nowhere near the power of one human conversation. That's why I wrote the *Guardian* piece: in the hope that it would help others going through the same thing to talk and be listened to. We don't always want concrete answers, or know how we want others to use our information—we just want to share it and feel it's heard, even for a second.

BLUE CURTAINS

L OVE, TWO CENTIMETRES FROM GRIEF," IS HOW MY friend Eva described the feeling she had for her new baby after she was born. Eva Wiseman is a columnist for the *Observer* and wrote about birth and babies (even though she had thought she wouldn't) because, as she said, how could she not? It was everything.

"Because they tell you: 'All that matters is that your baby is healthy,' but without wanting to make you feel bad, baby, asleep here next to me with your snore like a faraway A-road, that's bullshit," she wrote. "That phrase is one that works to embarrass and silence us. It doesn't mean to, but it does. So five months on it's considered pretty gauche to still be talking about the birth."

I saw Eva a lot in those months, her baby a most perfect seashell, and we talked about it all. The opinions people have that snake through your belly; the loneliness; the guilt of not feeling serene and cocooned the way the adverts tell you you'll feel, and instead pace-y, lonely and mad—feelings made even scarier because it's all love.

I could only empathize with the newness and weight of it all. She was my first friend to have a baby (Kate followed shortly), and while she never sought treatment for postnatal depression and was able to hold on to some very strong mental foundations, my bearing witness to all that big emotion happening in a small space made me think about how thin the membrane is between coping with that adjustment and not coping.

PERINATAL MENTAL HEALTH illnesses ("perinatal" means the period between getting pregnant and the baby being a year old) are incredibly common, thought to affect at least one in ten women in developed countries. Sally Hogg's 2013 report, *Prevention in Mind*, for the NSPCC (National Society of Prevention of Cruelty to Children) estimated that in England alone, 284,890 women are affected each year. Over a quarter of a million women. Every year. According to the American Psychological Association, up to one in seven women experience postpartum depression.

These are astonishing numbers, particularly when you consider that nearly half of all women live in places where there are no perinatal mental health provisions. Of the services that exist elsewhere in the UK, few met national quality standards as of April 2015. Pregnancy and giving birth, it seems, are still so often seen as a physical passage for the mother, rather than a physical *and* psychological one. But when perinatal mental health problems can range from anxiety and panic attacks to depression, PTSD and even postpartum psychosis, it makes those statistics—over a *quarter of a million people* in England alone—scream.

Figures released in December 2015 by the Royal College of Midwives (RCM) suggested that the number is more like 20 percent of *all* women who experience perinatal mental illness. For many of these women, the main problem is anxiety. The National Institute for Health and Care Excellence (NICE) has said that 13 percent of women experience anxiety during pregnancy, and around 12 percent experience depression—with many affected by both.

Yet perinatal anxiety is little discussed and too rarely recognized. The RCM estimates that only around half the cases are identified. "We have designed our programs to tackle anxiety early on because it's such a big issue," Rachel Jenkins, occupational therapist and leader of the therapeutic group courses at Bluebell, a Bristol-based charity supporting families affected by perinatal mental illness, told the *Guardian* in an interview.

"'Perinatal depression' is misleading as a term. Far and away the most prevalent condition I see is anxiety," she says. "It is common to catastrophize. Often women worry something is wrong with the baby." Women referred to Bluebell (by a GP or health visitor, usually) frequently reported insomnia, feeling tense and irritable, social paranoia, sickness, trembling, blurred sight, breathlessness and a racing heart—all classic presentations of anxiety.

Without the right help, low-level anxiety and depression can become disabling. However, the fact is that there isn't a mental health nurse in every maternity unit, and health visitors are not rigorously trained to spot or ask about subtle changes in a woman's mental state. Women can find themselves drowning in anxious and depressive ruminations, not knowing who to ask for help.

The cuts to local health authorities implemented by David Cameron's Tory government produced one of the worst mental health care crises in the UK in history, and perinatal mental health was no exception—despite George Osborne's pre-2015 General Election pledge that "those who suffer from [children's and maternal mental health] illnesses have been forgotten for too long. Not anymore. We stand for opportunity for all."

A review by the King's Fund think tank in November 2015 found that there was now "widespread evidence of poor quality care" and that more than two-thirds of mental health trusts had recently overhauled services. Of those, more than half had plans to reduce staffing levels, or the skills mix, in its workforce. It doesn't take a master economist to attribute this to the use of unproven, cheaper services in a bid to balance the books. Oh, George, David, Jeremy Hunt—you've had women's backs all along, haven't you?

As part of the *VICE* Guide to Mental Health, I commissioned journalist Jude Rogers to write about her experience with postpartum depression, which she says was more a slow-burning, shape-shifting anxiety that wound up leaving her feeling very unwell indeed. Her piece, which detailed how difficult she found it to get help, sparked great conversation across social media networks.

"It started slowly, almost imperceptibly, when Evan was tiny," she wrote. "The worries about his health, his breathing, our bond. In snatches of sleep I'd be back on the Caesarean table, asking the doctors if our baby, silent in the respirator, had made it. Their lack of answers, the silence, the three minutes that lasted eras, are still as vivid as life." A few months after Evan was born, the panic spread to her days.

"I felt anxious, heavy, sick. A long-winded referral process through a health visitor recommended a support group. It started in four months." She didn't have four months. Anxiety was seeping into every waking minute. "I called up a mental health coordinator. My call wasn't returned. I went to my GP in tears, who suggested antidepressants, dismissing my suggestion of having someone professional to talk to—I just needed someone to talk to—as the support 'wasn't there.' "

Fifteen weeks after Rogers first asked for help, she found a different support group, by chance, at a children's centre a kilometre or so from her home. Now, almost a year on, she says she is a "different person entirely" after reaching a point of feeling very unwell and finding that she had to use all her resources, "repeatedly," to get help with postnatal depression, "as if it was an unknown, relatively easy condition." This was despite living in an area rated "One" (the best) on the UK Specialist Community Perinatal Mental Health provision map.

These are not unknown or easy conditions at all, and it's usually only the more extreme cases of perinatal mental illness that are picked up by the media. In December 2014 we were confronted daily by the story of Charlotte Bevan, the Bristol mother who left hospital with her four-day-old daughter, Zaani Tiana Bevan Malbrouck, and committed suicide by throwing herself off a cliff while clutching her baby in her arms. Their bodies were found days later at the bottom of Avon Gorge—a tragedy so chilling, so unthinkable, it seeped into conversations everywhere. The grainy CCTV footage stills of Bevan leaving the hospital with her daughter in her arms make my insides drop.

It is essential to consider the bigger picture behind Bevan's mental state—she was schizophrenic, with a care team already in place, and had stopped taking her antipsychotic meds over fear she wouldn't be able to breastfeed. She later agreed to take them again after giving birth, but the inquest last October said that a "chain of failures" had left thirty-year-old Bevan suffering an undiagnosed psychotic relapse.

Avon coroner Maria Voisin said health professionals treating Bevan should have, considering her history of mental illness, organized a multidisciplinary meeting about her care, and that a proper postbirth plan of action had not been put into place. The system failed her: "Zaani's death was contributed to by a chain of failures in her mother's care."

Cases like Bevan's are rare, but they run the risk of making many women feel that something similar could happen to them, that their fall might not be caught. Speaking after the inquest, Bevan's mother, Rachel Fortune, stated: "Following on from what has been said and heard in evidence, the family would urge the commissioners to fund a dedicated perinatal mental health service."

In a joint statement NHS England, Bristol Clinical Commissioning Group, University Hospitals Bristol NHS Foundation Trust and the Avon and Wiltshire Mental Health Partnership Trust expressed their "deepest concerns" to Bevan's family. They said they would act on the coroner's findings to "see what other actions we can take to improve services for vulnerable mothers, their babies and their wider family." Because of course it isn't just the mother's life perinatal mental illness affects—it's the lives of those around them, their relationships, even the economy.

In October 2014, a report by the Maternal Mental Health Alliance (MMHA) conducted in association with the London School of Economics found that £8.1 billion (about

C\$13.6 billion) is lost every year due to women and their babies not getting the right support during pregnancy and beyond. Describing mental health issues in such stark economic terms feels quite dystopian, but the numbers are essential to kick a desperately needed national overhaul into gear.

Since July 2001, the MMHA have been working with the Department of Health and the Royal College of General Practitioners on just this: the #everyonesbusiness campaign. It's an essential move to ensure doctors like Jude Rogers's start to change their attitude. The campaign's approach is about raising what they call ACT: Accountability for perinatal mental health care being clearly set at a national level, and complied with; Community specialist services meeting national quality standards and being available for women nationwide; and Training in perinatal mental health being delivered to all professionals involved in the care of women during pregnancy and the first year after birth. Sobering maps highlighting the gaps in provision are published on the campaign website.

Caregivers still aren't giving parity to physical and mental health care, which has a lot to do with the meagre funds (always under threat of being cut even further) local authorities have to spread across all health services, despite the way our government spins the figures to claim the contrary.

The gulf between people's experiences and the provision of care draws a big red arrow to the word we always come back to when we discuss mental health: "stigma." Struggling mothers are afraid to admit to professionals how they're really feeling in case they're seen as crazy, as mothers who can't look after their babies properly.

In addition, the image of new parenthood, which bludgeons us through advertising and culture, is one cast in soft-focus pastels, twinkling night lights and cute gurgles. What Rogers refers to as "the torture of sleep deprivation and the leaden weight of new responsibility" isn't part of that picture. Too often, the struggling new mum feels, and appears, so removed from the blissful trance we're sold that even when she does seek help, she has to confront two layers of stigma: society's and her own.

These women (remember, a quarter million of them in England alone every year) need greater reassurance that it's okay to feel mentally unwell, that they can be helped through it and that feeling consumed by anxious or depressive thoughts does not in any way mean they have failed anyone—especially the human being who grew inside their body for the better part of a year.

A woman in this situation needs to be helped to not feel alone, to know that there are millions of other women across the world feeling the same thing at the same time. She needs to know that no one will look at her and infer that she can't do well by her child if she says she's struggling to leave the house. We're only at the beginning of really changing the landscape of perinatal mental health care, but hopefully, with the kind of campaigning the MMHA and other bodies are doing, it *will* become everyone's business—fast.

Stigma surrounding mental illness of any kind is still a stubborn splinter in our society that must be cleverly, doggedly extracted. The dichotomy between how prevalent mental health problems are and the stigma that persists is both fascinating and infuriating. Things *are* changing. Over the past few years people have, tentatively, become better at talking about their mental health problems than ever before.

People of my generation are finding it easier to open up than the previous generation was and the generation before that, because wider dialogue is being encouraged and celebrated in all sorts of ways. Hopefully for my children's generation it will be easier still. I can imagine a time in the future when we just talk about "health" rather than dividing it into physical and mental elements, a time when we examine the whole of a person's functioning, rather than the parts. But we're not quite there yet.

STIGMA, LANGUAGE AND
HOW WE CODIFY THINGS

A Brief History of "Madness"
Stigma (noun): A mark of disgrace associated with a
particular circumstance, quality or person

I<small>T'S HARD TO KNOW WHERE TO START WITH STIGMA</small>,
because it's hard to think of any aspect of any mental health
problem that doesn't relate back to it somehow.

If we look at rumination, one of the defining elements of
anxiety—although "spiralling" or "quietly losing your shit" are
probably more realistic terms—self-stigma is often the tie that
binds the thought loops. It takes the form of a question: Why
can't I just be normal?

Those of us who have a problem with anxiety probably
find this question as familiar as our own reflection. Sometimes,
it *is* the reflection. The flesh of our face, the jut of our bones—
they *become* those words, the rawest form of stigma there is, the
irrational belief that our anxiety and the symptoms that come
with it are worthy of not just society's scorn but our own.

Self-stigma (often referred to as "perceived stigma") is
the internalizing of our perceptions of what we should or
shouldn't be based on society's "rules." My rational brain
knows this isn't right or helpful, but when I'm having a bad

run with anxiety, rationality is on too high a shelf. The "normal" question lives in the silt of my mind like a flatfish, always ready to surface when my resources are low. But why? Why does the information-loaded, educated part of me still get worn down sometimes by the idea that I should be ashamed? It feels so base, so larval, considering what I know when I'm not feeling anxious. Are anyone's membranes tough enough to not let society's attitudes seep through, even a little bit?

The truth cannot be sugar-coated: in 2016, despite there now being a far greater acceptance and inclusivity of the whole spectrum of human life and the way people live it, there are still uncomfortable attitudes towards those with mental health problems. These attitudes stir up social stigma, which can be loud or quiet.

The quiet kind is the most unsettling, I think, because it usually involves deception. When someone starts talking about a mental health problem for the first time, discrimination and exclusion may occur in all kinds of disguised ways among friends, family, even at work, because people are wary—even if they can't put their finger on why. This can make the person who "came out" feel worse than before: that the shame was justified and that he or she will forever be branded by the problem. The danger with shame, though, is that it's so often a barrier between people feeling unwell and their getting the treatment to help them feel better. Delays in treatment often cause the getting-back-on-your-feet process to take longer. Anxiety in particular, as we know, can become very deeply ingrained, and I am a testament to how having little—or lousy—treatment can make things very tricky.

To better understand where the stigma surrounding mental illness has come from, we need to examine the history of mental illness itself: how mental illness has been treated, how treatment has progressed with better knowledge and how all these things, together with increased awareness and education, have impacted society's perceptions.

When we talk about stigma, we are talking about separating a person, about ascribing otherness: being the black sheep, the pariah. The etymology of stigma is *stigmata*, a sixteenth-century Latin word all about branding. It was used through the ages to describe the mark left by a branding iron on the skin of a criminal or slave; or in medicine, to describe the physical marks characteristic of a certain disease: the stigmata of leprosy, for example.

Stigmata is, of course, also the word for marks resembling the wounds of the crucified body of Christ, said to be supernaturally impressed on the bodies of nuns and monks. These are all such powerful images, but they don't really hold true with the way we use "stigma" these days. Today, we use the term broadly in relation to persons or groups perceived to be at odds with social or cultural norms—different, basically. Not "normal." We probably use it most in relation to mental health.

We know that mental illness is as ancient as humanity itself. It is as much a part of the human condition as our capacity for all emotion. But when we consider the history of how people with mental illness have been treated, it's easy to see where the otherness and the fear we still know today come from. In the beginning, though, we were just trying to work out what might help reverse a kind suffering no one really understood.

One early explanation for mental illness was that it related to the movements and phases of the moon—it was the Latin word *luna* that gave us "lunacy" and "lunatic." The earliest treatments for mental illness seem primitive and barbaric to us now, but existence *was* primitive.

Evidence of trepanning has been found in prehistoric human remains across the world. Cave paintings depicting people hammering sharp tools into another's skull suggest that people believed it would cure any kind of discomfort in the head, so everything from mental distress to migraines and seizures.

In some lizardy part of my mind, the idea of trepanning makes sense. It's almost a fantasy, actually. The physical pressure of anxiety has made me imagine taking a hammer to my head many times over the years. I'm pretty sure I'll be able to continue resisting that temptation, however.

Our ancestors believed that mental distress was the result of supernatural phenomena. Neolithic people didn't know about the multicausality of mental health issues; they only knew of their own discomfort. Without any other reference point, it's likely that they believed the symptoms of anxiety were the result of an invasion of some kind. A possession. (Which is precisely what a panic attack feels like.)

Trepanning made sense. It seemed logical, this creating an opening; neolithic surgeons may have hoped that the evil spirits inhabiting one's head would be released and the person would be "cured." Knowledge of brain structure was rudimentary and not all patients survived. But many trepanned skulls found show signs of healing. You wonder how those people turned out. If by some miracle they weren't left severely brain damaged, could the placebo effect of believing all the bad stuff had left their head be great enough to positively affect their symptoms? We can't know.

TREPANNING WAS KNOWN to have taken place throughout the Greek and Roman periods. Greek physician Hippocrates gave directions on trepanning that were later elaborated on by Galen, the most prominent Greek physician in the Roman Empire.

The practice prevailed right up to the 1800s, and, even when modern medical science started to emerge around the 1830s, creating an opening in the skull was still considered a therapeutic intervention for mental distress.

Rather than just having a chisel smashed through the head with a stone, though, the Victorian patient would be given the works. It was basically a spa treatment! The patient was sat on a chair and secured in place with straps before the necessary portion of the head was shaved smooth and a Y-shaped cut was made in the scalp, which was then peeled back. A mark was then made on the bare skull and the drill carefully placed on it. You can imagine the rest.

Modern surgeons still drill into brains today to treat traumatic brain injuries like hematomas (blood clots) and to monitor intracranial pressure, but they generally use the term "craniotomy" and replace the cut-out piece of skull as soon as possible. Trepanning is a ghost of psychiatry now.

In earlier times, those who survived the process and stayed *compos mentis* would often keep the piece of removed bone and wear it as a charm. Modern science would scoff at such an idea, but reading about it made me think a lot about superstition. We're generally a less mystic lot these days, which is what happens when scientific discovery gives us binaries and absolutes. I like those defined edges and how the entire planet, the existence of everything, is chemistry.

I get a dizzy, contented feeling looking at bees swarming over their honeycomb, knowing as I do that there is so much biochemistry and *essence* in the golden geometric hexagons. It's a feeling so clean, so sharp, it almost makes me sick. I have the same sensation when looking at snake scales, the marbling of fat through a piece of beef or the gills of a mushroom. I think having an anxious mind does make me appreciate these things more—not just the majesty of nature but the order and pattern, especially when I often feel disordered.

However, I also think that mental health problems can make us go the other way. When we feel chaos in our own skins, magic and symbolism can be comforting. I generally have a knee-jerk skepticism of much of what fits into the bracket some might refer to as "hippy shit," but have always found the idea of talismans quite nice. If I had been trepanned, I'd sure as shit want to keep the bone. I'd wear it on a massive earring.

I've had a few superstitious relationships with physical objects throughout my anxious years—usually things I've worn or used when I've felt terrible. I don't like eating Quorn sausages much now, because I associate them with depression and struggling to eat. The item that sticks out, though, is the pair of trainers I bought when I began to turn the corner from depression and felt able to start running again. Those trainers definitely took on a spiritual quality in my mind. Stop laughing.

Buying those neon-yellow Nike LunarGlides meant feeling panic-free enough to *go to a giant shopping mall like Westfield*—something I never believed would be possible again.

Westfield, with all its perfumed people, gaping shark-mouth shop fronts, weird lighting and fried-food smells, was a big test for my anxiety and I passed it. I felt like a don walking out of there that day. The trainers also meant that I felt capable of fast physical movement—something anyone who has been stuck in one place with anxiety or depression for a while will recognize as a big deal.

Having a new pair of running shoes meant I was committed to moving and capable of setting goals and achieving them, even if that goal was running three kilometres without stopping because I had to work through associating the tight chest-ness of aerobic exercise with the tight chest-ness of anxiety. When I threw them out recently after hanging on for far, far longer than I should have, it made me a bit sad. They'd taken on a smell headier than a wheel of Vieux Boulogne cheese, but those shoes were my back-in-the-game charms. I said a private goodbye in my head when I put them in the bin.

Mental illness had been very wrapped up in superstition and folklore, but this started to change towards the end of the 1700s, due to the advance of science and medicine. A deeper understanding of "the lunatic" was sought. We began to ask more questions about what caused someone to "go mad" and what to do with them. For a long time, keeping vulnerable individuals rested and calm was thought to be the responsibility of loved ones. The very ill, who couldn't be kept at home, wandered, begging for food and shelter and often, like Shakespeare's Ophelia, found none. In the Middle Ages, Christian institutions that sheltered "the insane" started popping up across Europe. London's Bedlam (the Bethlem Royal Hospital) was one such institution, and probably still is the most famous, centuries after its founding.

Despite the advance of scientific study, mental illness was still not understood in Victorian times and, as in many institutions run by a singular power—as the Bethlem Hospital was for a very long time, by a "keeper" or "master"—things went awry. Descriptions of the conditions there in the early 1800s make for very upsetting reading. The Victorians weren't primitive human beings trying to work themselves out; they knew barbaric from humane. Yet reports from inspectors speak of conditions that call to mind animals in badly kept zoos: squalor, raw sewage, nakedness, the ringing of chains, and hundreds of unanswered screams. It was these reports that ultimately brought about a change in the system (often referred to as the lunacy reform).

We are a very long way from this kind of horror now, but the Bethlem Hospital and other large public asylums of the Victorian era still haunt the history of psychiatry. Although hailed as places of refuge for the mentally unwell, they earned a reputation as dehumanizing prisons, run by greedy Machiavellian bastards. The historian Roy Porter called the Bethlem Hospital "a symbol for man's inhumanity to man, for callousness and cruelty," and when you read about things like men being restrained in harness apparatuses with iron rings around their necks for ten years at a time, sitting in their own excrement and breathing the burn of their electrocuted scalps, it's easy to see why.

You can imagine how the idea of "otherness" surrounding mental illness took shape in our society, can't you? If you were living in Victorian Britain, the asylums would have been terrifying. By default, mental illness was terrifying. Of course there would have been more humane and caring practices, but the overwhelming message was: If you become sick in the head, this is what's waiting for you.

In some parts of the world, a version of this fearful way of thinking still exists. Mental illness carries a huge social stigma across several African countries, particularly in remote communities with high illiteracy rates, and is still wrapped up in theories about demonic possession. The kinds of treatments offered in more developed countries are not on people's radars in these communities.

Low literacy, compounded by lack of access to services and affordable health care that could help educate people, means that those suffering from mental health problems will often seek help from—or be pushed to see—traditional healers to exorcise the cause of their distress.

My neighbour Alfred is from a remote village outside Lagos, Nigeria. Recently, he told me about how, outside the main cities where there are modern psychiatrists and mental health care facilities (although not enough: with an estimated population of 170 million people, there are less than 150 practising psychiatrists in Nigeria), many people who are suffering just don't have the language to describe the way they feel.

He told me that before he moved to London, a neighbour of his had been talking about having a "constricted heart" and doing "too much thinking." His family took him to see the voodoo priest, a figure Alfred says was "surrounded in reverence" within the community.

Alfred hasn't stayed in touch with his neighbour, because he never goes back to the village, but says he knew the next step would have been some kind of exorcism, where the priest would "directly communicate" with the "demon" inside this man, making him experience symptoms more developed societies would recognize as those of anxiety or depression.

Alfred also told me about a twenty-something man he knew who had been having delusional thoughts about being monitored by his mobile phone network (likely a first episode of psychosis). His family "dumped" him at the gates of a Pentecostal church that specialized in "prayers and deliverance" for the "possessed." I felt shocked by this, but as Alfred said, people of the church are so often the first responders for emotionally distressed people. Families just don't know what else to do.

The church is often the first point of call for ethnic communities in more developed parts of the world, too. When I spoke to Dr. Salter, who works with many individuals from black and minority ethnic communities, he told me how hard it can be for some people to speak out. He talked about how, despite there being no conclusive evidence that black and minority ethnic (BME) groups have a biological predisposition to serious mental illness, they are startlingly overrepresented in the UK's long-term psychiatric care.

Again, this delay in getting the right treatment speaks to both stigma and a genuine lack of knowledge. In a piece I ran as part of the *VICE* Guide to Mental Health, which tried to widen the discussion surrounding BME mental health issues, the writer spoke to a young man. At twenty-six, he had been sectioned and detained in a psychiatric intensive care unit during an acute episode of schizophrenia. The delay in addressing his issues stemmed from an ingrained sense of shame surrounding mental illness. "There's a stigma within the black community around mental illness, which I think is a fear of looking weak," he said. "As a black man, on one hand you've got all this pride around not asking for anyone's help, but then you've got a big pressure to make something of yourself, to not be the stereotype." He said that "paths to traditional help" were "never on the table," that "you'd turn to the church or you'd turn to family before you think: *Ahh, I need therapy.*"

EVEN IF WE LIKE to view ourselves as knowledgeable and empathetic, I think there's a strange irony sometimes in the way the ostensibly worldly-wise apply their knowledge and feelings in real-life situations, and I think it probably happens with mental health problems a lot. We make assumptions about what anxiety disorders, depression, bipolar disorder and schizophrenia look like, which are just not reflected in reality. It's likely that everyone knows someone who's struggled with mental health at times, but if something hasn't happened within our direct vicinity, it's easy to plod along with surface-level understanding. The words "anxiety disorder" may not fit with the image of a woman like me, and I can see how some of the things I've talked about might sound surprising if you looked at me and the footprint of my life. It frustrates and angers me how much I can see it. But this disconnect between what we *think* mental illness looks like and what it actually looks like comes from somewhere.

That there were so few clear diagnostic categories in mental health for so long is a major factor. Victorian patients at Bethlem, for example, were not classified in any logical manner. The severely mentally ill (likely in psychotic states, potentially dangerous to themselves and others) were indiscriminately mixed with the more quiet and quiescent—likely the depressed or "hysterical" (anxious). There was only "curable" and "incurable," "mad" and "not mad."

Someone having panic attacks may have been treated in the same way as someone having psychotic hallucinations—i.e., with a lot of drugs and restraining devices. The idea of restraining and drugging someone having a panic attack is obviously unthinkable today. However, this way of thinking has trickled through generations, and somewhere in the back of some minds, the words "mental illness" still mean danger: people forever bent out of shape with strange, mysterious sicknesses.

I have felt really unwell with anxiety often over the years and twice with depression, but I have never felt like a dangerous person. Any danger represented by a nauseated, exhausted woman of five-foot-six in her dad's baggy Gap rugby shirt, smeared on the sofa watching *Friends* repeats, is probably minimal.

In the first half of the 1900s, mental illness was still a frightening concept because of the way it was treated. Straitjackets, segregation and drugs like bromides were used liberally to sedate the unruly, and the asylums effectively became testing labs for controversial treatments like ECT (electroconvulsive therapy) and lobotomy.

If we think of society as a sand-art sculpture, the worse that the asylums got for the people inside (a fear I'm not sure can be quantified in today's terms), the more that layers of fear and social stigma would build on the outside. All this was compounded by the poor success rate of the new treatments. Some individuals benefited from them, but many didn't and were irreparably damaged. If you learn that people have become untreatable for a particular illness, you sure as hell don't want to "catch" it, in case you end up like them, too.

Eventually, by the 1970s, pressure from many areas—feminist criticism, the antipsychiatry movement, activism from past patients and a general political suspicion of massive institutions—saw most of the asylums closing. Other mental hospitals were converted to "short stay" treatment centres—in the UK this was called "care in the community." But not everyone could be helped. Many people were left homeless, with the responsibility to care for the mentally ill once more falling on loved ones or charity. When those resources weren't available, people became lost again as they had in the Middle Ages, thousands of wandering Ophelias.

So right up until the 1970s, when the emphasis was shifting to getting people back on their feet and into the community, there was still a strong sense of "us" and "them" regarding the mentally unwell. *Them*. The lunatics. The nutters! The 1970s weren't that long ago, really, and it makes sense that some of us haven't caught up with the reality that *anyone* can become mentally unwell; that a person can live with a mental health problem while being incredibly high-functioning, successful and capable of great things. That anxiety, for example, is just one part of what makes up a person—that even if people are hospitalized for a mental health problem once, twice, three times in their life, their problem does not define them any more than had they been admitted for a nasty chest infection. That no one, but *no one*, is immune.

It's a strange bind we're in with mental health in 2017. Ignorance still exists. Ill-informed perceptions and attitudes prevail in several pockets of society. But we also know more than we ever have. Hard facts tell us that every third or fourth one of us will experience a mental health problem in any given year, and that anxiety is one of the most common issues.

There has been extraordinary progress in the way treatments for mental health issues are now centred on getting people back into the rhythm of day-to-day life as quickly as possible—even in the most severe crises. This has, over time, shifted our attitudes towards seeing problems in the mind as less of a stigma and more a part of what it means to be a human being; a bump in the road, rather than the end of it.

We *are* getting better at not allowing the way things once were to blinker us to progress that has happened. *Is* happening. But there are things that don't help at all. A big one is the way we're often warned against telling our bosses about our mental health problems. I wrote a Comment Is Free piece in the *Guardian* about this, based on something Ruby Wax said in an interview with the *Times*: "When people say, 'Should you tell them at work?' I say, 'Are you crazy?' You have to lie. If you have someone who is physically ill, they can't fire you. They can't fire you for mental health problems, but they'll say it's for another reason. Just say you have emphysema." Mental illness, she added, "is like the situation used to be with gay rights. Like being in the closet, but mental illness is now the taboo, instead."

I had a problem with this. For Wax, a prominent advocate of mental health awareness and visibility, to urge people to lie seemed a significant regression. Clearly, many of us are still ashamed of reaching out when we're not feeling right. We fear being judged and what being honest will do to our image. Yet attitudes are improving everywhere. If a colleague struggles with depression, we're less likely now to describe this person as "mad" or "a bit nutty," drawing an imaginary spiral near our temple. Our codes are different. I really don't think it helps that campaigners like Wax, who has battled depression herself over the years, are telling us to keep our mouths shut. But at least her comments generated conversation.

I went on three separate radio shows to talk about the piece—two in the UK and one in the US. In the *Guardian* comments section, I'd say, half the responders rejected Wax's stance and half supported it. I was told repeatedly that I was naive, and I can see how it looks that way. But research by charities like Mind, the UK's biggest mental health charity, suggests that a culture of fear and silence around mental health in fact represents a cost to employers.

One in five people Mind recently surveyed said they take days off work for stress; one in ten had resigned from a job because of stress; one in four had considered resigning due to stress; and one in five felt unable to speak to managers about stress.

Reinforcing the idea that we should lie about the nature of our health problems just doesn't work. The suicide statistics tell us that. No one is 100 percent "well" all the time, but unless stigma is challenged with openness, the wider conversation will never change. As I've said, we should just be talking about "health" full stop. In discouraging people from telling employers they're unwell—because that's what depression or anxiety is, a blip in our overall health—people like Wax are feeding the very stigma they're warning against.

WORDS AND PICTURES: HOW THE MEDIA FEEDS OUR HEADS

Everybody in our debauched culture invites us
to simplify reality, to despise wisdom.
—SUSAN SONTAG, AT THE SAME TIME: ESSAYS AND SPEECHES

FRANKLY, I DON'T CARE IF HE WAS MAD, BAD OR sad," Piers Morgan wrote in his *Daily Mail* column in March 2015, after Andreas Lubitz, co-pilot of the Germanwings plane he crashed into the Alps in March, killing 149 passengers, was thought to have a history of recurrent depression.

Let's just let that sink in for a minute.

The pink-sea-anemone-in-a-wig is never shy of using tragedy to push his personal brand, but despite the snide horror of Morgan's words in light of such great loss of life, his was just one voice in the tabloid frenzy after an event that shook the world.

"Killer Pilot Suffered from Depression," shouted the *Mirror*. "Madman in Cockpit" was the *Sun*'s headline (a paper you'd have thought would have pulled its socks up after its notorious "Bonkers Bruno Locked Up" headline in 2003, when it "reported" on Frank Bruno's sectioning under the Mental

Health Act because of his bipolar depression. The headline was only thought too extreme by then-editor Rebekah Brooks after she'd left the office). CNN's home page splashed an image of Lubitz beneath the headline "Unfit to Work." The headline for Morgan's column was "Why Was He Allowed to Fly?"

UNFIT.

KILLER.

MADMAN.

BAD.

With a great tragedy—one that will have affected thousands of people—in the foreground, mental illness was thrust into public discussion in ready-made sound bites. If you offer up words as ammunition, some people will use them as such. It was hard to believe we were capable of this kind of shit anymore. Depression was directly being linked with murder. Whenever a major disaster happens, it's a perfectly normal human reaction to search for a cause. We scramble like eggs when we don't have clarity. But the way some of the press covered the news of the Germanwings crash was abhorrent and unforgivable.

The Internet was a strange place that week. Beneath the layers of outrage in opinion sections of newspapers and "good" online media outlets was a current of really horrible stuff. I browsed Twitter and Facebook intermittently to get an idea of what the public was saying in relation to the articles but had to stop. There are only so many variations of "PEOPLE WITH MENTAL ILLNESS SHOULD BE KEPT AN EYE ON AT ALL TIMES IMO" or "TBH THE SICK SHOULD BE TREATED LIKE THEY'RE SICK" you can stomach if you are, for all intents and purposes, someone who fits into that category. I felt the stigma I have towards myself being ever-so-gently plucked, and can only imagine how it made others in a worse position feel.

The way mental illness is portrayed and reported in the media is incredibly powerful in educating and influencing the public. It may be *the* most powerful teacher. It wasn't just the simplistic reporting about the Germanwings crash that was dangerous, though. More alarming was how it had absolutely no basis. That mental health charities, psychiatrists, MPs and other public figures had to remind people how very few depressed people become murderers was very sad indeed. You could almost hear the creaking of vertebrae as heads fell in disbelief.

When it comes to making sense of the media and how their language informs the way we codify things, we have to talk about responsibility. The writer, teacher and political activist Susan Sontag spent a lifetime examining the role of writing—both the internal world of the writer and the external one of those reading the material. She had chided the reduction of culture to "content" more than fifty years before the term became tender in today's media. In a piercing lecture she delivered before her death in 2004 on South African Nobel laureate Nadine Gordimer, Sontag said: "To tell a story is to say: *This* is the important story. It is to reduce the spread of simultaneity of everything to something linear, a path."

The responsibility of the media wasn't just to direct the reader to a narrative when it became public knowledge that Lubitz had suffered from a history of depression—it was to try not to rewind decades of growing enlightenment. Sadly, what happened will probably be taught in future media studies classes as one of the most short-sighted showers of bullshit we've seen in many years. Sadder still is how the outlets in question have been allowed to get away with it. What we say on our sofas at home is very different from what can be said in public spaces, and newspaper editors need to stop treating front pages like their front rooms.

It should go without saying that we can do better in our private, day-to-day conversations surrounding mental health, but being more conscious of the language we use around mental health in public is not, as the clarion calls of the "PC gone mad" brigade would have it, putting the boot to free speech. It's basic humanity.

Newspapers have more power to change ignorance of mental illness than ever, but some choose, instead, to carry on reinforcing it. Something that amazes me daily is how tired and basic the circulation of stock images for stories on mental health are. How many more times must we see a side-on picture of someone staring out of a rainy window if the story is about depression? The silhouette of a figure in a dark room, someone clutching her head with both hands or sitting with his arms folded on his thighs, staring at the ground? Stories on OCD illustrated with a picture of someone washing her hands? Every article on suicide seems to have pictures of a cliff or a bridge. What good is this doing to make people think even a little bit more about what mental health problems are in fact like?

Headlines are an incredibly important subject, too. They're not just read at kitchen tables or on public transport and forgotten: they spread across the Internet and social media like a rash. Very often, the headline and subhead are all people read. Everyone is guilty of digesting stories like this sometimes—

among the sheer volume and pace of information, a headline tells us all we think we need to know—and it takes seconds for a statement to explode on Twitter. Then come the hot takes, the opinion pieces, the long reads. All the while, the incendiary language stays in circulation, breathing its sour breath through our computers and touch screens.

The current system of press regulation in the UK is a sham. Jo Brand, a former mental health nurse, told the *Guardian* that press watchdog IPSO (Independent Press Standards Organisation)—"a toy town regulator," in her words—has so far achieved "square root of sweet FA" in tackling negative reporting about mental illness in the tabloids.

I fucking love Jo Brand. But we shouldn't just be looking at tabloids. Women's magazines are often no better. I've worked for most of the major glossy titles in some capacity, both as a freelance writer or on contract, and I've seen—and regretfully been complicit in—the way people's experiences with mental health problems are engineered to fit an already written, attention-grabbing headline.

EDITORS HAVE TO TREAD a fine line between writing headlines that make someone want to read a story and writing something gratuitous. This is a line that I know well. When I worked at *VICE*, a media company once famous for its no-bullshit (read: often incredibly offensive) headlines, we constantly had meetings about how to make headlines—and therefore the entire business model—work for pieces about mental illness or tragic experiences without detracting from the subtleties of the story. It's a process of fine tuning that isn't effective every time, but every single media organization has a responsibility to the public to have at least some kind of process in place when discussing mental health. Particularly if it's a publication with a massive audience.

I often wonder, too, about the nature of our appetite for stories about people on the supposed fringes of society, the ones who clearly have mental health problems, who papers like the *Daily Mail* can't just get away with calling PSYCHOS. How much would we really want to gawp at articles about hoarders with houses full of old newspapers spilling out into the neighbour's garden, for example, if journalists weren't forever on the hunt for the pot of gold that is a vulnerable person who can be convinced to have his picture taken for a couple of hundred quid? Those pieces are usually very "successful" (i.e., read and commented on by a lot of people), but if the paper stopped actively looking for and publishing so many, would we really be so hungry for them?

One story the *Mail* published in 2015 really stuck with me. It was about a thirty-five-year-old woman from Ireland whose "suitors" kept leaving her because she had two reborn dolls—dolls made to look exactly like newborn babies, down to every skin fold and fingernail. "Single woman who treats her two 'reborn dolls' as though they are real babies and even changes their nappies says she would choose THEM over any man" was the headline. They ran picture after picture of her pushing the dolls around in prams and holding them as if they were fragile newborn babies, supporting their necks and gently kissing their faces. Only towards the very end of the story were we told that she had spent years trying to conceive, and when she did fall pregnant had to be induced at thirty-two weeks because her baby boy's heart had stopped beating. "I don't think I will ever get over losing Jamie, but the reborn babies bring me so much comfort" was one of her quotes. "They will never replace him, but at least now I can finally go out and buy baby clothes and do things other parents do."

Do things other parents do.

Here was a woman obviously trying to cope with a horrendous trauma, whose mental health was so clearly fragile and in need of care, being reduced in a huge public forum to a "creepy" habit that makes blokes feel weird. The piece wasn't very successful—the Mail handily displays underneath the headline how many times a story has been shared—and the comments beneath the story were largely nonjudgmental, kind and understanding, which makes you wonder what the editors were thinking. Clearly, they wanted to provoke people into saying things like, "Whoa, what a freak!" But if that doesn't happen, where do they look next? For someone in even more mental distress? Where's the duty of care? The awareness of how these things only serve to reinforce stigma about mental health, vulnerability and the infinite variation in the way human beings cope with pain?

Gratuitousness like this is repulsive, but cack-handedness can be unforgivable, too. Particularly when the media are reporting on something as serious as suicide. As Brand noted in her interview with the Guardian, what we're fed is often appalling. We hear all the time about people who have been "driven to suicide" by something—charities bombarding old people with requests for donations, traveller communities living on people's doorsteps (a recent *Daily Express* headline)—and if it's a famous person who has taken his or her life, we're given every single little detail about how it was done: the drugs, the to-the-minute timings.

Now we have websites like TMZ that scramble camera crews to the scene, probably before some family members learn of the news, so we can watch victims' bodies being carried out of homes or hotel rooms, covered in white sheets.

This kind of zooming-in isn't just grotesque—it's perilous. People who are depressed, living with acute anxiety or any other mental health problem that makes them feel desperate may not necessarily have the drive or information to kill themselves. Wall-to-wall coverage on front pages and across the Internet of celebrity suicides can change that. Years ago, the Samaritans charity wrote a set of guidelines, in collaboration with journalists, with the knowledge that there is genuine and understandable public interest in asking why people kill themselves. We'll probably never get to the stage of media blackouts when famous people take their lives, but all mental health groups—Samaritans, Mind, Time to Change, Rethink—say that releasing too many details about a suicide might give someone who is unwell the impetus to put his or her own thoughts into action. In the rush to report the minutiae of a suicide like Robin Williams's, for example, those basic rules are so often ignored. The details explode through social media like fireworks until they're everywhere. Un-ignorable. Burning.

THE MEDIA ARE OBSESSED with how social media are affecting our mental health, which is ironic when most outlets push their stories through Twitter and Facebook throughout the day. Headlines like "Too Much Instagram Causes Anxiety" or "Bread Can Make You Depressed" pop up *all* the time. The stories themselves may link to a small study showing some causal connection between social media and increased levels of anxiety that is worthy of conversation, but the headlines give false conclusions right off the bat.

I've had several conversations during which, when I've said I'm writing a book about anxiety, people have responded with things like, "Well, yes, social media can make you very anxious." So let's be perfectly clear here: too much Instagram, Twitter or Facebook does *not* "cause" anxiety, because people do not "get" anxiety from any one thing. As I hope I explain in this book, brains are far too complicated to be tipped or swayed into a particular state by a single thing. Social media can *contribute* to the state of our mental health, because how could it not? It's become the way we absorb everything that's going on in the world.

Stories are broken on Twitter before "traditional" media—newspapers and TV, for example—can get anywhere near them. Society is largely filtered through social media now. They are a mirror for ourselves and the way we live, and may make aspects of certain people's problems worse. Or they might, in the way experience and information can be shared, make them better. The mental health of every single one of us exists on a sliding scale and can be affected by an infinite number of things.

I have a funny relationship with Instagram. I find it fun and silly and spend a disproportionate amount of my spare time tagging friends under close-up pictures of monkey bums and stuff. My friend Morwenna and I have been tagging each other beneath *National Geographic* pictures of bulging-eyed reptiles and livid-looking birds for a good couple of years now. It's like a private Morse code: an electronic doff of the cap through beaks, angry red baboon arses, @ symbols and emojis. Instagram can also be incredibly informative. I follow loads of medical, science-y and natural-world accounts that make me feel more connected to things I'm interested in. The flip side is that Instagram can, on occasion, send me into an anxious whirl.

That we're able to diarize our lives in cherry-picked, golden-filtered snapshots with something like Instagram means we can effectively choose how people see us. We can present the best, shiniest versions of ourselves. But if we're constantly looking at people whose lives seem more fun or successful than ours, it's very easy to start looking inwards. If someone posts a hotdog-legs picture on holiday somewhere exotic, we might think: *God, I wish my circumstances meant I could do that*, and then start examining our lot and how it's not good enough and how, yeah, we really need to do better.

If you are someone already prone to anxiety and being a bit reclusive sometimes, seeing endless pictures of people you know socializing in restaurants and pubs and at dinner parties can reinforce all kinds of thoughts. The worst thing is how compulsive it can become. Even if we don't really want to see life galloping on without us, we can't stop looking. Well, it's hard. I find it hard.

Even when I don't want to be in a pub on a Friday night and am very comfortable sniffing the dog's ears while lying on the sofa dressed in trackies with socks pulled over the pant legs, if I see pictures of my friends out doing stuff, I think: *Huh, I should probably be doing that, because that's what people do.*

Depending on my mood, I might ponder my choice for hours: *Why don't you just go out? You spend way too much time stuck in your head to just stay in and fester. Is this really who you're going to be from now on? A thirty-something Netflix binger who just posts pictures of her dog sleeping on a Friday night? Look at everyone you know mucking about and making moments count.* It's a difficult balance to strike with anxiety, this FOMO. (If you're reading this, Dad, that means "fear of missing out.")

On the one hand, I am pretty comfortable with having done *a lot* of going out and partying over the years—at some stages, far too much—and admitting to myself that I just can't be arsed. I am firmly of the position that all of us should regularly admit to not being arsed. On the other, part of getting better at dealing with, and accepting, anxiety means pushing out of your comfort zone—to feel the fear and do it anyway.

I am always saying to my therapist that I struggle to find the sweet spot between allowing myself to relax and pushing myself to do more. There's no right answer, but his response largely centres on being kind to myself. That if I really wanted to do something and couldn't bear the idea of not doing it, I'd do it. And if I say no, I have to practise sticking by my decision and accepting that it's really okay. "You are not going to revert to feeling helpless every day, and like you can't cope if you don't go for a pint one Friday night," he says. "And try to stop looking at your phone so much."

That's the nail on the head for me. Worrying that if I don't take every single opportunity to be an active, three-dimensional person, I'll go backwards. It's the time conundrum again: the fear of not filling each moment with MAXIMUM LIFE, in case I wake up and realize I've done nothing. That I've wasted the good, capable version of me by doing sod all.

I am naturally a lazy-ish person who likes to stay at home and read, cook and have baths. My tolerance for the phrase "old soul" is wafer thin, but inside I really, truly, am an eighty-seven-year-old woman. I like nice blankets, having my face lit up by TV light and fingering books. However, I do agonize over saying no to doing things a lot more than I ever used to. Because I'm better at enjoying myself now, and spend less time monitoring my body for even the slightest twinge that might suggest I'm about to go—to use a term my friend Tom, who has terrible panic attacks—"full cunt," there's a part of me that thinks I should be saying yes to absolutely every offer of social or professional engagement.

Nobody says yes to everything. It's impossible. But that dilemma is one of the prices I've paid, I suppose, for improving how I deal with anxiety. The pessimist in me would say it's just a new hook for my anxiety to hang itself on and that I will be unconsciously looking for things to be anxious about for as long as I live—but I know better than to go down that road.

This is very easy to say, and a lot harder to actually do. I've spoken to a lot of anxious people who identify with this push-pull thing, and I think the key probably *is* to practise being kind to ourselves and treat it like we're learning a new skill. It's all well and good for the media to bray at people to stay off their phones or laptops and to just bloody well stop following people online if it makes them feel bad, but there's a risk of creating more compulsion there. What we *can* do is work on our reactions. There's no need to get all life coach-y about it, but it's good to practise saying things like, "I'm perfectly happy where I am tonight" or "I can choose not to examine my contentment based on what other people are doing."

It *is* good to practise leaving our phones face down for longer stretches of time. It doesn't mean you're turning into the human embodiment of a Keep Calm and Carry On coaster—it just means you're trying something. And the brain *loves* to practise.

Rather than thinking in absolutes, it's a far more realistic strategy for our overall mental well-being to try to let things be. Social media can make that very difficult if we're tapping into them on our phones from the second we wake up until we go to sleep, but people are going to go out and post sunset selfies, and pictures of clinking margarita glasses at the top of the Heron Tower, and images of their glistening breastbones at the gym, and there really isn't much you can do about it. It's all gotten too big. Instagram can set me off on anxiety spirals, but rather than being all ARGHIAMGOINGTODELETETHEFUCKING-THINGANDNEVERLOOKATITAGAIN, I have worked at rationing my compulsive scrolling and practised (literally) saying out loud things like, "Cooking and staying on the sofa all night are exactly what I want to be doing," or "I don't need to see that film this weekend just because everybody else is."

If you'd told me five years ago that talking to myself in the kitchen about a computer program would be in any way beneficial to my mental well-being, I'd have turned into a puddle of frog spawn. But you know what? Sometimes it does help, and having a thing that helps at least some of the time is better than flapping and festering. Anxiety works like a line of dominoes, and if you can prevent the whole lot falling down by stopping the momentum after two or three have gone—i.e., get better at responding to your triggers in the first instance—you're less likely to start losing your shit so easily.

FACES AND NAMES

FOR ALL THE PROBLEMS THAT THE MEDIA CREATE IN conversations about mental health, they are also the means by which famous voices can cast influence. When a public figure talks about having struggled with mental health, the effect can be seismic. We know that shared experience is one of the most powerful, binding things between people. We might not be able to sit down and talk to the people we follow on Twitter, but when their experiences find their way into our phones, computers, newspapers, magazines and televisions, it doesn't just help crack the shell of isolation, it also gives us something to use as a jumping-off point in conversation. This can be very helpful and is particularly true for young people, I think.

When YouTube star Zoella—aka British vlogger Zoe Sugg—posted a video in 2014 about her experience with panic attacks and anxiety, I didn't really know much about her except that she had an enormous following. A colleague at the time said something like, "Oh, even *she's* talking about anxiety now," screwing up his nose. But I saw the video and, over a few days, watched the viewing numbers rise in the hundreds every minute.

The video was an honest account of incredibly uncomfortable symptoms—feeling sick, heaving, needing the toilet—which she prefaced by saying how the young woman people see talking about "material things" and "fashion" every day might not chime with what she was about to explain but how that was sort of the point.

Challenging notions about how anxiety disorders "look" and who has them is exactly the point. At this writing, the video has been watched three and a half million times and is still being commented on every day. Sugg has nearly ten million subscribers across her YouTube channels (more than Beyoncé) and over four million Twitter followers, the majority of them likely young adults. She said in her video that if she helped even one person to talk about similar issues, she'd be happy, but of course it has ended up being *slightly* more than that.

"I know just how isolating it can feel to experience severe anxiety. However, the overwhelming response I've received every time I've spoken out online shows just how many young people confront it every day," said Sugg as her role as a digital ambassador for Mind was announced shortly after the video went out.

This colleague of mine suggested that she was courting likes and shares by talking about something so of the moment. (He said the same of another big vlogger, Ingrid Nilsen, when she used her channel to come out as gay, saying something like, "Doesn't sit right with me.") I can't bear that kind of knee-jerk cynicism, particularly directed at a young woman like Sugg who is talking about her vulnerabilities and, you know, just: *Christ.* Why would she make it up? It would take a sagacious con artist to summon the kind of detail Zoella did in subsequent written pieces and videos, including one of her actually having a panic attack.

Being honest in front of so many people about a condition so densely packed with shame and misconception wasn't just commendable; it was likely ground-shifting for the thousands of young people who have commented—are still commenting—to say how watching her video helped them begin having their own conversations. I have no vested interest in Zoella as a "brand," because she is not appealing to my demographic, and thank god for that: teenagers are entitled to their private cultural spaces that older people don't get. I am, however, interested in her as a human being. I'm interested in the numbers and in seeing that one young woman has potentially given more people than live in the whole of London something to talk about with regard to anxiety.

I am not a famous person, but I did get a small insight into the power public disclosures can have when I wrote a piece on my anxiety for *VICE*—the one that spurred the writing of this book. Hundreds of people from across the world got in touch with me via Twitter, Facebook, email, text, phone, even through my parents, to tell me that they now had something to show people around them and say: "This is how I feel."

That I'd longed for something similar myself for so many years was the main drive behind writing about something I'd kept hidden for so long. So often in the past I've looked for articles and essays about anxiety in an effort to find my reflection. I've also typed things like "celebrity panic attacks," "celebrity anxiety," "celebrity depression" and "celebrity antidepressants" into Google more times than I can count, particularly before I started to be open with the people around me about my anxiety. What was I looking for? Some cosmetic reassurance that because people I thought were cool and smart and highly successful had experienced something similar, I was less of an oddity? Probably. If that sounds base, well, it is. Sometimes it's not a scholarly essay about the brain you want to read; it's someone else's story of suffering where you might not have expected it. It's the "Huh, even *she* has it" thing. Can any of us say with complete honesty that we're bigger or cleverer than the comfort of that feeling?

When anxiety got the better of me a few years ago and I became depressed, there were several stories that helped me. The comedian Rob Delaney's balls-out account of his depression made me cry and then laugh. Steve Coogan and his experience with panic attacks and anxiety. Sarah Silverman—another comedian, bit of a running theme—has spoken openly over the years about taking antidepressants for anxiety and cyclical depression, and using them to stay functional, which made me feel a lot less scared about taking them. Same for Lena Dunham, who has been very candid about her ongoing issues with anxiety—particularly the social kind—and about taking medication. Jennifer Lawrence (eternal swoons) has given interviews about having a propensity for intense social anxiety and how she has addressed it with medication and therapy in the past.

When I felt really unwell, Google told me that actor Kim Basinger had experienced crippling anxiety throughout her life. I can't say I was especially interested in her previously, besides the way she looks in *L.A. Confidential*, but during this period of acute distress I spent hours reading about and watching her. In a documentary Basinger made with HBO called *Panic: A Film about Coping* she talks about reaching her own tipping point, nudged over the edge by a panic attack that happened in a grocery store. She spoke of how her hands were suddenly shaking and how she began sweating profusely. She remembers being hardly able to move. She drove on the back roads to her home and didn't leave the house for six months.

I think Basinger's story resonated with me so much because celebrities don't talk very often about being *really* on their knees, or about how living with anxiety or depression is a process. We hear about rehab clinics and transparent stories about people being treated for "exhaustion," but they so often steer towards a redemptive ending, various shades of "BUT I'M FINE NOW!" This can be frustrating for the person living with anxiety because, in reality, even though we can get better and improve every day, there is rarely a cinematic moment of retribution and clarity—you know, the sort you see in movies—when a camera zooms into someone's iris and all the joy and bigness of life suddenly explodes: cutaways to crashing of waves, people laughing, speed-motion sunrises and blooming of flowers, dancing, women orgasming loudly, comets roaring through space, wolves howling in the pines, window-smashing operatic high notes. Yeah, I don't think they happen very often.

In the HBO documentary, Basinger was very open about how being anxious, shy and vulnerable to panic attacks and agoraphobia was a daily process—not something that she'd ever been able to "cure." Even though I watched the film before I was anywhere near accepting the whole process, it struck a chord somewhere. It roused a little voice that said: "She got up and so can you."

Another unlikely source of comfort I found, when at the peak of depression, was ex-footballer and now commentator Stan Collymore. I say "unlikely" because I couldn't have told you anything about the man other than how he violently attacked Ulrika Jonsson, and I generally don't seek out the advice of men like that. But on one of my worst days, when I had positioned myself in the most sun-scorched area of the garden with my phone and headphones to try to burn a hole through some of the static in my head, I remembered that someone on Twitter had linked to a (now quite famous) blog post Collymore wrote in 2010 about a horrible bout of depression.

I read it out of curiosity. In truth his words could have been anyone's, but I remember bursting into thick, gagging tears as I made my way through it. It described the mortifying stasis of the thing with crystal clarity, the feeling of being so aggressively booted off the treadmill of life. I'll never forget how reading some of those lines affected me that day. Particularly his account of how the ability for fast movement left him: how fit he had kept himself, how running had enabled him to remain on an even keel and how all that energy had left him like a sneeze.

I had been someone who usually ran at least three times a week, and at that point just couldn't reconcile the image of my body moving, marking the earth and occupying space, with how I was feeling then. Also affecting was his account of how anxiety had set it all off ("I started to feel anxiety, which grew into irrational fear") and the velocity of his deterioration. "I went from last Saturday at the gym, running 10 k as I normally do, looking forward to working, to Tuesday morning being unable to lift my head from the pillow, feeling like my body had been drained of any life, my brain 'full' and foggy, and a body that felt like it was carrying an anvil around," he wrote. "This to me is the most frightening of experiences, and one fellow sufferers I'm sure will agree is the 'thud' that sets the depression rolling."

The word "thud" was so sickeningly right.

For men, I think the power of a public male figure talking about mental illness and challenging stigma can be particularly strong. Suicide is the biggest single killer of men under the age of forty-five in the UK. The numbers are very frightening. In 2014, male suicides accounted for 76 percent of all suicides. Per the American Foundation for Suicide Prevention (AFSP), men die by suicide 3.5 times more often than women. In 2014, white males accounted for seven of ten suicides. In Canada, the suicide rate for men is three times higher than the rate for women—17.9 compared with 5.3 per 100,000, according to Statistics Canada.

Stigma around becoming mentally unwell doesn't just leave men suffering in silence—it kills.

What does this say? That the partners of men want them to be more open about how they feel emotionally, but that when they do, when they cry and are vulnerable and say they're struggling mentally, that women don't like it? That men get uncomfortable when other men lay themselves bare, and think the men should just shrug and get on with it? When the thirty-five-year-old Labour MP John Woodcock publicly announced in December 2013 that he was depressed, he confronted stigma not just as a politician discussing the personal reality of an issue often muddied in sweeping political rhetoric but as a man talking about mental health.

"I've been really struck by the number of men who have come up to me—often in my constituency—like ex-shipyard workers who have struggled for ten years, who have been keeping it quiet," he told Owen Jones of the *Guardian*. "We do operate in a culture where men, by and large, talk about their feelings less. They're self-conscious about talking about weakness."

Just like Woodcock saw in his constituency, the more public male figures are open about their vulnerabilities, the more men might feel confident talking about their own. And that "might" is massive. One conversation might lead to another, and another, and another, in pubs, staff rooms, front rooms, football pitches, changing rooms—words becoming tools to whittle out blockages. Conversations save lives.

In 2015, the reality of the prevalence of male suicide became clear when the Office for National Statistics released data showing that the male suicide rate in the UK was at its highest since 2001. Of the 5,981 suicides in 2012, a staggering 4,590 were men. Conversely, female suicides fell by almost 40 percent between 1981 and 2014.

CALM's Jane Powell has suggested that the drop of female suicides could be the result of improved life for women and their ability to fulfil themselves—in the workplace and at home—and that, while women have felt more liberated, men have been left unsure of their role. So, how do you reach men and tell them that it's okay to be vulnerable? That if they are suffering from anxiety or depression, they are one of millions—billions—and can get help? That mental health problems aren't weaknesses? Britain has high-profile campaigns on testicular cancer and driving safely, but where is the biggest killer of men under fifty getting the attention it so desperately needs? Where is the issue being named?

We can't just rely on public figures speaking out when they feel able to. We can't rely on news hooks and think pieces and the discussions that happen *afterwards*. Powell made a strong statement that while breast cancer does kill men, too, society focuses on it as a female disease, because far more women are affected by it than are men. She says suicide prevention must focus on men in the same way.

According to research by Mind, just 23 percent of men said they would visit their GP if they felt low for more than two weeks, compared with 33 percent of women. It is hammered into us all the time, by books, television programs and films dealing with mental health, that it's crucial to talk and not let things ferment inside us. But still, it seems, without making sure the ways we reach out to men are such that they'll actually respond, it's easy for men to plow on under the misconception that the talking rule only applies to others.

A man I'll call Sam, a thirty-five-year-old mechanic who lives in the north of England, says going to his GP to get help for anxiety wasn't the hard part—it was talking about it with his friends. "I had problems with social anxiety as a kid, where I'd get unbelievably homesick at parties and have to be picked up from sleepovers and stuff," he tells me. "I had a bit of a stammer and was worried all the time that people were thinking I was a freak and watching me, which turned into an obsession about what people think of me generally."

He went to see his GP at age twenty-one, because he'd begun experiencing panic attacks when out socializing with his friends. "I only have the tiniest hint of a stammer now, but when I was out, I'd revert to my teenage ways and start thinking that everyone was watching," he says. "Once I started thinking like that I'd turn inwards, focusing on everything my body was doing, always aware of what people would be thinking."

One night, he "lost it" in the pub. "I'd got so worked up at the table about whether I was sweating or blushing in a way that my mates could notice and all of a sudden felt boiling hot, dizzy and like I was going to puke. I went and stood in the carpark, feeling like I'd just had one too many, but was only on my second pint. I knew it couldn't be that. My arms felt like they were on fire and my head like it was being crushed in a vice."

Sam had heard about panic attacks before but didn't associate anything he knew with how he was feeling in the carpark. "This was like I was physically ill," he says. "I didn't hyperventilate or feel my heart going or anything; it was all temperature, head and stomach."

After it started happening "again and again" and making him "sack off going out all the time" and even worry about going to work, he went to the GP, saying he was having suicidal thoughts because he felt so out of control. His GP recommended CBT, which was something he "actually enjoyed" and "really improved with," but talking to his mates was another matter.

"I just couldn't find the words to tell them what was going on. How do you start that conversation? We're a group of working class lads who left school at sixteen; we don't really know about this stuff." Eventually, because his GP had encouraged him to cut back on the booze, he used that as a way in. "We were in the pub and I just said, 'Lads, I'm doing halves tonight because I've been having these panic attacks and the doc reckons it might help to ease up a bit,' and they were dead shifty. Didn't know what to say to me. One asked what I had to panic about and another said he knew someone who had them, but that was that. The subject was changed awkwardly. It took months to actually have a proper chat about it, and I only really started to get my confidence back when we did."

I spoke to another man, who I'll call Richard. He's twenty-six and works for a publishing company in London, and has experienced anxiety and depression from a young age. "I can remember being eight and just having this inexplicable feeling of dread," he says. "It then started to become tied to working out when everyone around me might die and how long I had left with them. I would work it out in actual mathematic estimates. My parents found me in my room crying a few times and I said it was because I was being bullied at school, so even at that early age I had a sense of shame."

When Richard was fourteen, his granddad died and those thoughts went into overdrive. "That's when I became obsessed with my own mortality and started having panic attacks, which made me even more anxious about life. The more anxious I got, the more depressive moods I had. It wasn't until I was twenty-one that I actually admitted to myself that words like "anxiety" and "depression" related to what goes on in my head. They were too big—how could I be someone who was *depressed*?"

This disconnect with feelings and words means Richard has never had any kind of therapy for his problems, even though he knows a lot about what's out there. "It comes from a fear of having nowhere to go afterwards if it doesn't work," he says. That it would be the point of no return. "It's the same when I tell people to an extent. The first couple of people I told I no longer speak to because it felt—perhaps just to me—that every conversation was framed by it: the sympathetic looks, the feeling that I was getting extra slack because I was a bit broken." He hasn't told his family or all his friends, and finds it "much easier" to talk to his female friends than the male ones, "which probably says a lot."

Towards the end of our chat, Richard tells me about the night he tried to kill himself. "Much to my shame, I tried to throw myself in front of a van late at night. It missed me, but I was battered and dazed as a result. I woke up in hospital with a hazy memory but left before the psychiatrist could come and see me. My face was all scraped up. I took a day off work and went back the day after, telling everyone I'd fallen over when light-headed. Don't think many believed me, but nobody pushed me on it."

No one from the hospital followed up with Richard save the paramedics, who strongly suggested he get some help. How do we reach men like him—who believe that evidence-based therapies don't apply to his flavour of suffering? One of the biggest sources of help for him currently is a depression thread on a Leeds United fan forum site.

"Loads of men use it to talk about their mental health and are really open with each other—something made easier with the anonymity you can have online." The apparent suicide of Welsh football legend Gary Speed in 2011 spurred wide discussion among men who use these kinds of forums, Richard says. It was also the case when ex-professional footballer Clarke Carlisle made an attempt on his life in 2014.

"These men sparked a huge wave of openness. I think when you have a direct mirror in men you've looked up to, in a sport as macho as football, it really hits home and makes you think: *Do I want to get to that point?* Being preached to by people in the media who claim to be 'cured' of mental health problems is a real issue for me, which is why I like how open Carlisle is about how he has to manage things on a daily basis. That is the reality for millions of us. You can be very well and functional, but still managing."

Richard suggests that men need more open, targeted spaces to discuss their problems, through things that interest them; and that forums or chat rooms on the Internet (he also sings the praises of the one on CALM's website) create a more realistic starting block than forever being told to talk to those around us or, indeed, a doctor. "They can be the first step on the ladder for men that feel otherwise battered by the pressure of life and what society is prescribing them."

If we look at male suicide rates and how they've gone up and down over time, we can see that it's not a biological fault that makes men kill themselves more than women—it's cultural. It's about what people expect and what's going on around them. According to research by Samaritans, people in the poorest socioeconomic bracket are ten times more likely to kill themselves than those in the richest.

Poverty is genderless, of course, but it is men who are more likely to commit suicide if they are poor. Having no money and no options can have a great impact on anyone's mental health, and while poverty isn't a guarantee of mental illness, it can certainly leave someone more susceptible.

Let's recap: male suicide rates are at their highest since 2001, in the middle of two consecutive Conservative governments, whose villainous spending cuts have seen more poverty and widespread suffering than Britain has experienced since Thatcher's reign. It doesn't take a genius to identify a causal link; if a man is already prone to anxiety or depression, what's going to happen when the rug is pulled from beneath his feet and he's left wondering how he'll eat in three days' time?

Statistically, men are also more likely than women to self-medicate with alcohol or drugs. The World Health Organization says that while overall rates of psychiatric disorder are almost identical for men and women, "striking gender differences are found in the patterns of mental illness." One of these differences is that in developed countries approximately one in five men develop alcohol dependence during their lives, compared with one in twelve women.

Johnny, a thirty-four-year-old musician from Edinburgh, has obsessive-compulsive disorder that's defined by intrusive thoughts and images of him fainting in public—although it has never actually happened. He says that drinking served to "block the general feelings of anxiety" he had on a day-to-day basis and helped curb the compulsions that made the obsessing less intense—"biting the skin around my nails, pulling at bits of my beard until it hurt, grinding my teeth, kicking my shin with the heel of my shoe"—and that even though drinking in excess made him feel dizzy (and therefore, you imagine, more prone to fainting), he found that the numbing buzz alcohol gave him made it easier to stop "thinking so fucking much.""It was: Go to the pub, drink, block feelings, feel better at hiding them, drink more, wake up hungover and feel anxious, go to work, go straight to the pub to drink more to not feel anxious," he says. "I was a fucking mess and it went on like that for about four years. In the end, alcohol dependency became a bigger problem than the OCD, which I'd had for years and never really done anything about. I was totally deluded, thinking that boozing was helping me function, while I kept quiet about how I felt with everyone I knew."

The tipping point came when Johnny went into a walk-in centre for an infected cut and a nurse gently commented on the smell of alcohol on him. "It was two in the fucking afternoon. She said, 'Do you drink a lot during the day?' and I just crumbled. I don't know why it was her that did it, on that day, or even that I'd really drunk that much, but I was so embarrassed. I just thought: *I can't do this anymore.* She told me to go and see my GP as soon as I could. When I did, he referred me to an addiction service and for a course of therapy. It took about a year, with many slip-ups, but I'm now off booze completely, taking an antidepressant and still seeing a therapist, and generally feel a lot better." When I asked Johnny what he thought might have changed the way anxiety took a hold on his life, his reply was a single word: "education."

Anxiety is something that can either creep or crash into our lives, for reasons I hope I've gone some way to explaining, and it can absolutely crush us before we try to understand, treat and accept it. Stigma makes that process harder, longer and more painful, because perceptions, and what we've been told we should or shouldn't be, are so woven into irrational thought patterns for every person who lives it.

There is no magic cure, or catch-all solution, but based on how knowledge has impacted society's attitudes towards mental illness over time, education *is* both what changes lives and what saves them. It *is* the tool with which to dismantle stigma, from the foundations up.

We all "have" mental health because we all have brains. The way that we feel influences how we act, what decisions we make, what we can do. It affects what we're capable of: our capacity for love, the way we use our knowledge, and our potential to learn and imprint our world. It determines the ease with which we're able to get up every morning and reckon with the fact that we're just . . . here. Here, with our autonomous bodily functions and our minds that can be affected by the slightest change in the wind.

We don't all have mood disorders like depression and anxiety, but mental health does exist on a spectrum in all of us. The questions are: How can we all get better at ensuring that people who *are* experiencing the pain those disorders can bring will feel able to talk—and therefore get better? Where do we start? How can we assuage the pain of anxiety when it creeps into our lives?

IN THE TIME between submitting my manuscript to my UK publisher and its printing, one of my oldest friends, Matt, took his life. June 2016. He was thirty-six.

As I type, I can't believe those words are truths.

Matt and I were club kids together in the early noughties. He worked the door at Trash, that genre and gender-dissolving Monday night sweatbox I wrote about earlier; there was no sexier crowd in London, a hurricane of asymmetric hair, fag smoke and fluid sexuality. It was less a club night and more an incubator of discovery. The music Erol Alkan, the DJ who founded the night, played—electroclash was in full throttle in 2003—sounded so forceful and sexy I felt I might erupt. Everyone was erupting, bursting out of daytime chrysalises into sweaty, jerking figures in a dark room. I didn't know Matt's mind despaired back then, and he didn't know mine did, either—but whenever he came inside for a dance in his Reebok Classics, we became transformed. Our only imperative was to see ourselves reflected in each other. We *needed* to be there, in the dark, not thinking. Only, years later, as an incredibly successful photographer who travelled the world shooting celebrities and high-profile fashion campaigns, Matt was doing a lot of thinking. Thinking alone. He was depressed. I knew, and we talked about it, often on iMessage late at night, but I didn't *know*. Not the ferocity of his thoughts, not that he desperately wanted help but didn't really know how to ask for it or, crushingly, believe he deserved it. No one knew but him. We know now. We read his thoughts made plain on a Word doc on his laptop screen. His death was all over the news.

We said goodbye to Matt in an East London crematorium on a hot June morning. His coffin disappeared under towers of flora: white roses like whipped cream; Asiatic lilies; peonies; hyacinths; succulents; cacti. It was a botanical garden, a burst of vitality, colour and scent. Exactly right, too, given how plant-obsessed he was. Walking into his flat was like entering a greenhouse at Kew Gardens; chlorophyll tickled every corner. The upkeep was intense. When he'd go away to some exotic location, someone would have to plant-sit, tend and keep watered his green, wall-climbing companions. Were they his children or his lovers? He could never decide.

Matt had made a funeral playlist—90 percent Kate Bush, 10 percent Debussy—and as the refrains of "Jig of Life" and "Moments of Pleasure" swam around the room, all we could see were the flowers. No casket. Just flowers.

I think of you all the time, you beautiful bastard. All the time. Your stupid laugh and the way your eyes crinkled when you smiled, your beef bourguignon, your kindness, your dancing, your soft head, your voice memos, your stinking trainers, the peace you felt in bleak natural spaces or with an animal in your hands. I have that, too. We like to imagine you growing now, like one of your ficus. You're the earth, the stems and the leaves.

THINKING ABOUT WHAT OTHER PEOPLE THINK

I N Scott Stossel's *My Age of Anxiety*, HE WRITES about how his hair-trigger shame reflex fires all the time. *That's him*, he imagines people thinking, *the one who can't control his own bodily functions.* That fear is one that we really anxious people are likely to have all the time: that people are sneering at our inability to hold it together, even though in all likelihood they haven't a clue how much our guts are hurting and threatening to explode, or how strong the feeling of pins and needles is in our arms.

I remember reading a *New York Times* review of Stossel's book and being struck by something the reviewer said. "Plaintive self-flagellation is a refrain in *My Age of Anxiety*— and, alas, the book's most tedious feature," it read. "In his fretting, Stossel sometimes overlooks the implications of his premise: If anxiety is a chemical disorder, then it shouldn't require any more apology than an epileptic's seizures."

Obviously, any book opens an author up to scrutiny, but that particular line stayed with me. No, one word: "tedious." Because no matter how tedious the constant rumination on shame and people's gazes are to someone on the outside, I know what Stossel is talking about and can guarantee that the tedium he will feel towards himself will be greater. Anxiety *is* tedium. Monotonous, infuriating tedium. I'm sure that living with him can be incredibly frustrating at times, as I'm sure living with me brings a great deal of annoyance. It always comes down to empathy and patience.

I've realized while writing this book that very few people I know have ever seen me *really* anxious or in the middle of a panic attack. I could count them on one hand. I always manage to get somewhere quiet if I'm going to have a panic attack, and my general, day-to-day ruminating usually happens when I'm alone. I have been and still get very anxious around other people sometimes, but I have been such a master of disguise, of the expert stealth exit, that I've never really had to say, "I feel incredibly anxious right now—bear with me."

Keeping my anxiety secret has not done me any favours, and I'm sure it's been obvious when I've thought it was perfectly disguised—after all, a mask often reveals more than it conceals. However, I'm getting better at just telling people I feel anxious if and when I do, because in all honesty, I've spent far too much of my life worrying myself sick about what other people think.

I think the tipping point for trying to curb that behaviour was when I became depressed and got very worked up over what Hanna, my partner, simply *must* have thought of me. It was as though fifteen years of shame and agonizing over what people would think if they saw the "real" me had been released in one giant *whoosh*, and it must have been an awful lot for her to deal with.

Going over and over, when we're vulnerable, what might be running through other people's minds about us does comes from stigma, but it's also another unfortunate part of being a human being with a huge capacity for emotion. We tend to act based on how we *think* people feel about us, but people's private thoughts are just that: private. We've not yet evolved to the point of achieving mind control.

Say you have a panic attack on the Tube. You're incredibly distressed, assuming what the people around you might be thinking. You actually have no idea, because you're unable to view their thoughts like a train station departure screen, but you carry on guessing and assuming anyway. This makes you feel worse.

The thing is, though, that people *will* look if there's even the merest whiff of a scene in an enclosed space. Of course they will. But just because people can't help looking doesn't mean they're sneering or disgusted. They're most likely thinking: *That person looks really uncomfortable. I wonder if he wants to be left alone or if I should say something.* And feel too awkward in themselves to do the latter. I think it would do every single person who lives with anxiety a world of good to practise telling herself that she can do precisely bugger all about what people think.

When we talk about changing attitudes and perceptions, what really matters is the membrane between our inner and outer monologues: how people transfer their thoughts into action. We all think unkind or stupid things sometimes about both the people we love and the strangers we come across, because we all have inner lives and knee-jerk reactions. Making an effort to remember that, I find, can be quite freeing.

PART IV

WHAT CAN WE DO?

DRUGS, DSM, DILEMMAS

C LINICAL TREATMENTS FOR ACUTE ANXIETY LARGELY
fall into two categories: psychological therapy and medication. Being such a kaleidoscopic condition means those categories have lots of variation and are only part of what we can
do to make living with the bastard easier.

In *The Concept of Anxiety*, Søren Kierkegaard captured the
infinitely varied expression of anxiety when he wrote:"Anxiety
can just as well express itself by muteness as by a scream." With
so many different manifestations of a condition, there can be
no perfect antidote and what works well for one person may
not work well for another.

According to the latest National Institute for Health and
Care Excellence (NICE) guidelines for anxiety, there is "no
significant difference in recovery rates for people using medication or psychological therapy." For this reason, it says, "all
patients should be offered a choice about the type of treatment
they receive."

The combination of medication and therapy is often said
to be the most effective treatment for getting over serious episodes of anxiety, and is something I can attest to, but it is up to
the individual what to try.

I have often found myself thinking: *Is this all there is?* when
it comes to interventions that could help me live with my anxiety better.

Dr. Kate Jeffery, the neuroscientist I met at UCL, told me, "I studied medicine in the 1980s, thirty years ago, and when I think about how far we've come since then, it's not far, really, in psychiatric terms. It's mostly still the same drugs being used for mood disorders, the SSRIs, which came along while I was a med student. We're still using more or less the same antipsychotics, with a few twiddles, but our medication options are still all basically hitting the dopamine system with a hammer."

Scientific researchers discovered the first antidepressants by accident in the 1950s. Scientists at the Münsterlingen Asylum in Switzerland found, while looking for a treatment for schizophrenia, that a drug that altered the balance of neurotransmitters in the brain (the chemicals that control our moods, the way we feel pain and many other sensations) could make patients feel episodic euphoria. That didn't do people with schizophrenia any good, but researchers thought it might work for people with depression. It did. Patients who first tried it in 1995 found themselves—not overnight, but over a shortish period—feeling more energetic and sociable. The drug was called imipramine and was marketed in 1958 as Tofranil. People called it a "miracle cure." Many rival drugs quickly followed as pharmaceutical companies saw the potential to capitalize on a rapidly growing market. These drugs were known as tricyclics, because of their three-ring chemical structure.

Many patients felt relief, but the side effects were hard. Weight gain, sluggishness, constipation and blurred vision were common—as was overdose. A better pill was needed and it didn't take long for scientists to produce a new, much more targeted type of antidepressant. Prozac was on the US market by 1987, Zoloft (sertraline) in 1992 and Paxil (paroxetine) in 1992.

By 1993, Prozac had been prescribed to ten million people across the world. In 1994, *Newsweek* said: "Prozac has attained the familiarity of Kleenex and the social status of spring water."

SSRIs weren't shooting at a broad range of brain chemicals; they were going for one: serotonin, one of those crucial neurotransmitters that carries signals between nerve cells. These drugs gave similar percentages of patients relief as the tricyclics—around 60 to 80 percent—but had far fewer side effects and less risk of overdose. But there are still side effects. Everyone tolerates SSRIs differently, but most people are started on a low dose to prevent side effects from being intolerable.

SSRIs can make your anxiety a bit worse before it gets better and the gradual increase must be done under the close supervision of your doctor, who is most likely to review you after the first month and possibly even on a month-to-month basis thereafter. No one should ever stop taking this kind of medication abruptly, even if the side effects are unpleasant, not just because most of the very uncomfortable ones disappear for most people but because going cold turkey with antidepressants is really not good. I've seen people do it and they've felt terrible.

I take a low dose of Citalopram (Celexa in the US) and did find it quite unpleasant at the very beginning. Tiredness was the main thing, but this wasn't a tiredness I had a reference point for. It was thick and synthetic, making me just want to rest my chin on my chest constantly for a couple of weeks. For the first few days this was a relief from the physical pressure of anxiety I'd been feeling in my head, which had been so strong I could taste it, like tin foil. I felt doped up and removed, which was actually nice, and in stark contrast to the blind fear and

repulsion I'd built up around taking an SSRI. Then the tiredness got so strong I "napped" for four or five hours during the
day. I kept feeling like I needed to cough, yawn or retch—a
weird urge in my chest that never quite realized itself. A few
times, my anxiety felt worse than ever, in spells that usually
lasted a couple of hours. Those days were quite bleak. After
about three weeks, though, the symptoms died down, and in
hindsight none was intolerable.

Over time, I stopped noticing anything save the odd
bout of that thick tiredness that would seemingly come from
nowhere. Side effects *can* be rough, but aren't a guarantee of
taking this type of drug and, as I've said, usually disappear eventually. SSRIs wouldn't exist if their therapeutic effect wasn't
considered greater than their potential side effects. However,
because it's the brain that is being targeted, we don't know
exactly how it will be affected by introducing a new chemical
until we try it.

I believe there is a metaphysics of anxiety, and that to understand it means to understand the human condition. But as someone who suffers from anxiety, I veer between being interested
in and able to ask those questions about the human condition
and just wanting something to take the anxiety away *now*. When
I'm walking down the street feeling like my ribs are piercing my
lungs, I can't do philosophy or existentialism. There's no room. I
just want the feeling to go away, because it's horrible.

No treatment can expunge anxiety overnight. I've had so
many fantasies about drinking one of those milky cocktails in
Clockwork Orange—a Moloko Plus or Knifey Moloko—one
night and waking up with a cleansed brain the next morning,
every cluster of frayed nerves smoothed down like frizzy hair

that's been oiled. But it's just that: fantasy. Both psychological therapy and medications like SSRIs take time to work, which can be a daunting prospect when you feel out of control of your mind and body. If you're anything like me, you'll even have had occasions when you've dreamed about being induced into a coma for a while.

A friend of mine who has experienced episodes of both acute anxiety and depression has a fantasy she calls "The White Room" when she's feeling bad. She's gently sedated in a room so bleached with sunlight that she's almost blinded, and is tended to by a matronly figure who shuffles in and out with sweet tea, toast and sedative top-ups. It is a chimera of stillness, of safety, that feels so far away when anxiety takes hold.

I think stillness is all anyone who knows the overwhelming nature of anxiety wants at the time, and there are substances that can give it to us. Alcohol, sleeping pills, codeine and cannabis are just a few examples of what some people I've known with anxiety have reached for when they felt terrible, most of them men. As I explained in part 3, addiction is common in men with anxiety and depression—alcohol and narcotics can provide a balm without the necessity of opening up about being mentally vulnerable. We know how perilous addiction can be, which is why it's so fascinating to learn how differently drugs for anxiety are used around the world. Not just the illicit sort, but the powerful ones prescribed by doctors.

Benzodiazepines are incredibly effective at providing relief for severe anxiety, and generally work within thirty minutes. On paper their sedative and muscle-relaxant effects read like a utopia, but they come with significant risk and are generally tightly controlled with anxiety disorders. The worry is that sufferers will either become addicted very quickly, finding themselves in a reinforcement circuit of feeling great and in control, then coming down, then taking more to feel great and in control again, then coming down again, building up tolerance, needing higher and higher doses, and eventually feeling that life would be intolerable without them. And things can quickly get to the stage where it actually is.

The withdrawal from benzodiazepines, my GP told me in her most serious voice, can be harder than coming off heroin. That these drugs work so well—I love looking around a flight to see people zonking out after they've dropped their pills—for anxiety can make any anxious person who knows about them think: *Shit, I need something like that.* They're such a delicious proposition, and the control over their dispensing seems to depend on where in the world you live.

Benzos are a group of drugs that have been used since the 1960s to treat anxiety, epileptic seizures, mania, alcohol withdrawal and sleeping problems. The most common ones are diazepam (Valium), lorazepam (Ativan), clonazepam (Klonopin) and alprazolam (Xanax). These drugs replaced the barbiturates that had been commonly prescribed for fifty years, up until the 1950s, but were incredibly addictive and posed a huge threat of overdose.

Benzos work in a similar way to those drugs and were greatly overused in the 1960s and 1970s. (We've all heard the stories of dosed-up, middle-class housewives, the kind Mick Jagger sang about in "Mother's Little Helper.") They boost the effect of the neurotransmitter GABA (gamma-aminobutyric acid), a chemical in the brain that controls the way messages move from one cell to another. GABA has a calming effect in the human brain. Obviously, this makes GABA drugs very addictive.

The Royal College of Psychiatrists says that around four in every ten people who take a benzo every day for more than six weeks will become addicted, and warns that benzos "should only be used for periods of up to four weeks."

When I went to my GP at the apex of the worst period of anxiety in my life, the one a few years back that led to depression, I had heard about drugs like Valium. I had never taken them, but knew that something existed that might bring the sleepy relief I was desperate for. Every night during this period I would look at my bed and think: *Fuck you.* Because I knew that the second I got in, the sheets would feel weird against my skin. That as soon as I closed my eyes, the static would start. That my sleep would be hot, fitful and nauseating.

I begged the doctor for something—a strong sleeping pill or *anything* that might loosen the invisible vice tightening around my head, even for one day. She said no.

"I am not going to prescribe you anything like diazepam because it won't do you any good," I remember her saying. She talked about addiction, reinforcement, that awful withdrawal, the comedowns and the side effects. I told her I was willing to take the risk. She said no again. I wanted to punch her.

I explained how I had never been addicted to anything in my life, that it had taken everything I had to get to her office that day (just under a kilometre from my front door) and that I was as desperate as I'd ever felt. I cried. I was shaking. But she held her ground.

Although it still seems harsh given such obvious distress, particularly since I know several people who have readily been prescribed short courses of benzos for all kinds of fabricated reasons, I now understand why she said no, although the most recently updated NICE guidelines say:"Do not offer a benzodiazepine for the treatment of GAD in primary or secondary care except as a short-term measure during crises." I was definitely in a crisis, but there we go. Instead, she prescribed the Citalopram that did go on to help me considerably, and a packet of beta blockers (propranalol)—the drug often prescribed after heart attacks, to keep a stable heart rhythm—to take when I needed them. Beta blockers carry no risk of addiction, and because they work on the adrenal system, they can be very useful for public speakers and people with social anxiety in that they calm both the heart and respiratory systems. I tried them and felt nothing. I'd later find them useful sometimes, as a preventive measure before a big social or professional event, but not then.

Psychiatrists have a reputation for adhering to the medical model of mood disorders—i.e., believing that anxiety is a chemical problem to be treated with chemical intervention. I certainly used to think that if you saw a psychiatrist, you'd leave with a mini pharmacy under your arm. Now that I've been in a position of speaking to some practitioners for this book, I no longer think that. But I've only met psychiatrists working in the UK.

Earlier I talked about the *Diagnostic and Statistical Manual of Mental Disorders* (DSM), and it's fair to say that not everyone believes in its worth. Not now that its newest edition (the DSM-5, updated in 2013, has 886 pages, compared with the modest 130 in its first edition) has created hundreds of new diagnosable, and therefore "treatable," disorders that could very well be explained as normal changes in mood and reactions to life events. Grief, for example. How can we medicalize grief?

The DSM is used in the UK, although less rigorously adhered to than in the US, and more often in addition to the more holistic International Statistical Classifications of Diseases and Related Health Problems (ICD), which is produced by the World Health Organization and used across Europe. Both effectively serve as dictionaries for mental health conditions and as a means of achieving a common language for those giving care. Or at least, that's why the DSM was created.

What exactly, you may ask, is the DSM and how is it relevant to me? How does the history of psychiatric drugs apply to me and my anxiety today? I tried to keep thoughts like this in mind throughout all my research because it's easy to feel swamped by history and information if you're suffering and just want relief.

I've been asking "Why?" about life since I first had a voice, much to my parents' frustration and often to my detriment as an adult. But so many of us sit opposite health professionals of all kinds and just take what they're saying at face value. To an extent this is completely expected—it would be hard to exist as a society without trusting experts in specific fields. But mistakes do happen and there is always an interesting history behind the words exchanged in any kind of care setting.

In terms of mental health, if you're someone who doesn't just want to take a diagnosis or treatment at face value, it is interesting to understand a treatment's history. If having a diagnosis helps you move on by giving words to your feelings, and if the treatment you've been offered makes you feel better and able to live, let no fucker argue with you: it's not about being clever or not clever; it's about living and knowing peace.

The diagnoses and common language we have today for anxiety and mood disorders all come from the DSM. It may now be a bulging digest surrounded with controversy, but the first edition was written to solve a problem that had plagued psychiatry for decades: no joined-up thinking.

In the book *Cracked: Why Psychiatry Is Doing More Harm Than Good* (2013), psychological therapist James Davies uses his expertise to guide the reader through the controversial history of psychiatry. "Until the 1950s, psychiatrists working in different places possessed no shared dictionary in which all the disorders were clearly defined and that carefully listed each disorder's core symptoms. Without this dictionary, the behaviour that one psychiatrist called 'melancholic' or 'depressive' another psychiatrist was likely to call something else," he explains. "So this made communication between psychiatrists in different places impossible."

The DSM was developed to try to identify and standardize the symptoms of any given mental health problem. All psychiatrists were expected to learn it so that they were all working from the same page. If your symptoms didn't neatly fit into a single category—in which case your problem would be called "comorbid"—the diagnostic process wouldn't really change. As Davies writes: "Your symptoms would still be matched as closely as possible to one of the diagnostic labels listed in the book."

Aside from organic disorders of the brain—like Alzheimer's, epilepsy and Huntington's disease, which all appear in the DSM—there are no biological markers for any of the others. Nevertheless, there are 886 pages' worth of diagnosable conditions that routinely have chemicals thrown at them.

In his book, Davies goes to meet Robert Spitzer, the psychiatrist who was a major force in the development of the DSM. "So let me get this clear," he begins, "there are no discovered biological causes for many of the remaining disorders in the DSM?" Spitzer's reply: "It's not for many, it's for *any*! No biological markers have been identified."

At that moment, Davies has a crucial realization. He remembers something the psychologist and activist Paula Caplan had said to him days earlier. "'Mental disorders,' she'd said, 'are nothing more than constellations.' At the time I'd not given the comment much thought, but now, having spoken to Spitzer, her analogy seemed suddenly perfect."

IT IS. THE DSM COMMITTEE didn't "discover" any mental disorders; it *engineered* them by drawing lines (constellations) between painful emotions (specific stars). They gave us the terms we know and use today within the anxiety bracket: "specific phobia," "generalized anxiety disorder," "panic disorder" and so on.

All the mental health conditions I list can be treated with drugs, should the sufferer decide to follow their doctor's advice if the doctor recommends medication. And therein lies much of the controversy. The DSM is relied upon by clinicians, researchers, psychiatric drug regulation agencies, pharmaceutical companies, health insurance companies and the legal system, and nowhere is this reliance so strong as in the US. This is what makes how anxiety is treated so interesting. For a start, of the American friends I have, I'd say 50 to 60 percent have been treated for anxiety at some point in their lives. Drugs like Xanax and Klonopin seem to be as easy to acquire as acetaminophen. When I spoke to Jon Ronson about his anxiety, he told me about how drugs like Xanax are helpful during his episodes of acute distress. When I told him about my experience with the unmoving GP, he said, "Seriously? You should try coming to New York. It's a different story." Then he told me a story that really shocked me.

"A couple of months ago I was doing a video for the *Guardian* about my public shaming book. I turned up at the studio where I was recording the video, somewhere in Brooklyn, and there was somebody who was recording her own video on before me. She was a doctor and said, 'What are you doing?' I said, 'Oh, I'm putting this book out about public shaming.' And she said, 'Did you see the article in the *New York Times* the other day about public shaming?' I told her I wrote it and she said, 'Oh, well, that piece is so great, you must be so happy.' I told her that actually I wasn't. That it had been very stressful. She said, 'What do you want?' There was this kind of long silence and I said Xanax. Then she got out her pad and wrote me a prescription for sixty Xanax."

Fucking *hell*, I say.

"That's how easy it is to get medication in America."

"But that's staggering, isn't it? That a perfect stranger who is not your doctor and knows nothing about you can just write you a prescription for a potent psychoactive drug?"

"Yep."

"Someone you've never met before in your life."

"Yep. And I've got worse stories than that."

I'm reminded of Scott Stossel's story. In *My Age of Anxiety*, he explains early on how much medication he has taken throughout his life to try to quell his anxiety and phobias: "Medication. Lots of medication. Thorazine. Imipramine. Desipramine. Chlorpheniramine. Nardil. BuSpar. Prozac. Zoloft. Paxil. Wellbutrin. Effexor. Celexa. Lexapro. Cymbalta. Luvox. Trazodone. Levoxyl. Propranolol. Tranxene. Serax. Centrax. St. John's wort. Zolpidem. Valium. Librium. Ativan. Xanax. Klonopin."

It's quite a list. When I read the book, I initially thought: *Christ, should I be trying all these drugs? Would my life be better if I had a stash of Xanax to fall back on when I feel like I can't cope?* Then it made me wonder in what ways drugs end up contributing to the problems of people who live with the kind of anxiety Stossel does. He has known nothing *but* medication. Powerful psychiatric medications that all come with their unique profile of side effects, weaning-on/off periods and withdrawal symptoms. He has twice been on antipsychotics, generally used in the treatment of schizophrenia or bipolar disorder. But if none of these medications provide the relief he needs, for as long as he needs them, what does this do for his belief in getting better? What do they make his vision of "better" look like? His thoughts about failure, helplessness and despair? You'd have to read his book—and really should: it's magnificent—to get a deeper insight into those emotions, but throughout it he uses his own frustrating experiences as a window into the checkered history of psychiatry and how, as he tells me on the phone from his office at the *Atlantic*, "as a society we are vastly overmedicated."

When I tell him about what medication had and hadn't been offered to me as someone presenting with acute anxiety, he is stunned. "Huh," he says. "That is fascinating. The American thing, which is probably a function of us not having a national health service and instead only health insurance that makes it cheaper for the insurance companies and basically everyone, is that doctors will make more money if they can have a fifteen-minute consult and throw drugs at someone. Pharmaceuticals are so often the first line of treatment for feeling blue or a little bit stressed." Of course, that so many with health insurance are over-medicated means many without it are at the other end of the spectrum. "There are plenty of people who are deeply emotionally distressed or have mental disorders who don't have access to the mental health system," Stossel says. "Insurance companies dominate health care in a way that might not make sense to someone outside the US."

I wonder, though: If Americans *are* as overmedicated for anxiety as Stossel and many others argue, propped up by quick chemical fixes, is the British model of *not* always using medication as a first-line response superior? Is my way of coping and living in any way superior to Stossel's? There's a strong argument that says anxious people who use anti-anxiety medication a lot will be experiencing nervousness because yesterday's drugs are wearing off. Benzodiazepines have a long half-life, which means they stay in your system for a long time. "You may lose sight of how much of your anxiety is just the rebound effect from the drug and how much of it is your underlying disorder," says Dr. Jeffery. The incentive structure with medication is completely different in America from the

UK and there is great moral debate to be had over doctors being seduced by huge pharmaceutical rewards, creating more and more disorders and prescribing more and more pills; over mass marketing, negative drug trials being routinely buried, research being regularly manipulated and the human cost of a field—no, industry—that has been helping itself rather than others. Big Pharma is a frightening business. But if we look at the British model, at least in terms of the state's approach, we find that people are routinely referred for the kind of therapy that will get them back on their feet and into productive work again as soon as possible. That sounds better than drugging people up to the eyeballs at the drop of a hat. Except, when we consider how the one-in-four rule for someone experiencing a mental health problem over any given year is generally used in both the US and the UK, can we be so sweeping about what "better" actually looks like?

As Stossel says on the phone to me, these cultural differences are fascinating to explore. "I mean, how much does the British 'stiff upper lip' approach to life in general apply to the structure of the health care system?" He tells me unequivocally that he depends heavily on, and wouldn't be able to cope without, anxiolytics, but we both agree on how coping is such a relative term. If one anxious person can be out and about in the world and able to pop something when he feels bad that keeps him out and about, he might feel like he's coping. Another anxious person might hate the idea of having to take something to cope. I used to be that person, but have come to terms with taking an SSRI and what it "means." I see the logic in everything I've been told about how drugs like diazepam wouldn't do me any good in the long run. But it doesn't stop me wondering sometimes what someone like Stossel is capable of that I'm not, given his access to a chemical crutch when the road feels unwalkable.

ASKING FOR HELP: WHAT DO WE GET?

I'M GOING TO FOCUS ON THE BRITISH HEALTH CARE system here, because Britain is where I live. The NHS is rightly envied as a framework that supports anyone, at any time, regardless of socioeconomic background. It doesn't matter who you are: If you need help, you can get it. Free. It is a magnificent structure full of clever, kind, selfless and dedicated people—and it's *ours*. It makes me inconceivably proud to be British. It's why I don't want to live anywhere else in the world. But blanket romanticism cannot always be justified, especially when we consider the problems our NHS has had in recent years in delivering good mental health care to everyone who needs it.

I HAVE HAD three experiences of going to a GP for help with my anxiety. The first time I was seventeen and clueless, which was when I was referred to the old woman with her elastic bands. The second time I was in my third year of university and went to my GP feeling like I was in a crisis. Looking back, I am uneasy about how quickly the doctor prescribed antidepressants, but I just took them because I was so desperate for something to help. He did refer me for therapy, but as I wrote about earlier, I very quickly became frustrated with the sweeping, box-ticking nature of it.

The third time was in 2013, during what I now refer to as The Bad Episode. The conversation I had this time with my GP was infinitely better. It was precisely that: a conversation. She asked me a lot about my previous experience with anxiety and how it had been treated; presented my options in a clear way and inquired what I knew about each; and stressed the whole while that although I was feeling unwell at the moment, I could be helped to get on with my life. She only suggested antidepressants when she knew about my history. I was angry at the time because she didn't give me drugs that would knock me out for a bit, but she looked after me very well. She took my panicky calls and for about a month would ring me once a week for a quick chat. This was above and beyond her call of duty, but she was responding with human kindness to someone who was very upset. I'll always be thankful for that. I turned down her referral for therapy because I already had S lined up, couldn't imagine myself being able to wait for the time she said it might take and, ultimately, could afford to pay for it privately. This financial bind is something I'll explore later.

As some of the attitudes and stigma about mental health change, services have to refocus, and I am a one-person testament to how they have, over time. I don't want to paint a picture of full doom, because many people across the country are receiving fantastic, compassionate care that is helping them get on with their lives. No one should ever be put off asking for help, because it *is* there. However, there's no use diluting reality: the speed with which we get help can be a major problem.

DAVID, THIRTY-EIGHT, lives in East London and has had periods of anxiety and depersonalization throughout his adult life. As a reminder: depersonalization is when you feel removed from your surroundings—as if everything is a hologram, an illusion. I have known it and can tell you that the sense of removal is frightening.

David recalls how he would be at work on his computer and feel like nothing around him was real: the computer, his stationery, the walls. People. He couldn't concentrate on faces or voices; in meetings he'd feel like he was wearing earplugs. It started to really affect his life.

The depersonalization was transient, but he would dread going to work or going out in case it happened. In summer 2015 he went to see his GP, who, he says, was "pretty good" in responding to his symptoms. Therapy was advised and he was referred to a clinical assessment service. He was to call and make a date for a telephone assessment, which—I called and checked with the assessment service he used—is supposed to happen within twenty-eight days. His happened on the twenty-eighth day, when he was "feeling terrible." They talked to him for around half an hour and called him back the same day to say that a course of CBT would be appropriate. Great, he thought. Only, they said it could take several months to see a therapist.

He put the phone down and cried.

"I didn't have months," he says. "I said to them, 'What am I supposed to do in the meantime?' And they said they were sorry and that I should look up local support groups or use the Internet. But my anxiety was so bad I felt like I was losing my mind. I didn't want to go to a support group—I wanted to talk to someone on my own." So, like me, he opted to find a private therapist and pay.

David's story is one of thousands. He says he was beginning to have suicidal thoughts and that, despite knowing on "a pretty deep level" that he needed help quickly, he didn't feel his problems warranted a visit to Emergency. Mental health services are the victim of years of neglect, and funding cuts have taken their toll. At a time of rising demand—which suggests both worsening circumstances and a greater confidence in seeking help for mental health issues, an unfortunate irony—waiting lists for treatment that's deemed non-urgent are criminally long.

Problems with oversubscribed local services are one (very big, frightening) thing, and although it is possible to self-refer to a mental health service, most people's first point of call is their GP. When the Care Quality Commission in the UK published a report in June 2015 about gaps in mental crisis care (extreme anxiety counts as a crisis), they found that 60 percent of people who'd visited their GP during a crisis were "satisfied with the experience" but pointed out how "vital" it was that GPs access specialist training to help them identify mental health conditions early, in order to prevent crises from occurring. Forty percent of dissatisfied patients is still a huge number. As Dr. Paul Lelliott, deputy chief inspector of hospitals, said: "It is not acceptable for people with mental health problems to be treated differently to those with physical health problems."

But for many people they still are.

How can it be that GPs have to *choose* to access specialist training about how to deal with presenting mental health problems, when they are so common and exist in absolutely every corner of society? How can it be that the way doctors might respond to someone with symptoms of an anxiety disorder might vary according to a practitioner's age, cultural background or whatever?

Speaking with the memory of my own experiences, I cannot bear the idea of a child or teenager being in crisis and feeling like help is either far away or not there at all, because I know how deeply embedded anxiety can become and, without the right treatment at the right time, how long it can take to chip away at later on.

BRITAIN'S MENTAL HEALTH CARE crisis seems to be getting worse and worse at the time of writing, with children bearing perhaps the greatest brunt. At the end of 2015, the dire state of care for children with mental health problems was revealed when figures showed that the number of children arriving at Emergency with symptoms of psychiatric conditions (incidents of self-harm are becoming more and more common) had risen to nearly twenty thousand a year—more than double the number four years before.

Experts said a chief cause was an absence of out-of-hours community care, with children being advised to go to Emergency after 5:00 p.m. The scale of the problem is a hefty burden on an already struggling system, but it should have been foreseen. Community support with Child and Adolescent Mental Health Services (CAMHS) needs to be provided for young people and their families when they start to struggle, so that the horrible suffering of a crisis can be prevented. As Sarah Brennan, chief executive of YoungMinds, a charity working with children with mental health problems, said: "They shouldn't have to turn to hospital services in desperation because there is no other support available."

UNWELL CHILDREN not getting the right help is unforgivable. Leaving things too late for the seriously ill can be disastrous—fatal, even. But failing the kids who are, I guess, in the middle—whose problems are not minor but not major enough to warrant immediate hospitalization—like I was, runs terrible risks. Self-esteem and stigma bloom when things aren't done well and in good time. And if a child had to work through stigma to get the care in the first place, a bad experience might lead that child or their family to believe that *all* experiences will be bad. As the NHS tells us itself in its online guidelines: "Teenagers with an anxiety disorder are more likely to develop clinical depression, misuse drugs and feel suicidal." Which speaks of retreat. Isolation. We have to get it right the first time, particularly for those who are already vulnerable.

I went to visit a single mother living with two teenagers in Tower Hamlets. This London borough is thought to contain some of the worst child poverty in Britain (figures published by the Campaign to End Child Poverty in 2014 revealed that one in two children there live in poverty). I discussed with

Suzanne the care that one of her children, a fifteen-year-old boy, received. Her son, who I'll call Daniel, has been diagnosed with obsessive-compulsive disorder and social anxiety. He has a history of self-harm.

Daniel had intrusive thoughts and fears about contamination, which seemed to happen most at school. He would be acutely aware of communal surfaces—desks, textbooks, banisters, science equipment—and carried a bottle of Boots hand sanitizer in his blazer pocket at all times. PE was his most uncomfortable subject, because a football or basketball not only slammed and rolled around in the dirt on the floor, it went from person to person and, in his mind, became a bomb of germs and disease.

His compulsions were the sanitizing, which had to be done within five seconds, but also a lot of counting: packing and repacking his pencil case five times, using his fingers to count out words when he had to talk to people, trying to keep his sentences in multiples of five.

He retreated into his own world at school and began actively protesting about attending. Suzanne tells me that she had just put it down to him being "a moody teenager." Getting to the bottom of how he was really feeling was a long and painful process. "It was a case of him hiding it and me not knowing what the signs were, what to look for. When your [financial] resources are low, all resources are low," she tells me at her kitchen table, drawing long and slow on an e-cigarette that smells exactly like Haribo gummy bears. Both her thirteen-year-old daughter and her son are at school. I ask her to elaborate.

"Well, when you're from a poor, uneducated background, all the odds are stacked against you. I'm a single mum who doesn't earn very much, doesn't know very much . . ." I stop her, saying she's being unnecessarily hard on herself. "Okay, well, I've never knowingly come across a mental health problem in my life, apart from the 'crazy' folk who used to wander around the streets outside our estate—this same one we're sat in now—so when my son started to act a bit strangely, I just put it down to his hormones. I didn't have a clue. One day I saw a small cut on his arm that looked too neat to be an accident. I asked him about it and he got so defensive. I thought: *Hmm, something's not right.*"

Suzanne asked Daniel what was going on and he eventually blurted out how "weird" he felt sometimes, especially at school. He said how cutting himself had "sort of made it better" because the way it hurt was "distracting." He promised never to do it again. But he did.

"I didn't feel a sense of urgency until he did it the second time," Suzanne says, wincing. "And I beat myself up about that every single day." This time she called to make a GP appointment straight away, but the next available one was in seven days. In the meantime, she kept an eye on Daniel, as much as a mother can keep an eye on her teenage son.

"It was the elephant in the room," she says.

The GP they saw said Daniel was likely suffering with an anxiety disorder, but didn't seem "overly concerned" about the self-harm. Instead of taking immediate action, he made a referral to their local CAMHS. Unfortunately, no doubt due to the perfect storm of reduced staffing levels (those cuts again) and oversubscription, it would take several weeks for the boy to be seen.

"Neither of us knew what we were dealing with. He only

knew that he felt strange and I only knew that he'd cut himself and that I wanted to stop him from doing that again, because he's my boy and I want to protect him," Suzanne says. Her eyes pool and glisten.

Sadly, before their meeting with a child psychotherapist came, Daniel cut himself badly enough to have to go to hospital for stitches. As his parent, Suzanne felt "a horrible mixture of terror and guilt." Daniel obviously needed to see a professional. Yet he had no choice but to wait. It was only after their Emergency visit that he was scooped up by the system and taken care of with a sense of urgency. A child shouldn't need to wound himself so badly that he requires eight stitches before his symptoms are recognized as urgent. Since then, Daniel has been having therapy and feels a lot better. He's even enjoying school again, particularly now that Suzanne has spoken to his teachers about what might be going on when he acts out of sorts.

Will it get better than this? It has to. A spokeswoman for NHS England admits that mental health services had been "the poor relation" in the past but insists there will be a turnaround. It's hard to imagine a service that needs prioritizing more. "The NHS is, for the first time in twenty-five years, planning on introducing clear waiting-times standards for mental health care, beginning in April 2016."

AT THIS POINT, let's be perfectly clear again: individual mental health care involving high-quality therapy does exist within the NHS, and around the world, and is making lives better for many people. I've met so many wonderful mental health professionals while researching this book, and there are millions of people getting the support they need from psychiatrists, psychologists, GPs, mental health nurses, peer support workers and social workers up and down the country—all free, because we have a democratic health system that looks after us. However, given our awareness of all the problems I've explored, it's a sad reality how often people believe that to get the best therapy they must pay for it. I've been privy to too many of those conversations and it's just not the case. But if you want good therapy *fast*, you are often better off looking for a private practitioner, who will have much shorter waiting times. It shouldn't be like this; we know it shouldn't. But it's a similar picture in any private health care system: you pay to get the same procedures you'd have done in an NHS hospital—only faster.

The idea of therapy may seem far away to some people because of their socioeconomic status. They may believe, through lack of knowledge or social stigma, that sitting in a room and talking to a stranger about their problems is either a self-indulgent waste of time or a privilege of the middle and upper classes—people who have money to spend. Their attitude may change once they actually get into that room and find relief in being honest about how they're feeling, but getting them there in the first place is the dilemma. The antidote to this sense of removal from talking therapies is, surely, improving public education and awareness of mental health problems in the first place. Learning what's available and might help if we become unwell is part of that.

One child in ten has a diagnosable mental health problem, which equates to around three in every classroom. Teaching children about mental health and emotional well-being from an early age, as part of their wider curriculum, seems so ridiculously obvious. I remember very little from my own PSHE (personal, social, health and economic) education, apart from very surface-level lessons about periods and sex. Lessons on mental health were non-existent. So, naturally, when I first started having panic attacks, I had absolutely no idea what was happening.

We know that childhood anxiety left untreated can lead to problems in adulthood (I am a walking case study), so what are we doing in terms of systemic practices that might prevent children and young adults from finding themselves in similar situations and not knowing what to do? We need to create a common language that tramples on awkwardness or ignorance about mental health. Young people are leading us in terms of acceptance of things like gender and sexuality, and they're doing it with mental health, too. Ensuring that mental health conversations happen in *every* classroom from an early age will make the picture even better.

An encouraging development in this area in the UK is a new series of guidelines for schools from the PSHE Association, which were released in July 2015. They cover preparing to teach about mental health, identifying emotions and developing coping strategies. Age-appropriate lesson plans have been written for every stage of education, from the five-year-olds in primary school to the seventeen-year-olds in sixth form.

I had a look at some of these plans and they are encouraging. Key Stage One (children between five and seven) plans involve dedicating time to thinking about feelings every day: making a conscious effort to name and identify feelings so that pupils will be better able to identify and manage their own as they arise. When you get to Key Stage Four (children between fourteen and sixteen), things become more specific: focusing on resilience and reframing failure; self-harm; eating disorders; anxiety and depression.

Workshops on healthy coping strategies and mindfulness are included, and there is a very strong emphasis on not teaching the lessons in isolation but rather as part of a general PSHE program. Crucially, it says, by the age of fourteen pupils should be taught "the characteristics of emotional and mental health and the causes, symptoms and treatments of some mental and emotional health disorders (including stress, anxiety and depression)," which will include proper information about talking therapies, medications and so forth.

What more can we do? More TV ads, billboards and information in pub toilets? More banner ads on websites and video sites like YouTube? It feels like there are so many platforms and so many ways to reach people that we could be utilizing. It's not about feeding people unnecessary fears that their mind could "go" at any minute. Nor is it about suggesting that everyone needs to be in therapy, because not everyone does. It's about saying, "Hey, problems like x, y or z happen to people sometimes—here's what you can do if it happens to you." But we need to target people in ways that make sense to them. For young people especially, this means using social media, school visits, new information websites and viral content.

RECENTLY, PIXAR RELEASED a film called *Inside Out*, which serves as a grand example of education through entertainment.

Inside Out took moviegoers through Riley's emotional roller coaster around relocating to San Francisco with her parents, and settling into a new life taught kids about the spectrum of feeling. It said: "It's okay to be sad and frightened sometimes, but that doesn't mean you'll feel sad and frightened forever." The film was praised by neuroscientists across the world for showing, moment by moment, how memories formed and influenced, and how they affect who we are and the way we respond to life's undulations. It created a jumping-off point for conversations about mood and mental health that made sense to everyone. While we can't always wait for beautiful films like Pixar's *Inside Out* to come along and help explain mental health to children, that doesn't mean we can't celebrate them when they do.

THE OBSTACLE TO GETTING the kind of campaigns I was just talking about off the ground is usually cost. Cost is something that informs *a lot* of conversations about mental health care today. We can start by looking at CBT—now the most common taxpayer-funded therapy in Britain for mood disorders like anxiety and depression, because it is evidence based and highly effective. However, CBT is also one of the cheapest types of therapy to deliver, which is where detractors have problems. As a cheap model that's focused on getting people back to work as quickly as possible, it has the whiff of something that might be favoured by budget-conscious governments holding the purse strings, who have considerable interest in people's ability to "contribute." As I said before, though, we can take whatever moral standpoint we like: CBT works. For many, many people.

Since CBT emerged in the 1960s, there have been countless studies that prove it is the one based on empirical fact; that the ways in which it helps people are quantifiable, both in society and with biology. Today, therapy referrals on the NHS will usually consist of a short course of structured meetings with a CBT therapist and/or online tasks to (hopefully) recognize and adapt our irrational thinking.

Freudian psychoanalysis once wore the crown of the talk therapies but has now sort of been put to the back of psychology's larder—at least, in terms of how most people are treated. It's not hard to see why. The practice of charging clients through the nose for years and years of pondering their childhoods, deeming every objection raised on the couch as "resistance" and something that needs even *more* analysis, seems like an expensive swizz. In CBT, by contrast, clients are encouraged to identify patterns of negative thinking and to develop the skills to adjust them as and when they arise—the objective being to get the clients back into the swing of day-to-day life as soon as possible and to help them feel in control.

In a *Guardian* piece at the beginning of 2015, Oliver Burkeman wrote a fascinating essay on the tension between the CBT and psychoanalytic models of therapy ("Therapy Wars: The Revenge of Freud," January 2016). He quotes the Nobel-prizewinning scientist Peter Medawar, who in 1975 called psychoanalysis "the most stupendous intellectual confidence trick of the twentieth century: and a terminal product as well—something akin to a dinosaur or Zeppelin in the history of ideas, a vast structure of radically unsound design and with no posterity." This "unsound design" is why CBT became so successful in Freud's wake. Psychoanalysis had nowhere as much empirical proof.

By the 1960s, advances in the science of psychology meant that the ambling conversations of psychoanalysis appeared less and less reliable or based on scientific fact. Behaviourists were showing that, like rodents', our behaviour could be predicted and manipulated in short periods. And when thousands of soldiers came back from World War II with profound mental health issues, this is exactly what was needed. These men didn't have time to lie on couches and free-associate—they were in emotional crises and needed fast treatments that wouldn't cost the earth. By 2012, over a million people had received therapy free because of the initiative economist Richard Layard, one of CBT's biggest champions, helped pass through Parliament with the Oxford psychologist David Clark. We can't argue with numbers like that. Or can we?

We have spent our entire history as humans trying to work out what this "life and existence" business means. The way we conduct ourselves in all our relationships and our working lives is the result of both unconscious and conscious imprinting. Every one of us has an inner life that is weird and mysterious, full of deeply buried images, fears, hopes and fantasies. So, as Burkeman asks: "Could the answer to our woes really be something as superficial-sounding as 'identifying automatic thoughts' or 'modifying your self-talk' or 'challenging your inner critic'? Could therapy really be so straightforward that you could receive it not from a human but from a book, or a computer?"

Computerized cognitive behavioural therapy (CCBT) is widely used in Britain today and, again, leads us to questions of cost. Devising a program that we can use on a computer, tablet or phone reduces the cost of care staff, building rent and all sorts of things. It's easy to be cynical. But there's an argument for giving us the option to integrate therapy into the pattern of our lives: not having to spend too much time in a clinical setting will benefit our ideas about what being mentally unwell means. Namely, that we can get treatment *and* carry on as normally as possible. I've seen examples of these computer programs and they're not as generalized or kindergarten-y as you might think—or as I thought they'd be. They're also most likely to be used as a bridge between meetings with an actual therapist who has skin, eyes, teeth and hair. But even so, can the loneliness and frustration of living with something like acute anxiety really be soothed by a voice coming through a laptop speaker and some cartoon sad faces?

Getting more control over my own anxiety has been markedly influenced by the rapport I have with my therapist. I am just one of many clients, but I feel like my well-being is his sole focus for the time that I'm in his office. It is a space I feel confident putting my vulnerability into, because I know it will be met with kindness. He is also available to me via email and phone between sessions—something that is part of the service I am paying for.

I want to briefly talk about the cost of seeing a therapist privately, because there is much variation. If you were thinking of going down to Harley Street, an area of London with a very high concentration of private doctors, you're looking at paying hundreds of pounds for an hour's therapy and not a whole lot less for the privilege of follow-up phone calls or Skype sessions. I have lots of thoughts about the private sector and the unfortunate us-and-them feeling it generates around many aspects of health: namely, the idea that having money will get you better care. But private health care also isn't going any-where fast, and it's pointless having a blanket disdain for anyone who has money and can genuinely afford to pay Harley Street prices. However, the credentials of the psychiatrists and ther-apists practising there are unlikely to be "better" than some-one you'd pay considerably less to see. In fact, most private psychiatrists and therapists also do NHS work, which says a lot.

BEYOND THE AFFLUENT ECHELONS of London, private psychotherapists usually charge between £40 and £100 (about C$70 to $170) for each hour-long session. If you are consid-ering having CBT privately, for example, you can ask your GP to suggest a local therapist. You can also visit the British Association for Behavioural and Cognitive Psychotherapies (BABCP), which keeps a register of all accredited therapists in the UK. Also, the British Psychological Society (BPS) has a directory of chartered psychologists, some of whom special-ize in CBT.

Not everyone knows the following—I didn't—but many private therapists will offer fees on a sliding scale, depending on income. One afternoon, I picked twenty-five random pri-vate therapists of varying disciplines across major UK cities and towns. Over a few days I called them all and asked if they'd offer a concessionary rate if someone's circumstances were difficult. All but one said yes. Twenty-four people is small fry when we're talking about an entire country's needs, I know, but it's some insight.

Taxpayer-funded CBT has a clear beginning and end, will be highly structured over its course—a minimum of five sessions but anywhere up to twenty—and inevitably includes lots of "homework" for the patient to do. It's not just plopping down in a chair and unloading—it takes work. It *is* work. And many people feel a lot better afterwards. However, recent studies have shown that CBT may have be less effective at treating long-term depression.

The results of the first big NHS study of long-term psychoanalysis were published by London's Tavistock Centre in October 2015 and showed that eighteen months of psychoanalysis had more of a long-lasting effect than the treatment you usually get on the NHS: largely CBT. After two years of analysis, 44 percent of patients didn't fit with the markers of major depression. For the others, the figure was 10 percent. Is Freud really having revenge? There is certainly weight to the opinion that psychoanalysis may alter our personalities in a longer lasting way, but can we really say that CBT is just a plaster, superficially holding together much deeper cracks in our psychic archaeology? Particularly given that any CBT therapist isn't going to hold up a director's clapperboard and shout "CUT!" every time someone mentions the past—the past is very much taken into account.

These so-called therapy wars aren't just about what's best for people. Much of the debate is coloured by people trying to protect their vested interests. Psychoanalysis, or psychodynamic therapies, and CBT are fundamentally different approaches. There are a lot of other models, too: humanistic, integrative,

person centred, gestalt. I refer back to what I said earlier about how anxiety often presents acutely compared with the slow burn of depression—although that, of course, can happen quickly—and how sufferers want immediate strategies to assist, rather than fart-arsing around the traumas of their childhood.

If you choose to see a private therapist who applies CBT techniques, the initial treatment will be very similar to that you'd get on the NHS—targeted, regimented and with lots of homework. But once the initial severity of the symptoms lessens, private therapists are likely to help you reflect in a much wider sense.

Arguments about what therapies are "right" or "wrong" cannot be ironed out with studies that contradict each other. Our individual minds are too complex and evolving for that. Different things work for different people. It's so difficult sometimes as a patient, client, whatever, to have conviction that something is wrong or unhelpful. We are not the "expert" of mental distress in a therapy setting—we're only an expert on our own suffering. With a comfortable, compassionate rapport, the sufferer's arguments, questions and beliefs can be acknowledged and challenged in a kind way. Being challenged is the whole point.

WHEN I LOOK BACK on my therapy with K, though, I do believe there was some wrongness there. I know she was trying to help me with approaches that came from her training and belief systems, and she was a mostly lovely woman with whom I enjoyed many conversations, but, with hindsight and

more knowledge, I think she behaved unethically; namely, by allowing her own bias around taking medication to enter our sessions. "Oh, you really don't want to put those chemicals in your body," she said—on many occasions. Towards the end of my time with her I had seriously started to wonder what else I should be contemplating for my increasingly anxious state, and obviously medication became a consideration, if an incredibly uncomfortable one. However, it is not a therapist's place to claim dogmatic authority on what medical treatments may or may not benefit someone.

Every time I mentioned medication and how, despite my fears and shame, maybe it would have to be an option at some point, she would shut me down. "No," she'd say. "No, I don't think so." Informative advice is one thing, but this was quite another. I emailed K while I was writing this book to try to get a sense of why she was so against medication, but she seemed to have a different recollection of events from me. "To respond to your interpretation that I was dogmatic about or against the use of medication, it's not that I don't believe in antidepressants or anti-anxiety medication, just that they don't cure the underlying problem," she replied. But she also reaffirmed that she does "see medication as a last resort." Many people do. I did. Still, I think she allowed her beliefs to reinforce mine, which wasn't fair when I was feeling so unwell. Of course I had agency, but I was vulnerable.

It's impossible to judge how much my taking medication contributed to my gaining more control over anxiety, alongside the new therapy I was having with S; or to work out whether earlier encouragement to explore my options would have stopped me falling so hard. But I do think some

of the conversations we had probably shouldn't have happened. Evaluations of whether medication is appropriate or not need to happen with a doctor.

If we can go back to the idea of what success and relief actually look like in therapy, it's important to remember that there is no cookie-cutter mould that everyone fits inside. In psychoanalysis, we may dredge up things that make us incredibly sad, but end up feeling we're more aware of the thought or behaviour patterns that relate to those painful things and can generally live with more awareness. It is less about the symptom and more about what the symptom *means*. But having an anxiety disorder so often means living daily with very uncomfortable symptoms, physical and mental. Sometimes we need to take our symptoms at face value and gain control of them, in order to have the capacity for deeper thinking.

To live is to feel pain. Every person knows pain and difficulty, because that's what the human condition is—even for the most optimistic, ostensibly happy-go-lucky types. As poet Rainer Maria Rilke famously said: "The purpose of life is to be defeated by greater and greater things." I believe that. Most of us just live for the good bits in between the shit. So, if psychoanalysis can help people feel they've found relief in the basement of their mind and therefore feel more adept at dealing with the present, it's not something I or anyone else can argue with, really.

Being "better" looks different for different people. Personally, I want to carry on developing my skills for working on relief in the present, and I'm lucky to have found a therapist who I feel helps me do that. I am more open than I've ever been to accepting that there are sedimented layers of thoughts and beliefs that haven't been washed away in the tide of the present and that affect who and how I am today, but I'm not going to seek out a psychoanalyst's couch anytime soon. Why? Because—and I'm going to be bold here—I think gaining relief, clarity and coping mechanisms from talking therapy probably depends on the therapist more than the type of therapy given. It depends on the human relationship, on rapport, compassion, patience and kindness. All these things significantly affect a person's commitment to change. As Oliver Burkeman notes in his *Guardian* piece: "If one therapy is better than all others for all or even most problems, it has yet to be discovered."

Burkeman met a psychoanalyst named David Pollens, who worked on the Upper East Side of Manhattan. He said something interesting: "There was a wonderful British analyst, Michael Balint, who was very involved in medical training, and he had a question he liked to pose [to doctors]. It was: 'What do you think is the most powerful medication you prescribe?' And people would try to answer that, and then eventually he'd say: 'The relationship.'"

If I could summarize everything I've written about therapy so far, it would be to tell you that you have options.

HELPING OURSELVES:
WHERE DO WE START?

Time's a goon right? You gonna let that goon push you around?
—JENNIFER EGAN, *A VISIT FROM THE GOON SQUAD*

WHERE DO WE START HELPING OURSELVES? THE million-dollar question, that. If I had put a quid—a toonie or so—in a jar every time I'd typed "anxiety symptoms and how to deal with them" into Google, I'd have enough by now to charter a private plane to plop me on that Caribbean island with the swimming pigs—the place I go to a lot in my dreams, where I somersault through liquid turquoise to a chorus of oinks. I'd probably have enough to buy the whole island.

I don't believe that anyone suffering with anxiety or depression should have to just try to "deal with it" alone. When I read Matt Haig's book *Reasons to Stay Alive*, parts of it moved me to tears. But I found it upsetting, both on his part and that of his readers, when he said that his "solution" was never medical—it was time.

No one's solution *has* to be medical, but equally, no one should think that the only solution is waiting and hoping things will get better. Mood disorders like anxiety and depression are illnesses, but they're not like infections that we can subtract a day of suffering from by taking an antibiotic. They're too complex and variable for that. I do often struggle with the concept of time—no biggie—but I don't want to let it just tick away.

People with a colourfulness in their mental health will have a different attitude towards whatever condition they have. You often hear those prone to depression say that because they've known such darkness, it makes them rejoice in the light so much more. I know people with anxiety who say that having such a propensity for fast thinking and nervous energy often helps them get shit done better. I know that my own issues have made me less judgmental of other people's vulnerabilities and how they manifest. I know that I feel with a big F and—this sounds cheesy as all hell, but it's true—that the world can surprise and enthrall me in the simplest of ways. The shiny oil fresh limes leave on my hands. Getting a good knot on a bin bag. Sand. When the sky is pink milk before the sun sets. It's like the gates to my senses have creaked wider and wider over time.

Caitlin Moran, the well-known and outspoken journalist and author, is someone who has been very open about having both panic disorder and a history of depression. She wrote about this sensory business in her contribution to Mind's Penguin book, *Dear Stranger*, which contained writing from all kinds of public figures about their mental health. Hers was a letter to "The Dark Place," and referred throughout to her imaginary dog—a tiny dachshund called Eric, now her touchstone for how she should be treating herself as someone who can be mentally vulnerable ("You must treat yourself as a loved one, or teammate. Or pet."):

The Dark Place is not all bad, you know. We learned to trust each other, in the Dark Place. We bonded, in the empty place. We've had some quality time there. And we also know why we end up there, now: because depression takes a layer of skin off, so you feel more of the world than most people. But, as I explained to Eric, that sentence changes, depending on how you say it. We feel more of the world than most people. WE FEEL MORE OF THE WORLD THAN MOST PEOPLE. That's amazing. That is why we end up in the Dark Place—but it is also why we cry with joy when we listen to David Bowie, and are obsessed with the moon, and can stare at the redness of cherry-juice on our fingers and imagine a whole world that is cherry-juice-red—with stained-glass trees and frosted crimson grass, and tiny, bright birds that fly out of scarlet oyster shells.

I don't want to praise anxiety for taking a layer of skin off—which really is how it feels sometimes. I don't always like being as sensitive as I am, or having to mute my mum on Facebook because she keeps posting too many videos of rescue dogs being found in inconceivable conditions. Even with their happy endings, I have to stop myself watching these videos because I carry them around with me for days, the dogs' sad onyx eyes like migraine halos. I can see the ways in which knowing anxiety, and the capacity the brain has to change states, has made me examine how I judge people and how important it is to listen. But it's not for me to comment on how my behaviour affects other people. Maybe I will get to a stage of my life where I can feel thankful or "blessed" for what anxiety has given me. But if that's even possible, it's not a part of the process I've reached yet.

302 | ELEANOR MORGAN

"Process" is a very important word when it comes to anxiety. We can have crises more than once. Recovery periods have peaks and then troughs—often referred to as "blips." We can have all sorts of epiphanies and turning points along the way. But finding a magic bullet that well and truly smashes anxiety forever is rare. However, we *can* change our narratives. Increasingly, it seems that mindfulness training might be something that helps us do that.

MINDFULNESS:
A MIND-BLOWING INDUSTRY?

MINDFULNESS HAS EXPLODED, WHICH IS A WEIRD sentence to write about something that encourages being quiet and still. We really have become obsessed with the concept of still thought. The ability to just *be*, in the moment, amid our busy, loud lives.

What actually *is* it, though? As a definition, Jon Kabat-Zinn, an eminent figure in the mindfulness field due to his founding of the mindfulness-based stress reduction program that has been applied in care settings across the world, says: "Mindfulness is awareness that arises through paying attention, on purpose, in the present moment, non-judgmentally. It's about knowing what is on your mind."

Of course, Buddhists have practised mindfulness for more than two thousand years—the gentle effort of being present with experience is at the core of the other *m*-word: "meditation." To offer another definition, mindfulness is, neurologist James H. Austin says in his book *Zen and the Brain* (1998), "a relaxed attentive state" that "helps relieve us from self-inflicted trains of thought"—all things anxious people find incredibly hard to do. But that's where the practise element comes in and, inevitably, the fact that most of us will need to be taught.

In the 1960s, meditation was placed firmly within the hippie-shit bracket, considered just one of the many "mystical" things people could become obsessed with. Over time, though, it went mainstream. Everyone knows about it now: the image of a person sitting with wrists on knees, eyes closed, hands poised as if to click; humming *ommmmm*. But it's not really about switching off. Nor is it quite as simple as sitting on a mat, chanting, or even about passivity. True meditation is more a fitness regime for the mind. And it's hard!

When I went to see S for the first time, he explained that he would be using mindfulness as part of my therapy, along with exposure, coping strategies, general relaxation and something called "acceptance and commitment therapy." Mindfulness was part of the latter. The hope was that it would encourage me to accept my thoughts rather than judge or react to them. This is something you have to practise and practise, like throwing a Malteser candy up in the air and trying to catch it in your mouth.

When S first mentioned mindfulness I initially thought: *Nah*. First, it took a while for me to listen to any of the familiar words coming out of his mouth and think they'd apply to me and *my* anxiety: secret, tangled and untouchable for the last fifteen years. Second, I was cynical about how an ancient practice, which required nothing but you and a quiet space, had been rebranded and watered down into a multimillion-pound industry.

I'd seen the apps, the colouring books that invited you to colour your way to inner peace, the adverts for the first "mindfulness opera," staged at the Barbican in autumn 2015 (an interactive four-hour show with a yoga session instead of an interval). That sort of thing. I mean, a mindfulness colouring book? An adult person sitting at a table, *colouring in*? Are we all going to drop to our knees one day and actually start crawling back to the dark goo of our mothers' wombs? It's not hard to see what Giles Coren meant when he wrote a column for *Time Out* magazine on the subject, calling mindfulness "cynical capitalist techno smegma."

And yet. Genuine escape takes fortitude. Whatever pursuits we have decided to follow, someone, somewhere, has found a way to make money from it. Is spending £7.95 (about C$14) a month on an app (this is what Headspace costs—downloaded over three million times since it started in 2012) that might help you relax better really that bad? That's the cost of two London pints.

I do struggle with the idea of adult colouring books, but also believe that if someone has the means to access something and it helps them, my judgment should probably be suspended. I do wonder if those who have dismissed mindfulness as a downloadable dummy—newspaper columnists, the inveterate contrarians who lurk in the bowels of social media waiting to pounce the SECOND anyone talks about something popular—know what they're talking about?

It's generally wise to be wary of any capitalist venture with cure-all claims—don't get me started on "wellness" and "clean eating"—but when you shut out all the noise surrounding mindfulness, what we're actually talking about is a practice with solid neurobiological authority and one that has been around free for a very long time. That there's a degree at Oxford University on the neuroscience of it suggests there *might* be a bit more going on than our surface-level, headline-fed understanding.

Ruby Wax studied it and couldn't be a louder proponent of mindfulness if she tried. I've struggled with things Wax has said in the past, and it's easy to be suspicious when we hear a celebrity shouting about anything supposedly transformative—genuinely shouting, in Wax's case—and to think: *Charlatan.* Particularly when it's in that person's vested interest to pack out public appearances and theatre shows or to sell books. But those who are able to shelve their hard-bitten cynicism for a second will also see a woman who has committed herself to studying the science of a practice that has helped her gain a new vantage point on real suffering, in the hope of turning that knowledge into something that might help others.

Having multiple episodes of depression means hard, skin-stripping suffering for anyone, regardless of fame or wealth. A person is not her bank account. It's not just the episodes of depression themselves, either; it's also the seasick buildup and the recovery, relearning your own language. Perhaps it takes knowing that kind of suffering to be more open to what people like Wax are saying in the public domain. But I think we can be wary and wiser at the same time.

Mindfulness *has* become hijacked by lifestyle gurus. Core Buddhist principles are watered down and spread thinly for corporate gain left, right and centre. But mindfulness is also an empirically grounded practice that can help people better live with mental health problems that may have previously left them feeling debilitated. Sure, there are half-baked lifestyle guru versions of mindfulness, but there is also the practice that has been recommended as an alternative to antidepressants by NICE, the UK's main regulator of medical treatments, for over a decade. This practice alters the actual physiology of the brain and is supported by heavyweight clinical trials; many universities (including Oxford) have set up entire research centres dedicated to studying it.

Neuroscientist Joseph LeDoux, one of the world's foremost experts on the science of anxiety and a man whose work I have quoted a lot in this book, says in *Anxious: The Modern Mind in the Age of Anxiety*: "In recent years meditation has become the subject of a great deal of research that is grounded in basic principles of modern neuroscience and cognitive psychology." He also says that learning to meditate can be "a challenging task," but is "obviously a skill that is within the capacity of our species." In fact, he believes that instruction in the use of controlled breathing exercises should be a major part of early education because it's an "easy and free way to have some power over anxiety."

Meditation is something that children can be trained to do to "the point that it becomes a habit that is simply expressed when tension arises" and is, he says, "a simple trick that, if built into one's life early, before major problems arise, could greatly reduce the adverse consequences of uncontrolled stress in childhood."

Schools are now starting to embrace mindfulness, and reports suggest that while every child's reaction will vary, most enjoy having some time to be still and quiet. If my childhood manifestations of stress could have been counteracted with breathing exercises rather than laughs, I wonder whether I might be in a different position today.

AT THIS POINT you might still be curious about what mindfulness *is*. For me, it was gaining a greater understanding of the anatomy of the brain that made me actually try it. So here's what goes on: We've discussed already that when we're spiralling and losing our shit with anxiety, it's because our amygdala has been activated and is firing out the fight-or-flight chemicals to prepare the body to attack or run. We know what those chemicals can do to us—the evidence is there in whatever symptoms of anxiety we have: a racing heart, a change in breathing, dizziness, a rumbling in the bowels. With mindfulness you practise directing your focus to one of these senses, and as soon as your attention is fixed on a physical sensation, a different part of the brain is activated: namely, the insula, a small region tucked away deep within the brain and thought to be where we read our physical state and instigate feelings that will make us take action—like feeling hungry, then eating—to keep an internal balance. When the insula is activated, the amygdala settles down and the stress hormones begin to shut off. Our heart rates go down, along with our blood pressure and so forth.

Mindfulness is not something that can be taught and done in a couple of minutes, because it's the practice and repetition of gently allowing our anxious thoughts to exist while we focus on a single sense that makes the insula stronger. It's brain body-building—you're actually building mental muscle. You can't make your biceps pop in one gym session, can you?

In one 2014 study, which looked at the way different brain regions in an individual respond to uncomfortable stimuli, researchers tested marines scheduled for pre-deployment training and deployment to Afghanistan. This was significant because military personnel are at increased risk for cognitive,

emotional and physiological problems after prolonged exposure to stressful environments and would, in theory, benefit from
mindfulness training (MT).

The marines were divided into two groups: those who
received their usual training (control) and those who received
an extra twenty hours of mindfulness-based mind fitness training (MMFT). All subjects completed tasks during a functional
MRI scan of the brain both before and after the MMFT. Those
who received the training showed significant strengthening
of their right anterior insula and the anterior cingulate cortex (ACC), which is located in the medial frontal lobe and is
another part of the brain involved in emotional regulation. It's
also vital in regulating heart rate and blood pressure. Studies
like this support the theory that mindfulness can change the
way our brain activates and responds to negative stimuli, which
may improve our resilience.

Basically, it works—although not everyone will have the
determination to stick out the practise part. I don't do it every
day but have noticed, in the three or so years I've been trying
to, that the time it takes for me to acknowledge and redirect my
anxious thoughts has shortened. I do it with an app—there are
so many out there to choose from now. I tried a couple before I
found one that hit my biting point of being both accessible and
challenging. I gave Headspace a go but couldn't carry on with it
because I found the guy's voice—a heady amalgam of transatlan-
tic Cliff Richard and faux cockney—too annoying, but I know
many people who like and have stuck with it.

For me, it was the mindfulness series by Jon Kabat-Zinn,
the guy famous for creating the mindfulness-based stress reduction program (MBSR) that is now taught across the world. (I

do not have shares in it or any connection to him whatsoever, before you ask.)

If you want to try mindfulness on your own with your phone, my advice is just try an app and see how you get on. There are plenty of online tutorials, and YouTube videos, too. Look for terms like MBSR, MT or "compassion and awareness" rather than just "meditation," to avoid anything *too* hemp-y. Or don't. It's up to you. The Internet and app stores aren't your only options, either. You could go to your local Buddhist centre and ask about instruction. If you're not near one, try your local community centre; it might be running courses. You could ask your GP to recommend a therapist who incorporates mindfulness into the treatment approach and have a chat with that person. To reiterate: Mindfulness is not a cure for anxiety. It obviously won't be for everyone, because it requires commitment and proper practice. But it is supported by solid science and has helped me and many other highly anxious people learn to get better at not reacting on a hair-trigger and to gain new perspectives—*man*. Stick that in your techno smegma pipe and smoke it.

EXERCISE, TREES AND HIPPOCAMPI

A S WE'RE REMINDED EVERY SINGLE DAY OF OUR lives, eating well and exercising are the twin pillars of health. There are all kinds of politics wrapped up in the way we're fed ideals about diet, body shape, stress levels, appetite and exercise—for both men and women—and it's both sad and frustrating to see just how vulnerable we are to any new craze that promises to change us for the better.

It feels like we're more out of sync with our bodies, from which our minds are not separate, than ever before. Susie Orbach wrote her revolutionary work *Fat Is a Feminist Issue* in 1978, but her exploration of how profoundly tied up women's relationships with their bodies are with the way people see them is as relevant today as it was then.

Too often, I think, our ultimate goal with exercise is still thinness: being lean, in control, occupying the smallest space possible. It's a drive that has been smudged into our psyches through decades of gender inequality, sexual politics, advertising and media. I am a woman. I am aware that not being overweight is better for my health all round and I exercise to keep my body a stable size. I have a pretty healthy relationship with my body but can't lie about the aesthetic drive behind my desire to sweat, either. I like to see the shape of my muscles and

what they can do. However, and it's a big however, I exercise—
have to exercise—for my brain. I feel so much better mentally
when I do and suffer when I don't.

Working out—running, cycling and doing weight training
in the gym—gives me a seize-the-day feeling that is absent
when I don't. I like feeling physically strong, like the fleshy
animal I am that's capable of extended or fast movement, but
the biggest payoff is what a tremendous buffer exercise is for
my anxiety.

It's not foolproof. I have clusters of days sometimes when
I don't feel able to work out, which leads to secondary feelings
of guilt, lower energy levels and irritability—all unhealthy
things that are ripe for triggering anxiety, which then makes
me feel even *less* like I want to go out and do some exercise.
But this is why having the discipline of a routine is so important to me.

Routines are fantastic for the anxious brain. Variables like
where I am on my menstrual cycle and whatever stress I'm
under with work all have an effect on my ability to stick to it,
but on the days that I set my alarm at 7:00 a.m. and get up and
go for a run, or go to the gym before sitting down to work, the
spirit level is far steadier.

I was so sporty as a kid, both a county swimmer and
hockey player right up until I left school, but that all went to
shit when I headed to university. When I rediscovered exercise
after becoming quite overweight for a while in my twenties, all
that happy flushing and muscle memory came back. I couldn't
run when I was depressed, but getting back into it was the best
feeling in the world and, I am certain, helped make my recovery a lot shorter than some I've come to read about.

I eased myself back into exercise by doing laps of London's Victoria Park on my bike—I could get home quicker if I needed to that way. The first few times were very strange. My anxiety levels were still so high and I felt as if there were a screen between me and the mechanics of the environment—the trees, people's normal and boring conversations, ice cream vans, the distant roar of the A12. I wasn't hallucinating, but it felt similar, like everything had been prewritten, *Truman Show* style.

I kept doing it, though, knowing something was shifting, and started having bigger and bigger gaps between the dissociative feelings. There are so many trees around Victoria Park's footways that, depending on the direction of the sun, you can be overshadowed or completely blinded. Feeling my face lit by the sun and closing my eyes against it one minute, only to lose the beam the next, made me consider the lack of permanence in anything. *I am organic matter,* I mused, *like the scorched grass of the football pitches or the canal and its summer chlorophyll duvet.* I thought about how the canal would look different in winter once the algae had gone, watching moorhens and coots swim through it, cutting the bloom open as they went.

The more I cycled, the more I looked; and the more I looked, the more I realized how quickly my moods could slip in and out; that my physical and mental states were malleable. I had flashes of realization that I was breaking free of the despair I'd been feeling—the coldest winter at the beginning of summer—and the harder I pedalled, the more I felt like my body was cheering on my mind. I tasted my sweat and it was spectacular. I was ready to run again.

The first few runs during that period were disgusting. Cycling is one thing, but nothing compares with the thudding impact of running. The physicality of it made me feel confused and sick. My body hadn't really gotten unfit, but the things I normally worked through—the immediate change in breathing, the first feverish beads of sweat, the activation of leg muscle—felt revolting. I would stop and stand against trees, convinced I'd never make it round. But I knew I had to keep going. More than anything, I didn't have the stomach for dealing with the failure of trying to do something and giving up. I remember the first run that felt good. It was after sunset sometime in June and I was going along Regent's Canal. The air was slightly stagnant and thick with cider and fag fumes, but everything shimmered. Everyone looked sexy in the gloaming. My torso was drenched with sweat, my breathing grew steady and short in the way that it does once you've hit a good rhythm, and I stuck my tits out and thought: *This is you. This is what you do.* Once home, I got in the bath and lay flat on my front completely submerged and still, like I did as a kid. Instead of imagining I was a crocodile, though, I focused on the silence. The hot thud of my heartbeat in my ears. Stillness, I was swallowing it.

In a caption beneath a recent Instagram photo of herself in a crop top and leggings, Lena Dunham said something so great about movement and mental health: "Promised myself I would not let exercise be the first thing to go by the wayside when I got busy with *Girls* Season 5 and here is why: it has helped with my anxiety in ways I never dreamed possible. To those struggling with anxiety, OCD, depression: I know it's mad annoying when people tell you to exercise, and it took me about sixteen medicated years to listen. I'm glad I did. It ain't about the ass, it's about the brain."

She's right: it *is* mad annoying when people tell you to exercise when you don't want to. That we're bombarded with new, conflicting information all the time about what exercise and how much of it is best for us is one thing, but the real issue is how do you get yourself to exercise when you're feeling anxious or depressed? How do you keep going if doing it takes such Herculean effort and the delay between effort and reward can be so substantial? How do you do something that will ultimately improve your energy, when you feel you have none?

The answer is, almost certainly, starting small. Psychologists studying how exercise can relieve anxiety and depression have suggested that ten- to fifteen-minute walks may be just as good as forty-five-minute workouts. Some studies show that even light exercise, like walking, can work really quickly to elevate low or anxious moods—like taking an ibuprofen for a headache. Even if it's temporary relief for a few hours, it's relief nonetheless. Sometimes, if I *really* don't feel like doing a proper workout, even doing some press-ups or sit-ups can make me red faced enough to knock the corners off the concrete block on my chest.

Mental health charities thoroughly recommend exercise as part of how we can help ourselves with anxiety and depression ("We can't emphasise enough the importance of exercise in using up excess adrenalin," say Anxiety UK), as do health professionals across the world. Science has also provided some evidence that physically active people have lower rates of anxiety and depression than sedentary people. Exercise may improve mental health by helping the brain cope better with stress. In some studies, researchers have found that people who did vigorous exercise were 25 percent less likely to develop depression or an anxiety disorder over the next five years. But what's actually going on in the brain when we do it?

We hear terms like "brain chemistry" all the time in relation to exercise, but let's try to make things a bit clearer: exercise is so effective at combating feelings of stress and anxiety because it causes *immediate* increases in the level of key neurotransmitters, including serotonin, noradrenalin, dopamine and endorphins—the very ones thought to be affected by anxiety and depression. It also does something nifty with cortisol—one of our major stress hormones.

Scientists have known for a long time that elevated cortisol levels can interfere with learning and memory; increase blood pressure, cholesterol and the risk of heart disease; and lower immune function, even affect bone density. Elevated cortisol can also increase the risk of mood disorders like anxiety and depression. When our fight-or-flight system is activated, cortisol floods our bodies and causes the anxiety symptoms we know and dearly love. A buildup of cortisol can wreak havoc on the mind, but any kind of aerobic activity can recreate the "flight" outlet and effectively burn up the excess (we all know the phrase "burn off some energy"—maybe that's where it comes from). Regular exercise means that cortisol is being lowered *all the time*. That is an equation that appeals to me.

Wendy A. Suzuki is a professor of neural science and psychology at New York University, the author of the book *Healthy Brain, Happy Life* and giver of good TED Talks. In a piece for *Quartz* at the beginning of 2016, she wrote about not just the short-term benefits of regular exercise, such as how it improves our ability to focus, but also what it can do for the way our brain activates in the long term.

"My favorite neuroscience-based motivation for exercise relates to its effects on the hippocampus—a key brain structure that's critical for long-term memory." We all have two hippocampi: one on each side of the brain. Suzuki says the hippocampus is unique because it is "one of only two brain areas where new brain cells continue to be generated throughout our lives—a process called adult hippocampal neurogenesis." She tells us that studies in rodents have demonstrated that increased levels of physical exercise can result in improved memory by enhancing both the birth rate and "the survival of new hippocampal brain cells." Exercise encourages the long-term growth of hippocampal cells by "immediately increasing levels of a key growth factor in the hippocampus called "brain-derived neurotrophic factor." When she exercises, she now imagines "BDNF levels surging in my hippocampi, encouraging all those new hippocampal cells to grow."

This idea hasn't been tested in people yet. But it's a hypothesis that suggests some very attractive benefits for society as a whole. Suzuki says it's also worth noting that one of the most profound long-term benefits of exercise on the brain is how it lowers our chances of suffering from conditions like dementia when we get older. "Part of this can be attributed to the buildup in the numbers of healthy young hippocampal cells as you exercise over the years," she says, with the caveat that such a long-term benefit, which might not be felt for decades, probably won't sound that sexy to a reluctant exerciser. "But if more people were to join the gym this month and actually stick to it, more of us would be able to avoid debilitating cognitive decline, which could save society billions of dollars as we enter old age."

Another thing I love about exercise is how it involves being in nature. Living in a city like London doesn't provide the most varied buffet of options, but I am lucky enough to have a huge park pretty much on my doorstep and to live within running or cycling distance from spaces like Walthamstow Marshes and the Lee Valley Nature Reserve, which, although only ten kilometres from central London, feel properly wild: the atmosphere changes.

I remember coming out of my depression in June-time and cycling to Walthamstow Marshes to collect some elder-flower heads to make some cordial. It was warm, the breeze gentle and grassy, and I felt more purpose stripping that tree than I'd felt in a long time.

I feel suffocated if I don't see trees and bodies of water or smell dirt for a few days. I've always been like that. Growing up in remote countryside probably has something to do with it. Our house was surrounded by rolling fields, the kind that look like patchwork quilts from a plane window, and our "garden" was basically just an acre of woodland full of rope swings my dad hung for us in it.

My sister, Kate, and I would leapfrog over the stream to get into the fields of high corn and press it down into "houses," with individual bedrooms, kitchens and bathrooms. We'd eat, snooze, pee and play out there all day, describing in immense detail the minutiae of our ideal homes and the meals we'd cook for our husbands. I remember talking about lime-green walls with huge, sponged-on sunflowers once—a vision, along with the husband thing, that hasn't been realized in adulthood.

If we got bored, we'd tramp the five hundred metres or so to the horse paddock on the farm, run by the young couple my mum and dad rented the cottage from, and just walk around and around the horses, breathing hard and smoothing down their hair when they came near. On the days that we'd be lucky enough to be invited by the farmer's wife to help groom them, we'd revel in getting up close in the confined space of a stable, even if it meant having your shoes shat on from a great height. The smell of their nose breath—leather and bonfire—was heavenly to me. I still love the smell of horse shit. It's childhood, Kate and the static haze of summer holidays. It's standing up on the backseats of my dad's red-and-white Citroën 2CV ("The Toad") on the deserted country lanes and singing along to "Under Pressure." It's me, Version 1.0.

When we get close to nature, we're doing our brains a solid. In a recent *National Geographic* piece ("This Is Your Brain on Nature," December 2015), the writer spent some time in the desert with David Strayer, a cognitive psychologist at the University of Utah who specializes in attention. His theory is that being in a natural environment allows the prefrontal cortex, the brain's command centre, to "dial down and rest, like an overused muscle." He's not alone in his hypothesis. If our prefrontal cortices can become like a pulled muscle, there is mounting evidence to suggest that nature can be its ice pack.

Researchers at the University of Exeter Medical School recently published data they had collected from ten thousand people living in major cities and used high-resolution maps to track where they'd lived over an eighteen-year period. They found that those living near green space reported fewer mental health problems, even after taking into account things like employment, education and income. With studies like this, it's hard to tell exactly why people have felt more okay mentally.

Could it be that people were using the green spaces to exercise in more? That lots of green flooding our vision triggers the activity of certain neurotransmitters?

These questions are why people like Strayer are examining how nature affects our brains and the rest of our bodies closer than ever before. As the *National Geographic* piece says: "Building on advances in neuroscience and psychology, they've begun to quantify what once seemed divine and mysterious. These measurements—of everything from stress hormones to heart rate to brain waves to protein markers—indicate that when we spend time in green space, 'there is something profound going on,' " as Strayer puts it.

It's funny how at odds this kind of research is with how disconnected we've become from nature in our digital age. Our fingers have become USB sticks, rather than tools to hold up flowers to sniff or to wrap around branches to climb trees. It's not just being glued to our computers or phones every day, either. Research by the Harvard School of Public Health says that American adults spend less time outdoors than they do inside their cars—less than 5 percent of their day. Most of us will know that ain't healthy.

What's going on in our brains to make us feel good when we look at nature? Quite a bit, according to neuroscience research over the past few years. A study published in the *Korean Journal of Radiology* in 2010 used fMRI scans to observe the difference in brain activity when subjects looked at urban or natural scenes. The results indicated that when people were looking at natural scenes, more activity showed up (remember what Dr. Jeffery said about the glowing orange blobs) in the anterior cingulate and the insula—areas we know play a big role in emotional regulation. When people looked at urban scenes, more activity was seen in the amygdala—anxiety's flight deck.

In terms of what's happening neurologically, it all sounds very much like mindfulness: allowing our senses to focus on visual, auditory and olfactory stimuli. Nice views, nice sounds and nice smells. Watching a mallard swim and chatter its way across a lake is a gentle focus. You can't really observe its movement and its quacking while you're ruminating on something else. Casting our gaze at any life form in a natural landscape takes us outside ourselves. I've lost count of the number of conversations I've had with people who are prone to anxiety, who say they fantasize about natural spaces, sand dunes, forests, mountains and orchards when they're feeling bad.

People say, "Fuck it, I'm going to quit my job and become a gardener," knowing they probably won't, but the fantasy of that quiet push-and-pull with the earth is so fine when the world feels dizzy and confusing.

TALK TO PEOPLE of my generation about working in an orchard and working with the hands, and they'll go all misty eyed. I think it has a lot to do with the feeling of awe that comes with being in nature. It renders us ageless, stirring the same reverence, fear and wonder we had with the world as children. But it's also the fantasy of our work being measurable and seen without Facebook comments, retweets or drawn-out meetings. Obviously, it would be incredibly unwise to tell people that standing by a lake and watching a load of ducks, or walking through a forest, will take away their anxiety or depression. God, but can it help. Ecotherapy—which includes everything from horticultural therapy to animal-assisted therapy—is widely recognized as bringing all kinds of health benefits. Mental health charity websites like Mind are full of stories of how natural therapeutic settings have not just helped people but in truth have saved their lives. It's not just sensory activation—it's purpose, community achievement.

I remember helping Hanna clear up the garden and rebuild a wall when I was coming out of my depression, and having that delicious feeling of realizing I'd not been aware of time passing. I was just slinging mud about and putting rocks on top of each other. But when our mental muscles are exhausted, simple tasks like this are wonderful. One of the most calming things I can do, especially when I'm anxious, is chop vegetables. I swear to god I can do a Michelin-standard *mirepoix*. If only I could carry a chopping board, a sharp knife and a bag of carrots around with me at all times.

We can read all the science in the world about why nature is so good for our brains, but until we fill our vision with green, it's easy to forget how wonderful it feels. If you're in the middle of a really tough period of anxiety or are feeling depressed, try as hard as you can to go for a short walk. Every day. It's not a lonely, sad or weird thing for people to do by themselves. Forget all that—you're looking after your brain. Start small and make an effort to walk a little bit farther each day. In my first session with S he encouraged me to do this, and as I said, it was the best suggestion anyone has ever given me.

Even if you live in an urban area with little green space, you can slowly walk around the block with the sole purpose of observing what's going on around you as you do, because there is nature everywhere: birds flapping and singing in the tops of trees or on telephone wires, squirrels bouncing along the ground like iridescent rats, cats turning their heads like owls and staring at you like your most important role on earth is regarding their majesty. Look at the condition of the buildings: How's the paint job on that garage? Is the paint cracking because of weather damage? Can you see what influence nature has had on man-made things as you walk? Look for moss, mushrooms growing where they shouldn't, oxidized copper, cobwebs in window frames, overgrown weeds in neglected gardens. That sort of thing. The next day, walk farther and look for more than you did the previous day. When you open up your vision, you'll be surprised what you see, and science tells us that your brain will be thanking you.

PAMELA

I MENTIONED ANIMAL-ASSISTED THERAPY IN THE LAST section, which cues me to talk about dogs for a bit. As you have probably already gleaned, dogs have always done something to me. I grew up with them, no fewer than two at a time. All the photos of me, from Brillo pad–haired toddler to teenager about to leave home, involve human limbs and furry legs intertwined in some way.

Our first dog, Sniff, was the special one. A black whippet-Labrador cross with a white diamond over her heart, she let me and my siblings ride her round the garden and suffered the endless tugging and twirling of her ears with a stretchy smile on her face. She would sit so still as I put her in flowery dresses and tied tea towels round her head to make her look like an old Italian *nonna*. Silly girl.

Sniff wasn't just a dog. They never are. Some people don't get the idea of attaching such profound emotion to an often stinking animal (I know one person who says "all dogs are Tories"), but if you know, you know. When your world fills with pain as a child—family separation, infidelity, arguing, courts, dramatic physical illness—being able to throw your body over something unfalteringly loyal, warm and with a heart beating just like your own, can drown out all the noise. And when you wake up in the morning and your dog is still there, looking at you, not getting up until you're ready, you feel safe. You want to make dogs feel the same kind of safe, too.

When Sniff died, my dad laid her out in a blanket on the back doorstep for us to say goodbye before he buried her. There was my best friend, lying stiff on her side with her tongue hanging out. She never let her tongue hang out, but her heart wasn't beating now, was it? She didn't care about being graceful anymore. Our other dog, Scruff, came and sniffed her up and down before running inside to hide. I couldn't stand upright. I had two days off school and I'm not sure I've known grief like it since.

The things animals can do for our mental health are well-documented. Across America, people are registering their dogs, cats and llamas (really) as service animals and taking them everywhere they go, for emotional support. I've seen people with lap dogs on internal US flights and it's always quite interesting, particularly when you watch them shitting into their owner's handbag and the subsequent clear-up operation, while everyone's desperately trying to pretend it didn't happen. Pet therapy is also used widely in settings such as residential homes, children's wards and psychiatric hospitals, particularly with dogs, because their presence is calming, highly sensory and does that basic thing of giving people something to talk about and respond to other than themselves or their care staff. Dogs have been shown to reduce the agitation of dementia patients, for example, and increase pleasure just by their presence. The patient may take the time to groom the animal, take it on a little walk or give it a treat, and with that comes all sorts of benefits: being outside, gentle exercise and a sense of purpose.

There are also studies that show significant reductions in anxiety scores after animal-assisted therapy sessions in hospitalized psychiatric patients. It doesn't surprise me at all. Nor does the success of companies like Borrow My Doggy, where people can sign up and be "matched" (like Tinder, without the awkward chats and disappointment!) to dogs they can walk or just have in their home for a few hours.

When I first started having panic attacks at seventeen, one of the only things that made me feel better when I got anxious at night was picking up our Jack Russell, Harry, when everyone had gone to sleep. I'd take him into bed with me. He wriggled and snored and dropped the kind of farts that can actually induce terror in a person. But it didn't matter. Listening to his breathing was the most soothing thing I knew. All through my subsequent anxious years I've quietly craved a bit more than the shimmer of human contact. I've had and still have cats, but it's not the same. Cats are beautiful, but they don't give a shit. I wanted a different four-legged friend, the kind that would make me have to leave the house even when I didn't want to. I wanted a dog again. Only it was never the right time because of, you know, work and life. When I left *VICE* in the summer of 2015 to write this book, I thought: *Sod it.*

Writing in isolation for extended periods of time is, I have to say, not the best thing for my anxious brain. I anticipated the mid-afternoon ruminating, the lack of human contact and the staring at the window thinking: *I don't know if I can do it.* There was room for a dog now. There had to be. I swore I'd get a rescue initially, but she came to me during an idle look online over breakfast one morning: a fuzzy picture of a three-month-old "cockapoo" (we've since found out she's a schnauzer–cocker spaniel cross), black as a crow, needing to be rehomed because her young owner was pregnant with her second child and didn't think she could handle a puppy anymore. We sent a few emails and I went to see her in Essex the next day. It had been a bad week anxiety-wise, but sitting on their kitchen floor as this Hairy Maclary ran rings around me, I clean forgot. The next day we went to get her to take her to London.

Pamela has brought more joy than I ever thought she could. It is a sickening yet crystalline love. Putting her dinner down on the floor makes me so happy. Amid the turds in their myriad consistencies, the chewing, the tapeworm (long gone now—Christ), the digging, the following, the jumping, the goose-shit eating, the dragging me into the fishmonger to lick ice fish water off the floor and get scales stuck in her paws, the farting—sweet Jesus the farting—I genuinely feel different with her in my life. She's given me routine and purpose and everything people with dogs say they give you, because I *have* to take her out.

In *Instrumental,* James Rhodes talks about how anxiety can make you revel in the banality of conversations with strangers, which is something I've truly come to appreciate more with her around. I meet and talk to people I'd never otherwise meet, every single day, and don't find it banal at all. I love it. Having a dog is one of the best social levellers in the world. Some of my favourite characters are the constantly squabbling cockney couple in their seventies who wear matching neon-yellow windcheaters every time they're out with their miniature schnauzer, Khan. Then there's ninety-year-old Gerry, who has approximately two teeth and a little grey bichon frise called Ruby. He must put at least a litre of Aramis on every morning and tells me the same story about Ray Davis being a tight, tax-dodging "CAHNT" every time I see him.

My favourite of all is a man whose name I don't actually know (what's a human name when dogs are around?), who is disabled and drives a mobility scooter around the park with an absolutely microscopic Chihuahua-type thing running along-side. Every time I see him he has another Grindr conquest to boast about. Once when I was talking to him his phone binged and he just zoomed off mid-sentence, shouting, "I'm about to get lucky, my girl!" I'm convinced he has more sex than anyone I know.

Most of all it's the telepathy. I honestly believe that the most tender part of our being blooms when we look a dog in the eyes. Nothing is questioned and nothing is revealed, but you are seen. A dog can't tell you, but you know you are. When I hold Pamela's gaze, smooth down her ears and tell her she's a good girl, it suspends me in time. When I lie with her in my arms in a quiet room and breathe her dusty, biscuit-tin smell, I don't ruminate. I can't. My senses are too busy with animal warmth. I asked her what she thought about it all, but she didn't have much to say.

HELPING SOMEONE WITH ANXIETY

Acording to Google Trends, the number of
people typing the phrase "how to help someone with
anxiety" into the search bar has increased year on year between
2004 and 2016. You could look at the graphs and attribute it to
anxiety increasing over time, but I'm not sure that's right. To me
it speaks of increased awareness and empathy, of people wanting to understand and help. I'm not sure a condition with such
varied manifestations can be condensed to a pamphlet-style
guide for partners, friends and families, but if, as an anxiety
sufferer, I can add anything to what the myriad mental health
charity guides or thousands of online resources are saying, it
would be quite simple. In a nutshell: Assume nothing; ask everything. Make both of you a cup of tea, give the other person the
best-looking one and say, "Tell me about it."

Seek out information on websites such as the NHS UK,
Mind, Rethink, Anxiety UK, No More Panic, the Anxiety
and Depression Association of America, Anxiety Disorders
Association of Canada, Canadian Mental Health Association
and CAMH, among others, so you can recognize what the
person might be thinking and feeling. Try to be patient. Talk
to friends about what's going on, because chances are someone
you know will have dealt with anxiety in some way. Keep in
mind that your anxious person realizes they're probably very

annoying sometimes. Try not to tell them what they should or shouldn't be doing, and instead ask how you can help in the moment, whether that's giving them space (this is usually what I need) at home or quickly getting somewhere quiet for a bit if you're out—a park, the back of a quiet café, even a car park, if it means separating from a crowded space.

If you do find yourself becoming frustrated by a resistance to seek help, which is completely justified, try to suspend judgment as much as you can and know that anxious people want to get on with their lives as much as—probably more than—you want them to but might be struggling with ideas of being beyond help, shame and not knowing what's best for them, so this is where researching stuff is good. Remind them that anxiety is just one part of who they are, that you still see them as the same person and not a victim. Try to make them laugh. For Christ's sake, try to make them laugh. Stick a whoopee cushion under them if you have to. Oh, and don't ever tell them they've got nothing to be anxious about. If you've gotten this far in the book, you'll know that's not how it works.

FUTURE TREATMENT

THE WAY ANXIETY AND OTHER MOOD DISORDERS are treated is going to change big-time. There are a lot of obstacles in the way, but research is starting to show that therapeutic interventions will become far more tailored to the individual than they are today. We're talking about actually rewriting traumatic memories; new psychoactive and anxiolytic (anxiety-reducing) drugs without the side-effect profiles they have now; targeted brain stimulation and gene-specific medication. These things are probably just the tip of the iceberg, and though some are closer to becoming applicable than others, they are, generally, a way off.

When I went to spend the afternoon with Dr. Jeffery at UCL, we talked a lot about neuroscience research and what the future of anxiety treatment might look like. One of her main points was how we are "in desperate need" of a new drug that provides an anxiolytic effect but without the habit-forming sedative effects benzodiazepines come with: "Drugs like diazepam are incredibly effective but come with a big price. They create a bubble that you just can't live in forever. They are dangerously addictive and you can't function when you take them away. Meanwhile, you're losing the opportunity to try other things that might have helped because you're dealing with the withdrawal."

Of course, creating a new drug isn't the magic bullet for dealing with such a multicausal condition, but as Jeffery says: "People with acute anxiety deserve to have the *option* of having a medication that they can take like a painkiller when they're suffering."

In the pharmaceutical world this hallowed drug is referred to as an "anxioselective anxiolytic" and is pretty much the Holy Grail. Imagine the possibilities. If a pill was created that could potentially provide relief to the millions of people who experience acute anxiety on a regular basis, and that had little abuse potential and dependence liabilities, it wouldn't just improve the quality of life for so many—it would be a gold mine. The market potential is absolutely massive. "Valium without the side effects" are words that make my heart sing arias.

When drugs like Valium first appeared, researchers knew nothing about how they interacted with gamma-aminobutyric (GABA) receptors. GABA is an important chemical that occurs naturally in the brain, where it functions as a neurotransmitter, helping regulate brain activity. It's also used in other parts of the body to regulate muscle tone. Unlike neurotransmitters like adrenalin, dopamine and serotonin, which have a stimulating or "up" function that makes neurons fire more quickly, GABA has an inhibitory function and tends to slow neurons down. Too little of it and things start firing too easily and too often. Coffee is a GABA inhibitor, which is why it can make you feel anxious and jittery if you have a lot. Too much GABA and you can't get up. However, despite the huge molecular tool box we have to work with now, we're none the wiser about the *precise* receptors that might be targeted to make a drug that works as well as a benzo without the side effects that come with attacking them

334 | ELEANOR MORGAN

all. The quest has been going on for about forty years. In the past five years, a relatively new drug called pregabalin (Lyrica), which has anticonvulsant properties and is used to treat fibromyalgia (a chronic pain condition) and epilepsy, has been proven in several significant studies to show great anxiolytic effects, which is interesting because it is a synthetic GABA. It's now viewed as a first-line medical treatment for anxiety in the UK, US and Canada, and will probably play a substantial role in the treatment of many psychiatric conditions in the future because of its calming effects. However, currently GPs are only prescribing it once SSRIs have been tried. It is worth asking about, though, if you're considering medication, as the side effects (remember, not everyone gets them) are reportedly similar to ones SSRIs can cause at the start of treatment (namely drowsiness), with less likelihood of gastrointestinal upset.

Dr. John Atack is professor of molecular pharmacology at Sussex University and head of the Translational Drug Discovery Group that's based there. His lab is just one of many trying to discover a "Valium without the side effects" drug and is focused on the role GABA plays and how it can be synthesized further. I went to Sussex to meet him. Atack is a tall, lean man with a very thick Lincolnshire accent and salt-and-pepper hair. He picks me up from the station, calling me en route to tell me what he's wearing—a pale blue shirt and "thin-framed specs." We walk through the Sussex campus towards the lab, stopping off at the medical block's canteen, because he insists I must need a coffee and a "bite" after my journey. The train from London took little over an hour. Anyway, we sit down on neon-orange chairs, some very milky lattes in hand, and talk about medication for anxiety.

"The drugs out there now are basically crap," he says. "Well, they're not, because they help a lot of people. But from a neurobiological perspective like mine they've not changed in so bloody long. We're still using antidepressants that are working in quite a general, mysterious way on the brain. We just know that they work. SSRIs are more selective because they're focusing on serotonin uptake, but even they haven't progressed for decades." And benzos? "Benzodiazepines come with risk, but they have helped researchers get a better hold on what's going on with anxiety in neurobiological terms."

We eventually make our way to the lab, through a series of heavy doors with combination locks. "Almost there," he says, as the smell of chemicals gets stronger. He shows me rooms full of silent pharmacists, their blue-gloved arms disappearing inside massive fume cupboards. He bumps into a male colleague, who I initially mistake for Bill Bailey. "Oh, John, remind me that I need to show you something later," he says. Atack looks at me and smirks. "You know I'm not that kind of doctor, Mark, but I'll have a look anyway." Mark shakes his head in that "bloody character we've got here, eh?" way. It is just the tip of the banter iceberg that follows us around throughout the afternoon.

I'm not allowed to go where the "animal work" is happening (i.e., the rats), but we wander around in lab coats looking at centrifuges, slides on the neurochemical basis of anxiety disorders, scans of glowing orange amygdalae and thousands of test tubes while we talk. I ask him why the research for such an important drug is taking so long, considering how advanced our science is now. "It's partly to do with the way the neuroanatomical basis of anxiety is still unknown," he replies with a sigh. "But it's also money."

I thought that might be coming.

"Generally speaking, antidepressants are cheap as chips to make. Something like Citalopram costs pennies to manufacture. It's fine to give everyone who has an anxiety disorder or depression a serotonin-acting drug because there's a huge market and we know they work for a lot of people, but there's not a huge amount of incentive to develop drugs with more specificity for something that is unfortunately still, despite how many antidepressant prescriptions are written every day, often seen as a minority problem."

"So there are issues to do with funding?" I ask.

He grimaces. "Yes."

I make a guess at what part of the problem might be: the lack of scientists among politicians, who have a simplistic, lay view of things like psychoactive drugs.

"I should be careful what I say here, but there are problems at the top, yes, and the allocation of money to bodies that fund drug discovery projects."

He won't be pushed further, but it must be immensely frustrating to a scientist with a significant interest in mental health (Atack has spent years studying schizophrenia) who knows that we have the power to crack the chemistry and yet hits a funding stumbling block at every turn. Because it's not just the initial experiments that need funding. Any new drug must first go through animal trials and then enough human trials to prove that it works better than a placebo—something that Atack says "is not an easy task" and can "take a very long time."

Every stage costs a lot of money. Also, you want to be the scientist who gets a drug to market. That really is the Holy Grail. I wonder when Atack sees this "Valium without the side effects" wonder drug in fact appearing in pharmacies around the world—even if he's not the one who gets it to market. "I'd like it to be in my lifetime," he says. "I'm cautiously optimistic that we'll make progress here, but I've been doing this a long time so I'm also realistic."

THE LAW AROUND doing clinical trials, a European law called the Clinical Trials Directive, impedes research because it puts in place huge cost-regulating thresholds for trials, which don't apply to treatments. In an interview with *VICE*, Professor David Nutt, a psychiatrist and neuropsychopharmacologist specializing in the research of drugs that affect the brain and conditions such as anxiety, addiction and sleep, said: "We've done trials where it has cost us £30,000 [about C$50,000] just to get a hundred placebo tablets, because even placebo tablets have to go through the same controls, largely based on the beyond-stupid fear that we might transfer mad cow disease. Then we've got to find a company that's also got a Schedule One licence [a licence to possess drugs], which takes a year. A year in terms of a grant is hundreds of thousands of pounds."

Nutt is a very interesting figure in how treatments for anxiety might look in the future. When I went to meet him at his office in Imperial College he said the same thing as Atack (an acquaintance of his): that he was determined to see, in his lifetime, a new kind of pharmaceuticals for people suffering with anxiety and depression. If anyone can do it, you'd believe he can. Nutt has become the voice of drug reform, not just in the UK but also internationally.

It's hard to think of another figure creating as much dialogue about the war on drugs as he is, which is impressive considering how little dialogue there's been, full stop, for so many years. Of course, speaking out is what got him sacked from his position as the government's chief drug adviser when he had the brass neck to report that, purely based on scientific statistics, LSD and ecstasy are less dangerous than alcohol. This is despite over half the British people thinking the government's approach to illegal drugs is bollocks. The tabloids had a field day, obviously, calling Nutt everything from "professor poison" to "the sacked drug tsar." I can tell you that the grey-haired man sitting in front of me in a linen suit looks about as much like a tsar as he does Ariana Grande.

For a long time Nutt has been interested in psilocybin, the active ingredient in magic mushrooms, for studies into whether it can help treat the depression that anxiety sufferers often feel. "Psychedelics like magic mushrooms and LSD are generally thought of as 'mind-expanding' drugs, but we have found that psilocybin actually decreases activity in certain areas of the brain that regulate the way we see and feel the world," he says. "It's very exciting." The areas he is talking about are the medial prefrontal cortex (mPFC) and the posterior cingulate cortex (PCC). The mPFC is known to be very active in depression, causing the negative rumination cycles and feelings of worthlessness, which gives weight to the theory that psilocybin may have significant antidepressant properties by decreasing action in the mPFC in the way current antidepressants do. In one study, Imperial College researchers found that people with anxiety who were given a single psilocybin treatment had decreased depression scores six months later.

Clearly, this is an ingredient with great potential as a future therapeutic tool. In 2013 Nutt was awarded a Medical Research Council grant to study the effects of psilocybin on patients with depression, but it became blocked by red tape relating to Britain's strict drugs laws. "It was immensely frustrating," says Nutt. "We urgently need more types of treatment for depression and anxiety, but the government keeps denying scientists access to what they need that could genuinely help people." What they need is access to Class A drugs, but the regulations that stop researchers getting them aren't just frustrating, Nutt says—they're "harmful."

On his website, Nutt explains that although psilocybin has potential for treating mood disorders, "attempts [now] to use magic mushrooms for self-treatment of any condition could be risky and is not advised." But people are doing it, in the form of micro-dosing.

There are online forums teeming with accounts of people taking teeny, tiny (like, a twentieth of a usual dose) bits of magic mushrooms and feeling the same—if not better—therapeutic effects as those from drugs they'd been taking previously for anxiety and depression, while experiencing very little in the way of hallucinations or tripping.

Reddit has a whole micro-dosing thread full of people doing it with not just mushrooms but also LSD and MDMA (methylenedioxymethamphetamine, or Molly)—the properties of which are being researched for the treatment of PTSD. Of course, the difficulty with self-prescribed micro-dosing is how the nature of street drugs has changed over the past few decades. There is little uniformity in purity or strength. One batch of mushrooms might work great; the next might be stronger and even at a low dose leave you in that horrible twilight zone between being not high and hallucinating. This would have quite the opposite of an anti-anxiety effect. Cannabis is another one. People have been smoking cannabis for its medicinal properties for over four thousand years—even Queen Victoria was prescribed it by her doctor, for period pain. Smoking a joint is synonymous with relaxation in popular culture and almost every anxious person I know has tried smoking weed at some point to see if it helps. I have and it does sometimes—but not too much. I'm only ever one misjudged drag away from spinning out.

In terms of anxiety, two chemicals in cannabis are interesting to scientists: tetrahydrocannabinol (THC) and cannabidiol (CBD). Studies have shown that THC increases anxiety and short-term psychotic symptoms, while CBD—which appears to have the most medical benefits in treating everything from pain to seizures, combating cancer cells, and reducing nausea and vomiting in chemotherapy patients or people with chronic GI disease, and of course anxiety and depression—has the opposite effect. It's not the bit that gets you high.

Most street varieties of cannabis, or skunk, are high in THC and very low in CBD, so you can see the problem. You can buy CBD online, but it's not something I think I'd ever do without having someone like Nutt either beside me or on speed-dial—I'm too chicken. I won't be micro-dosing with mushrooms anytime soon, either, although I sort of wish I had the balls to try. These days, two glasses of wine have me on my back like a woodlouse.

In reality, until the drug laws Nutt says are "moronic" change, the likelihood of any ingredient from a Class A drug being synthesized for therapeutic use in the general public is slim. You wonder if it might end up that anxiety and depression sufferers themselves provide overwhelming evidence that micro-dosing works, before the drug classification system changes and scientists like Nutt can expedite such important research. We're only dealing with people's quality of life, after all. The glaring irony in all this is that it's in the government's interest to get new drugs on the market to help people function better and carry on contributing to society.

Our individual genetic profiles might provide great scope for individualized mental health treatment in the future. When I met Dr. Jeffery, she talked about breast cancer and how we can now genetically subtype breast cancers—something that we couldn't do even a few years ago. "We know some people are going to respond to Herceptin [a medicine used to treat some types of breast cancers] and that some people aren't," she says, "and I think we'll end up doing the same with psychoactive drugs." How? "Well, it's going to take a lot of research, but we hope that one day we'll be able to look at someone's genetic profile and have a better idea of which drugs they'll respond to, or if they might respond better to CBT. There are so many variations in personality types and people are immensely variable in how they react to things, which includes propensities for anxiety and depression. So much of that is genetic." I ask what the main roadblock would be to this kind of research. She smiles. "Probably funding."

What if you don't want to take medication?

As I have said, I am not "pro pills." I'm pro anything that works for people and helps them live how they want to. I'm sure we'll eventually get to a stage when the moralizing around psychoactive drugs like antidepressants starts to go away, and when people who know little about mental health problems won't talk about things like "happy pills," "masking the real problem" or "putting chemicals in your body," because education about mental health in general *is* getting so much better. But there will always be people who don't like the idea of introducing a chemical that's going to alter the way their brain works, and who will want to work on their problems without drugs in the picture. Studies to improve the effectiveness of talking therapies for anxiety disorders will continue, but the future of other drug-free treatments could be very interesting. "Something like brain stimulation will likely turn out to be something we could be doing a lot more," says Dr. Jeffery. Like ECT? "No. Something minimally invasive."

Dr. Jeffery has been researching this stuff for years, but for those of us who are relatively new to the world of brain stimulation: ECT (electroconvulsive therapy) is a treatment that sends a small electric current through the brain, which in turn stimulates a short seizure. The procedure is usually done under general anesthetic and is used far less now than in the past, due to better psychological and drug treatments. No one is certain exactly how ECT works, but according to the Royal College of Psychiatrists, it is likely down to changes in blood patterns through the brain, which can alter the metabolism of areas that may be affected by depression. There is also evidence that ECT can affect brain chemistry and, recent research has shown, can help the growth of new cells and nerve pathways in certain areas of the brain.

Types of non-invasive, targeted brain stimulation are already happening. Transcranial direct current stimulation (tDCS) has made researchers very excited because of its ease of use, low cost, very few side effects and encouraging results. The pain-less procedure uses weak electrical currents to deliver targeted stimulation to the brain via electrodes on the scalp. It has already shown promise in treating mood, anxiety, cognition and certain symptoms of Parkinson's disease but is still in the experimental stage—no one in the general public is using it. A different type of non-invasive brain stimulation is in use, however.

Repetitive transcranial magnetic stimulation (rTMS) is a groundbreaking non-pharmacological treatment for depres-sion, with mounting evidence suggesting it may also work very well for anxiety disorders. It is currently recommended as a last resort to people for whom all other forms of treatment have failed to bring relief, not because it's dangerous or invasive—far from it—but likely because of how much it costs, which I'm coming to.

On paper, rTMS really does seem like the dream treatment: no needles or anesthetic, no pain, no side effects, the ability to carry on completely as normal afterwards—even driving. You just sit for half an hour in a comfy chair with some light machinery on your head and feel a gentle pulse. The positive response rate is thought to be in the 70 to 80 percent region—i.e., huge. In treating depression (or anxiety), rTMS therapy dir-ectly addresses the left dorsolateral prefrontal cortex (DLPFC), an area a few inches above the left temple. It has strong connec-tions with the limbic system, which plays an important role in the regulation of mood. rTMS runs a magnetic current in the DLPFC to regulate the flow of interactions between brain cells, with stimulations lasting under a millisecond. Studies have also shown that rTMS increases levels of serotonin and dopamine, and we know what they do.

If 80 percent of people who have done rTMS have felt vast improvements in their mood, why can't we all have access to it? Because, as I've said, it costs a bloody fortune, that's why. rTMS is obscenely expensive and currently only delivered at a handful of clinics across the world. The treatment is short but intense: five sessions each week, for three to six weeks, with benefits felt after just seven days. At the London Psychiatry Centre, one of only two UK clinics doing rTMS, the treatment costs £2,000 (about C$3,350) a week. An average treatment lasts four weeks so would set you back £8,000 (about C$13,500). In Canada, rTMS is not available on most province health insurance plans, but some clinics provide the treatment for free. For example, rTMS is not currently covered by the Ontario Health Insurance Plan (OHIP) but is available cost-free at the University Health Network (UHN), a health care and medical research organization in Toronto, including the MRI, visits to the psychiatrist and the treatment sessions themselves.

STUDIES KEEP PROVING how effective rTMS is, which makes it incredibly attractive, along with the zero-side-effects thing, but being able to spend that kind of money is a joke for most people. £8,000! The London Psychiatry Centre say on their website that although the treatment is very expensive, "when we consider the benefits, the cost pales in comparison . . . For many patients, it has proven to be the most significant investment they have ever made."

Sure, we spend that kind of money on cars and plastic surgery, and if something is going to improve our mental health significantly for a long time, the argument for spending a big chunk of money is there, but ... *£8,000.*

The comments underneath the centre's Facebook post about the treatment say it all: "People are drawn in by its high success rate and feel devastated when they learn it's something only the rich will be able to afford. Maybe in the future, if more funds are ploughed into improving treatment options for *everyone* with depression or anxiety, this groundbreaking technique won't just be reserved for those with loads of zeros in their bank balances."

Another promising, yet slightly scary, *Clockwork Orange–*sounding treatment for anxiety disorders, particularly PTSD, might exist in something called "memory reconsolidation: the unmaking of traumatic memories." A person garnering interest in this area is Dr. Daniela Schiller, who directs the Laboratory of Affective Neuroscience at the Mount Sinai School of Medicine in New York. In 2004, the year Schiller received her doctorate in cognitive neuroscience from Tel Aviv University, she was awarded a Fulbright fellowship and joined the laboratory of Elizabeth Phelps at New York University.

Phelps is a colleague of Joseph LeDoux and both are among the world's leading investigators of what's going on with the neural systems involved in emotion, learning and memory—all things that inform anxiety disorders. The year 2004 was, coincidentally, also the year *Eternal Sunshine of the Spotless Mind* came out, exploring what might happen when two people have all their memories of each other erased. This is pure science fiction and in real life is impossible: You can't stick a pipette into someone's brain and suck out a few neurons, or "erase" single memories without damaging others. We're not yet able to examine individual neurons directly. But fMRI has, as we know, helped neuroscientists monitor activity in certain parts of the human brain, and what Schiller and her colleagues are interested in is rewriting frightening, upsetting memories so they can be recalled without the distress attached to them. We know that trauma can be part of what causes anxiety disorders, particularly PTSD, and that memories can inform the present in all kinds of painful ways.

Schiller has seen first-hand the impact trauma can have on a person. Her father, Sigmund, spent the first two years of World War II in the Horodenka ghetto, in Ukraine, and the next two on the run, hiding in bunkers across Eastern Europe. In 1942, he was captured by the Germans and sent to a concentration camp, where he survived the war. Sigmund has never spoken about his time in the camp to his family. In an interview with the *New Yorker*, Schiller said: "I long ago concluded that his silence would last forever . . . I grew up wondering which of all the horrifying things we learned about at school the Germans did to him."

We need memories of fear to survive. We spend our infancy learning about things we can't touch because they'll hurt us—fire, sharp knives, boiling water—but for people with disordered anxiety, fear takes over in an irrational way. Our fear memories begin to concern even the *memories* of fear. With something like panic disorder, people can spend their days worrying about having another panic attack. They avoid any situation that might be "dangerous"—which can end up being the world beyond the front door—and a reinforcement circuit is made. People like me struggle (but can relearn) to extinguish conditioned fear. The amygdala, where our fearful memories are stored, can activate even at the *thought* of having a panic attack. According to Schiller, there's more we could be doing for people with these kinds of activations.

In order to understand how reconsolidation might work— i.e., saving a better version of a file over a corrupt one—we need to understand the bones of how memories are formed and affected. Our brains are electrical—we have full-on Van de Graaff generators going on up there. Every memory we have depends on the strength of the chemical reactions that connect *millions* of neurons, which are electrically "excitable" cells, to one another. Neurons communicate through synapses, which are like tiny alleyways between the cells. But to do this they need something called dendrites, which are like loads of little branches that look a bit like seaweed. The dendrites pick up the chemical signals and carry information across the synapses into other cells. In terms of memory and learning something new—a word, name or sum, for example—we "remember" when those synapse connections are strengthened. This usually happens through repetition. When neurons can communicate more easily, so, too, can memories be more readily recalled. The strengthening process is fragile, though, and can go to pot if interrupted.

You know how it is when you're trying to remember something—a name, say—and you keep getting interrupted. It's so much harder. When this happens, memories don't have time to form. Dr. Jeffery tells me it takes "several hours" for a new experience to go through all the chemical and electrical processes required to transition from a short-term memory to a long-term one.

As time passes, long-term memories become less susceptible

to being interfered with, because they become embedded in our brain circuits. This is consolidation. But the process has shown to be less straightforward than it seems and can be interrupted by all sort of things. Scientists have tried it with drugs on rats, but they're too toxic to use in humans. So, Schiller wondered if memories could be *re*consolidated with behavioural therapy, instead.

In a study that was published in *Nature* in 2010, Schiller "trained" sixty-five people to fear a blue sphere by associating it with an electric shock. The next day, even looking at the sphere without the shock was enough to set off anticipatory anxiety and fearful reactions. The shock itself was nowhere near as uncomfortable as the fear of it happening. Then Schiller divided the subjects into three groups. By presenting the spheres repeatedly, without a shock, she was trying to "teach" them to overcome their fear. The results were dramatic and interesting: Those who saw the spheres that following day within ten minutes of having their memories revived forgot their fear completely. The others, who were not shown the spheres again until hours later, remained frightened. Clearly, timing was crucial.

Schiller spoke to me about the project on the phone from New York, where the line was crackly and it sounded like she was in the back of a car. "Is this not the Pavlov's dog–esque technique we're already doing with exposure and extinction therapy?" I ask.

"Well, yes," she says, her Israeli accent soft, and with the inflections of someone who's been working in America for a long time. "Extinction therapy—or exposure therapy, as it's known—has been an effective treatment for anxiety disorders like PTSD and phobias for quite a while now. The more you're confronted with the thing you fear without feeling anything bad, the less fear you have of it. Over time, experiencing less and less fear associated with what you fear makes it much easier to deal with."

But isn't the problem with anxiety disorders that our memories of the things we fear, even when we've associated them with being relaxed, are always competing? I tell her about my panic attacks and how, even though I have recalled the feelings in a therapeutic setting and tried to associate them with being there, relaxed, in the chair, it feels like there's a true fight going on sometimes.

"Yes, but the real key in making them join together, as it were, is timing. If we catch it at the right time, we can make a different memory. We are not erasing anything. You'll still be able to recall what has happened, whether it's looking at a coloured shape or, like you say, a panic attack, but the uncomfortable emotion won't be there."

WHEN SCHILLER'S RESEARCHERS tested the subjects again a year later, the fear responses still hadn't returned. The work has provided the most promising clue yet that people with PTSD or other anxiety disorders may have another long-term solution on the horizon that doesn't involve drugs. Is she optimistic? "Well, you don't want to get too overexcited about it, because getting things out of the research stage and into actually making people's lives better is hard. But I think we have the power to make anxiety disorders less terrible for people."

Her research continues.

I FORGET SOMETIMES that there was a time when I didn't have to deal with some anxiety symptom every day. I often have this vision of a fifteen-year-old me, sitting in a school bus on the way to play a hockey match. My friends and I are willing on the independence we're certain adulthood will bring us. We talk about dinner parties, getting into the pub and, "*Godddd*, just being able to do whatever we want." Then we'd play our match, get back to our houses and go through it all over again on our parents' landlines.

You hear people say how it's a shame that teenagers wish their lives away, but I think it's how we cope. We're transitioning into our adult selves every day: weird, gangly butterflies emerging from the chrysalises of our young skins, and this state of flux makes us look for certainty, something we can think of as fixed. The fifteen-year-old me didn't want to go back to being a baby. She wanted the next bit, to see her wingspan. I didn't know on the bus that day that I'd spend as much time as I have in adulthood wanting to press rewind.

As well as the acute episodes of anxiety that leave me overcome with nausea, vertigo, tingling, gut ache, a chest-bursting sensation and a feeling that I'm skidding down an imaginary verge, there are the waves of that nameless dread that come and go all the time. Sometimes it's like a bruise being gently pressed. Other times it feels like knowing one of Kim Jong-un's nuclear bombs is going to go off and wipe us all off the face of the earth, but I don't know when. I just *know*. Except I don't. It's a dance of feelings both precise and unnameable.

Anxiety has been disabling for me at points over the years.

When it's not acute, I can be buffeted by any kind of "real" worry that I can hang the undefinable foreboding on: work, my family and friends' health, my own health, running out of money, what kind of neighbours are going to move in upstairs, missing trains, being late, the dog being bored, the dog dying, the tone of someone's email, whether I've annoyed someone, food going off, not ringing my mobile phone network to ask why the Internet is so slow, whether I'll make a good mum one day. I worry little and I worry big, about everything and nothing. How much that worry impacts my day-to-day life and my movement varies. Sometimes, when I can strategize and catch the thoughts like gnats, it doesn't impact me at all.

How I might have become this way is something I hoped I'd answer while writing this book, and I think I have a better idea now than I ever have before. But any conclusion we try to make about anxiety is going to end up being as muddled as the condition itself. The kind of anxiety I have—that is: disordered, clinical, whatever word you want to use—isn't any one "type" of condition. It is medical, psychological, philosophical, spiritual and cultural: the product of my biology, my environment and simply being a human being.

Many things have contributed to the red, screaming ball of raw life my parents took home from the hospital over three decades ago becoming me today, sitting at my laptop, contemplating. Through the research I've done and the people I've talked to, including the therapist I continue to see, I am aware of the confluence of factors inside and around me, the individual: the influence of my genes and being attached to Betty in my first two years of cognitive development; the childhood anxiousness that was mostly dismissed; the significant lack of stability throughout my teenage years after my parents' messy separation; a traumatic brush with death, and the transient state of consciousness in intensive care, coupled with loss of bodily control and a long recovery period, during which I lacked the opportunity to emotionally process my experience; the years of subsequent physical problems that have required further hospital treatment and that provoke symptoms often indistinguishable from the ones I feel when I'm very anxious; the stigma; a fear of forever being seen differently if I told people the "truth"; the shame.

I have found that investigating the science of the brain and what systems are implicated in anxiety has given me a feeling of power I didn't have previously, because when anxiety hits and the chaos of time rushes over, under, around and through me, it can feel so disorientating. Exploring my assumptions, and why they may not be right, is power. So is knowing—*really* knowing—that there is not a soul on earth who is mentally stable all the time and that I don't need to pathologize every variation in my mood or emotional state, trying to work out what it *means* in the wider picture of my health.

It's been enlightening to see how neuroscientists aren't just open to but *recognize* the power of talking therapy and mindfulness to affect the physical structures of our brains—changes that are as measurable as ones produced by medication—because it shows the number of options we have. Looking at the stigma that still surrounds mental health has been an uncomfortable reality check, but it helps me examine why I felt I had to live my anxiety in complete secrecy right from the beginning, and why that made it worse in the long run. In turn, it's made me see how fucking critical it is to help young people become more emotionally literate and know what mental health problems might look like, in case such problems ever affect them.

We are animals who lucked out and got these big brains— elaborate and with limitless malleability, capable of so much. But to be human is to be involved in constant internal dialogue. Sometimes, for some of us, the lack of clarity in life and our endless quest for the "true" or "pure" versions of ourselves are profound distractions from whatever is in front of us. Those who live with anxiety spend so much time lamenting purity or stillness, but maybe, in order to work towards living with it better, we need to try to accept the idea that a complete removal of all our neuroses would not leave a gleaming, crystalline core. Normal doesn't exist. Anxiety need not define us. I have to remind myself of this often.

In *My Age of Anxiety*, Stossel quotes the author Angela Carter: "Anxiety is the beginning of conscience." I've thought about that a lot and think she might be right. Without anxiety, nothing would get done. It propels us to ask questions, to not always be satisfied. It commands movement, emotional intelligence. But for some people, people like me, it can go beyond the point of being useful and become disordered. At times, the way my mind has short-circuited has made me feel hopeless, heartbroken and so frustrated—as though I've been cauterized from joy, while thinking myself inside out. Rationally, I know this isn't the case at all. I have remained, with two notable time-outs, a high-functioning, contributing person who has travelled, has a lot to be proud of and knows a lot of love. There are traits I have—inquisitiveness, compassion, pretty good judgment (I think) and an instinctive desire to listen to people—that exist alongside my anxiety and, who knows, might also be because of it, in some way.

When I tell people about this book, many say, "Oh, that's brave," and I always bristle. All I've been is honest. I wish "brave" wasn't ascribed to conversations about mental health so often, but there we are. It won't always be this way. See, this is the thing about being human beings: we don't stay the same! Our codes change. *We* change. We're forever adapting to the squally waves of life. Anxiety can strip us of rationality, confidence and spark, but in learning to accept it as part of who we are, we can learn to see our moods and thoughts as tides. In and out, in and out, in and out they go. No mental state is fixed, because brains aren't fixed—we're highly evolved like that. We're spectacular.

ACKNOWLEDGEMENTS

Thank you to Mum, Dad, Kate, James and all the many, many animals buried in the Essex countryside that we have loved over the years. To Kate Merry, for continuing to give me the freest moments I've ever known, in laughter and ketchup. To all the friends I laugh with, especially Nell, Morwenna, Eva, Hattie and James. To Jackey, I wish you could have known your impact. Maybe you do. To Jon Elek at United Agents, for making shit happen. To Hanna and to Pamela, thank you for the stream of sunlight while I wrote this book.

RESOURCES

Anxiety Disorders Association of Canada

WWW.ANXIETYCANADA.CA

ADAC works to improve lives by promoting the prevention, treatment and management of Canada's most common mental health concern: anxiety disorders.

Bell Let's Talk

WWW.LETSTALK.BELL.CA

Bell Let's Talk is a multiyear charitable campaign that funds research and engages with the public to break down stigma, spread awareness and encourage accessibility to help.

Canadian Alliance on Mental Illness and Mental Health

WWW.CAMIMH.CA

CAMIMH is an alliance of health care providers and people with mental illness working together to get Canadians involved in a national conversation by battling the stigma around mental illness and offering information on available support.

Canadian Association for Suicide Prevention

WWW.SUICIDEPREVENTION.CA

While not itself offering direct therapeutic or mental health services, CASP's website will point you in the right direction if you are considering suicide, trying to help someone who is or grieving a death by suicide.

Canadian Coalition of Alternative Mental Health Resources

WWW.CCAMHR.CA

The CCAMHR is a national consumer-oriented forum that brings people from different organizations together to discuss and generate policy on mental health issues like stigma, employment barriers, housing and other services and supports.

Canadian Mental Health Association
WWW.CMHA.CA
Founded in 1918, the CMHA provides direct service to more than 100,000 Canadians annually in over 120 communities, with a focus on helping people with mental illness develop the personal skills and tools necessary to lead meaningful and productive lives.

Centre for Addiction and Mental Health
WWW.CAMH.CA
CAMH is Canada's largest addiction and mental health teaching hospital, offering an array of services that aim to meet a wide variety of patient needs, including assessment, brief early intervention, residential programs, day treatment, continuing care and support for families.

Centre for Suicide Prevention
WWW.SUICIDEINFO.CA
CSP is an education centre within the Canadian Mental Health Association, offering online and print resources to caregivers, survivors, researchers, professionals and community members across Canada and around the world.

eMentalHealth.ca
WWW.EMENTALHEALTH.CA
Dedicated to improving the mental health of children, youth and families, eMentalHealth.ca provides anonymous, confidential and trustworthy online information around the clock and connects those in need with counselling and other services.

Institut universitaire en santé mentale de Montréal
WWW.IUSMM.CA/INSTITUT.HTML
The IUSMD is Canada's largest francophone psychiatric hospital in Canada, with a variety of programs that offer care, research and teaching.

Kids Help Phone
ORG.KIDSHELPPHONE.CA
Kids Help Phone offers free and anonymous help to young people who need it, including an array of counselling options, extensive online resources and advocacy on behalf of young people locally, nationally and globally.

mind*your*mind

WWW.MINDYOURMIND.CA

mind*your*mind is a non-profit mental health program that gets young people and the professionals who serve them involved in co-developing reliable, relevant mental health resources with the aim of reducing stigma and increasing access to and use of community support.

Mood Disorders Society of Canada

WWW.MOODDISORDERSCANADA.CA

The MDSC's central goal is to give a voice to people with mood disorders and to make that voice understood on a national level, gathering information, raising awareness and advocating on behalf of the mood disorder community.

National Network for Mental Health

WWW.NNMH.CA

Run by and for mental health consumers/survivors, the NNMH brings other consumers/survivors together, along with their families and supporters, for resource sharing, information distribution and mental health education.

Ontario Shores Centre for Mental Health Sciences

WWW.ONTARIOSHORES.CA

This public teaching hospital provides a range of specialized assessment and treatment services to people dealing with complex and serious mental health issues and is home to the Bell Canada Youth Mental Health Outreach Clinic.

PTSD Association of Canada

WWW.PTSDASSOCIATION.COM

The PTSD Association of Canada offers coping strategies and resources for individuals living with PTSD and provides an array of educational materials ranging from medical research to personal stories.

Teen Mental Health

WWW.TEENMENTALHEALTH.ORG

TMH uses the best scientific knowledge available to develop training programs, publications, tools and resources for teens and educators, all aimed at improving the mental health of youth.

The LifeLine Suicide Prevention and Awareness Mobile App
WWW.THELIFELINECANADA.CA
This mobile app connects individuals in crisis with support and guidance 24-7, aids in suicide prevention and offers guidance to those bereaved through suicide.

There are many additional local resources available for those living with mental health issues and those seeking help for a loved one—so many, in fact, that we cannot possibly list them all here. People across the country dedicate their lives to caring and finding help for those community members living with mental illness. We encourage you to seek them out. Though many suffer from depression at some point in their lives, depression—as is true of all other mental health issues—is anything but trivial. Call. Write. Find someone who will listen. They will understand. They are out there waiting to help.

FURTHER READING

BOOKS

American Psychiatric Association. *Diagnostic and Statistical Manual of Mental Disorders*. 5th edition. (DSM-5). Arlington, VA: American Psychiatric Publishing, 2003.

Austin, James H. *Zen and the Brain*. Cambridge, MA: MIT Press, 1999.

Bretécher, Rose. *Pure*. London: Unbound, 2015.

Burton, Robert. *The Anatomy of Melancholy*. Ann Arbor, MI: University of Michigan, 2001. First published in 1621.

Davies, James. *Cracked: Why Psychiatry Is Doing More Harm Than Good*. London: Icon Books, 2013.

Egan, Jennifer. *A Visit from the Goon Squad*. New York: Alfred A. Knopf, 2010.

Freud, Sigmund. *Introductory Lectures on Psychoanalysis, 1916–17*. The Standard Edition. New York: Liveright: 1989.

Gray, John, *Straw Dogs: Thoughts on Humans and Other Animals*. London: Granta Books, 2003.

Haig, Matt. *Reasons to Stay Alive*. Toronto: HarperCollins, 2016.

Kagan, Jerome. *The Temperamental Thread: How Genes, Culture, Time, and Luck Make Us Who We Are*. New York: Dana Press, 2010.

Kagan, Jerome, and Howard A. Moss. *Birth to Maturity: A Study in Psychological Development*. New Haven, CT: Yale University Press, 1983.

Kierkegaard, Søren. *The Concept of Anxiety: A Simple Psychologically Oriented Deliberation*. Translated by Alastair Hannay. New York: Liveright, 2015. Reprint edition. Originally published in Danish in 1844, under the title *Begrebet Angest*.

LeDoux, Joseph. *Anxious: The Modern Mind in the Age of Anxiety*. London: Oneworld Publications, 2015.

Manguso, Sarah. *Ongoingness: The End of a Diary*. Minneapolis: Graywolf Press, 2015.

Orbach, Susie. *Fat Is a Feminist Issue*. Melbourne: Arrow, 2006.

Proust, Marcel. *In Search of Lost Time*. Volume 2. Paris: Grasset and Gallimard, 1913.

Rhodes, James. *Instrumental: A Memoir of Madness, Medication and Music*. Edinburgh: Canongate, 2005.

Ronson, Jon. *The Psychopath Test*. London: Picador, 2012.

Smith, Patti. *M Train*. London: Bloomsbury, 2015.

Sonnenburg, Justin, and Erica Sonnenburg. *The Good Gut: Taking Control of Your Weight, Your Mood, and Your Long-Term Health*. New York: Bantam Press, 2015.

Sontag, Susan. *At the Same Time: Essays and Speeches*. New York: Farrar, Straus and Giroux, 2007.

———. *Illness as Metaphor*. New York: Farrar, Straus and Giroux, 1978.

Stossel, Scott. *My Age of Anxiety: Fear, Hope, Dread, and the Search for Peace of Mind*. London: William Heinemann, 2014.

Various contributors. *Dear Stranger: Letters on the Subject of Happiness*. London: Penguin, 2005.

Williams, Mark, and Danny Penman. *Mindfulness: A Practical Guide to Finding Peace in a Frantic World*. London: Piaktus, 2011.

ARTICLES, PAPERS AND REPORTS

Bauer, Annette, Michael Parsonage, Martin Knapp, Valentina Iemmi and Bayo Adelaja. *The Cost of Perinatal Mental Health Problems*. LSE & Centre for Mental Health, October 2014.

Baxter, A. J., K. M. Scott, T. Vos and H. A. Whiteford. "Global Prevalence of Anxiety Disorders: A Systematic Review and Metaregression." *Psychological Medicine*, vol. 43, no. 5 (May 2013): 897–910.

Brooker, Charlie. "Here's How to Avoid the Norovirus." *Guardian*, January 14, 2008. https://www.theguardian.com/commentisfree/2008/jan/14/comment.charliebrooker.

Burkeman, Oliver. "Therapy Wars: The Revenge of Freud." *Guardian*, January 7, 2016. https://www.theguardian.com/science/2016/jan/07/therapy-wars-revenge-of-freud-cognitive-behavioural-therapy.

———. "This Column Will Change Your Life: Sudden Exposure." *Guardian*, October 31, 2009. https://www.theguardian.com/lifeandstyle/2009/oct/31/change-your-life-sudden-exposure.

Care Quality Commission. *Right Here, Right Now—Help, Care and Support During a Mental Health Crisis.* June 2015.

Danziger, Shai, Jonathan Levav and Liora Avnaim-Pesso. "Extraneous Factors in Judicial Decisions." *Proceedings of the National Academy of Sciences of the United States of America*, vol. 108, no. 17 (April 26, 2011): 6889–92.

Daskalakis, Nikolaos P., Linda M. Bierer, Heather N. Bader, Torsten Klengel, Florian Holsboer and Elisabeth B. Binder. "Holocaust Exposure Induced Intergenerational Effects on FKBP5 Methylation." *Biological Psychiatry*, vol. 80, no. 5 (August 2015): 372–380.

Dunham, Lena. "Difficult Girl: Growing Up, with Help." *New Yorker*, September 1, 2014. http://www.newyorker.com/magazine/2014/09/01/difficult-girl.

Fuertes-Knight, Joanna. "When Are We Going to Stop Marginalising Black and Minority Ethnic Mental Health Patients?" *VICE UK*, May 1, 2015. https://www.vice.com/en_us/article/when-are-we-going-to-stop-marginalising-black-and-bme-mental-health-patients-181.

Gwang-Won Kim, Gwang-Woo Jeong, Tae-Hoon Kim, Han-Su Baek, Seok-Kyun Oh, Heoung-Keun Kang, Sam-Gyu Lee, Yoon Soo Kim and Jin-Kyu Song. "Functional Neuroanatomy Associated with Natural and Urban Scenic Views in the Human Brain: 3.0T Functional MR Imaging." *Korean Journal of Radiology*, vol. 11, no. 5 (August 27, 2010): 507–13.

Haase, Lori, Nathaniel J. Thom, Akanksha Shukla, Paul W. Davenport, Alan N. Simmons, Martin P. Paulus and Douglas C. Johnson. "Mindfulness-Based Training Attenuates Insula Response to an Aversive Interoceptive Challenge." *Social Cognitive and Affective Neuroscience*, vol. 11, no. 1 (April 8, 2014): 182–90.

Hodgkin, Emily. "Single Woman Who Treats Her Two 'Reborn Dolls' as Though They Are Real Babies and Even Changes Their Nappies Says She Would Choose THEM over Any Man." *Daily Mail*, November 24, 2015. http://www.dailymail.co.uk/femail/article-3331668/Single-woman-treats-two-reborn-dolls-real-babies-changes-nappies-says-choose-man.html.

Hogg, Sally (for the NSPCC). *Prevention in Mind: All Babies Count; Spotlight on Perinatal Mental Health*. NSPCC, June 2013.

Kohn, David. "When Gut Bacteria Changes Brain Function." *Atlantic*, June 24, 2015. http://www.theatlantic.com/health/archive/2015/06/gut-bacteria-on-the-brain/395918/.

LeDoux, Joseph. "Emotion, Memory and the Brain." *Scientific American*, June 1, 1994.

Navaneelan, Tanya. "Suicide Rates: An Overview." Statistics Canada, catalogue no. 82-624-X (November 27, 2015). http://www.statcan.gc.ca/pub/82-624-x/2012001/article/11696-eng.htm.

Owen, David. "Beyond Taste Buds: The Science of Delicious." *National Geographic*, December 2015. http://ngm.nationalgeographic.com/2015/12/food-science-of-taste-text.

Rogers, Jude. "The 'Hidden' Illness of Post-Natal Depression." *VICE UK*, April 27, 2015. https://www.vice.com/en_ca/article/more-than-half-a-million-women-experience-perinatal-mental-illness-190.

Rosenbloom, Stephanie. "Moody? Cranky? Tired? Feed Me!" *New York Times*, December 1, 2005. http://www.nytimes.com/2005/12/01/fashion/thursdaystyles/moody-cranky-tired-feed-me.html.

Schiller, Daniela, Marie-H. Monfils, Candace M. Raio, David C. Johnson, Joseph E. LeDoux and Elizabeth A. Phelps. "Preventing the Return of

Fear in Humans Using Reconsolidation Update Mechanisms." *Nature*, vol. 463 (January 7, 2016): 49–53.

Shea, Matt. "Professor David Nutt Is Still Fighting Against the UK's 'Moronic' Drugs Laws. *VICE UK,* May 16, 2013. https://www.vice .com/en_dk/article/david-nutt-magic-mushrooms-interview.

Spechler, Diana. "This Is My Brain on PMS." *New York Times*, May 5, 2015. https://opinionator.blogs.nytimes.com/2015/05/05/this-is-my-brain-on-pms/.

Specter, Michael. "Partial Recall: Can Neuroscience Help Us Rewrite Our Most Traumatic Memories?" *New Yorker,* May 19, 2014. http:// www.newyorker.com/magazine/2014/05/19/partial-recall.

Suzuki, Wendy A. "Acute Exercise Improves Prefrontal Cortex but Not Hippocampal Function in Healthy Adults." *Journal of the International Neuropsychological Society*, vol. 21, no. 10 (November 2015): 791–801.

Williams, Florence. "This Is Your Brain on Nature." *National Geographic*, January 2016. http://ngm.nationalgeographic.com/2016/01/call-to-wild-text.

Woolverton, Frederick. "Are We Born into Trauma?" *Psychology Today*, September 15, 2011. https://www.psychologytoday.com/blog/the-trauma-addiction-connection/201109/are-we-born-trauma.